# Investigating gender

D0387972

# Investigating gender
Contemporary perspectives
in education

*Edited by*
*Becky Francis and Christine Skelton*

**Open University Press**
Buckingham · Philadelphia

Open University Press
Celtic Court
22 Ballmoor
Buckingham
MK18 1XW

email: enquiries@openup.co.uk
world wide web: www.openup.co.uk

and
325 Chestnut Street
Philadelphia, PA 19106, uSA

First Published 2001

A catalogue record of this book is available from the British Library

ISBN 0 335 20787 1 (pb)      0 335 20788 X (hb)

**Library of Congress Cataloging-in-Publication Data**
Investigating gender: contemporary perspectives in education/edited by
Becky Francis and Christine Skelton.
    p.   cm.
    Includes bibliographical references (p.   ) and index.
    ISBN 0-335-20788-X – ISBN 0-335-20787-1 (pbk.)
    1. Gender identity in education. 2. Educational equalization.
    I. Francis, Becky. II. Skelton, Christine.

    LC212.9 I59 2001
    305.3–dc21
                                                2001036255

Typeset by Type Study, Scarborough
Printed in Great Britain by St Edmundsbury Press, Bury St Edmunds, Suffolk

# Contents

# List of contributors

*Stephen Baron* is Senior Lecturer in Education at the University of Glasgow. He has researched issues of community and education since the 1970s, and is currently part of the team evaluating the City of Glasgow's pilot reorganization of its schools into 'Learning Communities'. He is presently completing the text of *Community and Control: Surveillance, Containment and the State*, due to be published by Pearson Education.

*Wendy Cealey Harrison* teaches in the School of Social Sciences at the University of Greenwich. She is the author, with John Hood-Williams of *Beyond Sex and Gender*, to be published by Sage during 2001. Her research interests centre on the fundamentals of theorizing in the social sciences and she is currently investigating the possibility of a productive interface between psychoanalysis and neuroscience.

*Jo-Anne Dillabough* is an assistant professor in the department of Curriculum, Teaching and Learning at the Ontario Institute for Studies in Education, University of Toronto. Her work focuses on identity debates in feminist theory, feminist political and social theory and their application to education, and the study of gender, politics and culture in education. She has published widely in international journals and edited collections on these topics. Her recent book (co-edited with M. Arnot) is entitled *Challenging Democracy: International Feminist Perspectives on Gender, Education and Citizenship* (2000) and is published by RoutledgeFalmer.

*Becky Francis* is Reader in Education at the Institute for Policy Studies in Education (IPSE) at the University of North London. Her research interests include the construction of gender identities in school, gender and achievement, and feminist theory. She is author of *Power Plays* (Trentham Books,

1998) and *Boys, Girls and Achievement: Addressing the Classroom Issues* (Routledge-Falmer 2000). She is joint editor (with Dr Christine Skelton) of the journal *Gender and Education*.

*Martyn Hammersley* is Professor of Educational and Social Research at the Open University. He has done empirical work on processes of social interaction in schools and also on the media. Much of his writing has dealt with methodological issues. His most recent books are *Taking Sides in Social Research* (Routledge, 2000) and *Case Study Method* (Sage, 2001), which was co-edited with Roger Gomm and Peter Foster.

*Mary Jane Kehily* is Lecturer in Childhood Studies at the Open University. She has a broad range of experience both as a teacher and a researcher in schools and universities and has written widely on issues of gender and sexuality, narrative and identity, and popular culture.

*Helen Lucey* is a research fellow in the School of Education at King's College London. Her research interests focus on the formation of identity, particularly in relation to social class and gender. She is currently researching children's experiences and perceptions of the transition to secondary school with Diane Reay. Together with June Melody and Valerie Walkerdine she has co-authored *Growing up Girl: Psychosocial Explorations of Gender and Class* (Palgrave, forthcoming).

*Anoop Nayak* is a lecturer in social and cultural geography at the University of Newcastle upon Tyne. He teaches courses on racial identities, globalization and theories of human geography. His current research interests concern ethnic and racial studies, youth subcultures, masculinities, work and schooling.

*Carrie Paechter* is Senior Lecturer at the department of Educational Studies, Goldsmiths College, London University. Her research interests, which have been developed out of her previous experience as a mathematics teacher in London secondary schools, include the intersection of gender, power and knowledge, the construction of identity, especially with regard to gender, and the processes of curriculum negotiation. Her most recent books are *Educating the Other: Gender, Power and Schooling* (Falmer Press, 1998) and *Changing School Subjects: Power, Gender and Curriculum* (Open University Press, 2000).

*Ann Phoenix* works as a senior lecturer in psychology at the Open University. Her research interests include motherhood and the social identities of young people (including those of 'race', ethnicity and gender). Her current research is an Economics and Social Research Council (ESRC) funded project (with Chris Griffin) on consumption and the construction of young people's identities. Her most recent publications include *Standpoints and Differences* (edited by Henwood, Griffin and Phoenix) (Sage, 1998) and *Young Masculinities* (with Frosh and Pattman) (Palgrave, 2001).

*Lynn Raphael Reed* is a principal lecturer at the University of the West of England. Her research interests are masculinities and schooling, gender, feminism and education in East Central Europe, and teacher professional development in urban schools. She has also written and published in the area of feminist methodology.

*Diane Reay* is a senior lecturer in research methods in the School of Social Science and Public Policy, King's College London. She has published widely in the areas of gender, social class and ethnicity. Recent publications include *Class Work: Mothers' Involvement in their Children's Schooling* (University College Press, 1998).

*Sheila Riddell* is a professor of social science, and works at the Strathclyde Centre for Disability Research, University of Glasgow. She has written extensively on gender identity (as well as social class and disability), and equal opportunities, including the production of a comprehensive report on equal opportunities in the Scottish education system for the Equal Opportunities Commission. Her recent, ESRC-funded work has focused on the experiences of adults with learning difficulties.

*Christine Skelton* is a senior lecturer at the University of Newcastle where she teaches courses on gender at undergraduate and postgraduate level. Together with Becky Francis she edits the international journal *Gender and Education*. She has published widely in the area of masculinities and education. Her most recent book is *Schooling the Boys: Masculinities and Primary Education* (Open University Press, 2001).

*Alastair Wilson* is a research fellow at the Strathclyde Centre for Disability Research, University of Glasgow. His research interests include education, training and empmloyment for adults with cognitive impairments, the experience of disability within higher education and professional assessment of children with special educational needs.

# Introduction

## Becky Francis and Christine Skelton

The feminist study of gender and education has built up a diverse body of dynamic and ground-breaking research over the last three decades. At various times during this period examples of contemporary work have been brought together in collections which seek to provide an overview of the field (see, for example, the influential collections by Arnot and Weiner 1987 and Weiner and Arnot 1987). These collections have provided useful introductions to the subject area for undergraduate students, and excellent sources of reference for postgraduates and academics. Recent shifts in focus around the theorization and study of gender and education, caused by social and policy changes, meant that we deemed it timely to produce a new collection of essays which would outline theoretical developments in the area, and showcase the cutting-edge research around different issues within the field.

During the 1970s and 80s, much feminist research on gender and education was motivated by concern at the underachievement, and marginalization, of girls. A perception of girls as underperforming in comparison to boys predominated at this time, and feminist researchers maintained this 'underachievement' was explained by the discrimination and marginalization that they demonstrated girls faced in the education system. Some feminist researchers attempted to call attention to girls' out-performance of boys at primary schools and at English and modern languages in secondary schools (for example Clarricoates 1980; Lee 1980; Spender 1982; Walkerdine 1988), but this point was largely ignored. In fact, even in the 1970s (prior to the replacement of O levels with GCSE examinations in England and Wales), slightly greater numbers of girls than boys were gaining five or more O-level A–C grades (Arnot et al. 1999). Yet because these often included low status, 'feminine' subjects such as home economics and so on, the pattern was not taken seriously. Boys were doing significantly better at subjects like maths and science, which were perceived as most important (by feminists, who saw these subjects as leading to the most highly remunerated careers; and by the public at large, who perceived these 'hard', traditionally masculine subjects as having more status than 'feminine' subjects such as languages).

When the Education Reform Act 1988 introduced the National Curriculum into England and Wales, all this was set to change. Girls and boys were now compelled to take the same core subjects. 'League tables' cataloguing pupils' GCSE results were introduced so that educationalists and parents could assess school performance, and these league tables revealed the extent of girls' success for the first time (Arnot *et al.* 1999). Although the performance of both sexes has been improving since the introduction of GCSE examinations, girls' improvements have been more rapid than those of boys. Girls have continued to out-perform boys at language subjects, and catch them up in maths and the sciences.

Few readers can have escaped awareness of the furore that this development has provoked among educationalists and in the national media. Rather than congratulating teachers or girls on improving girls' achievement, the GCSE results created what Epstein *et al.* (1998) refer to as a 'moral panic' about boys. This concern at boys underachievement is by no means limited to Britain: similar patterns are evident in many Organization for Economic Cooperation and Development (OECD) countries (Yates 1997; Epstein *et al.* 1998). Of course, feminists have been at the forefront of those pointing out that the claim that boys are underachieving is over-simplistic (variables such as social class and ethnicity continue to have a bigger impact on achievement than does gender). Moreover, many feminists compare the public and official concern at boys' performance with the lack of interest given to girls' underachievement in the past (when the design of strategies to improve girls' performance was largely left to committed feminist teachers). Now, reams of newspaper commentary and hundreds of thousands of pounds of government money are devoted to exploring possible strategies to raise boys' achievement. However, this public concern has also, to some extent, served to raise the profile of gender research. Further, it has impacted on the focus of research in gender and education: where in the 1980s the vast majority of research in gender and education focused on girls, in recent years the proportion of research focusing on boys' constructions of gender has markedly increased.

This new focus on boys has reflected and drawn on a rapidly growing body of work on masculinity, which developed throughout the 1990s. Indeed, there are now journals specifically dedicated to work in this area. Much of the work on masculinity draws on feminist research and often adopts a pro-feminist stance. As Skelton (1998) has observed, such research is welcome: many feminists have in the past have drawn attention to the lack of regard for gender issues by men, and to the way in which masculinity was assumed to reflect the unproblematic 'norm'. Others have pointed out that as gender is a relational construction, one needs to study femininity in relation to masculinity, and vice versa (Stanley and Wise 1993; Kelly *et al.* 1994; Francis 1998). As such, the study of masculinity has much to contribute to the field.

On the other hand, as Skelton (1998) points out, not all the work on masculinity takes a pro-feminist approach. A focus on the minutiae of identity in this work has sometimes been at the expense of adequate analyses of power relationships, hence masking continuing gender inequalities (Skelton 1998; Francis, forthcoming). Some studies appear to ignore the large body of work on gender which has been developed by feminists over the latter decades of the twentieth century. Finally, some writers on masculinity take an anti-feminist (even anti-women) stance. Examples of the latter approach can be found in the work produced by members of the 'men's movement', which draws on essentialist notions of 'natural sex differences' to argue that men are being unnaturally feminized (and discriminated against) in modern society, resulting in a 'crisis of masculinity' (see Skelton 1998; Whitehead 2001). Yet ironically, it is arguable that the current interest in masculinity and, in educational research, the concern with boys' 'underachievement', have served somewhat to legitimize the study of gender and education in the eyes of the (mainly male) academic and media 'powers that be'.

Besides the continuing explorations around notions of boys' under-achievement, gender analyses continue to be applied to studies of classroom behaviour, curriculum, the teaching profession, educational policy and a multitude of other topics. Such research has demonstrated that, despite their improved achievement, many facets of girls' educational experience remain negatively affected by the masculinist values and expectations reflected in educational institutions. Research has highlighted the continuing prioritization of male experience and masculine values in the curriculum (Paechter 1998a). It has noted the continuing domination of top educational positions by men (David and Woodward 1998; Meehan 1999). It has demon-strated how boys continue to dominate classroom space and teacher attention (Francis 2000a; Warrington and Younger 2000; Skelton 2001) and to belittle girls' contributions (Lees 1993; Skelton 2001). Sexual harassment remains a problem (Herbert 1989), and work by Lees (1993) and Francis (2000a) suggests that the surveillance and policing of girls' sexualities in the school environment remains intense. Further, the gender constructions among both primary and secondary school pupils remain strongly polarized (Davies 1989; Thorne 1993; Francis 1998, 2000a). This is reflected in the continuing divergence in subject choice according to gender, once pupils have completed their GCSEs (where all students must pursue the same subjects). At A level and degree level, males continue to favour science subjects, while females largely opt for humanities and arts subjects (Whitehead 1996; Francis 2000b). This gendered divergence is also evident in vocational training (Equal Opportunities Commission 1997). As Rees (1999) observes, the sub-ject areas which are adopted more frequently by males tend also to be those in which it is easiest to find jobs, and where jobs are most highly remunerated.

Although boys and men continue to dominate the educational environment, research in gender and education has not failed to highlight the negative consequences of the construction of masculinity for many boys in education. Boys' constructions of 'macho' masculinity often conflict directly with the culture of the school, which brings many boys into conflict with teachers and other authorities (Skelton 2001). 'Laddish' constructions of masculinity have been linked to underachievement (Epstein 1998; Francis 2000a; Warrington *et al.* 2000). The jockeying for position which a hierarchy of masculinity entails can be extremely intimidating and frightening for individual boys, involving as it does the 'othering' of particular boys who can be positioned as effeminate (Salisbury and Jackson 1996; Connolly 1998; Epstein 1998).

The problematization and investigation of the dominant group which 'others' those outside it has not been limited to the study of masculinity. The ways in which dominant societal constructions present middle-class, white, able-bodied and heterosexual values as 'normal' and unproblematic have been increasingly scrutinized by researchers in the 1990s and early 2000s. As such, 'whiteness', heterosexuality and the middle class are growing areas of study within and outside research in education. Such research and its findings have implications for the study of gender constructions and relations, and are consequently represented in this collection. This extension of analyses of identity to new areas illustrates the focus on identity and diversity which has proliferated within gender studies and the social sciences generally over the last decade. The concern with identity is reflected in the design and contents of this book: rather than examine research on specific educational issues, or in different sectors and levels of education, we have taken gender identity as a starting point. We have attempted to highlight the different and diverse areas of gender identity research taking place within the educational setting (for example, 'race' and gender, sexuality and gender, and so on). However, as a number of researchers have noted, the fragmentation of foci on different variables such as 'race', class, gender and so on is potentially limitless (Cealey Harrison and Hood-Williams 1998), and can impede the generalization across social groups which is often necessary in order to promote social change.

This attention of researchers to diversity rather than similarity within social groups, and to contradiction rather than consistency in the presentation of self, has been encouraged by two factors. These are the criticisms of identity politics which developed in the early 1980s and have continued to the present, and the simultaneous impact of poststructuralist and postmodernist theory in the social sciences. However, many feminist theorists have been deeply sceptical concerning the implications of poststructuralist theory from the outset (for example, Bordo 1990; Hartstock 1990; Soper 1990; Spretnack 1993) and the extent of its potential to contribute to emancipatory projects continues to be closely debated. All of these elements, from the factors impacting on and shaping gender identity to theoretical issues, are considered by the contributors to this book, in order to present a contemporary picture of research in gender and education.

## Outline of the book

Our intention in designing this book was to bring together examples of some of the latest research and theoretical developments in the field of gender and education which would provide a thorough overview of the construction of gender identities within education, and the consequences of such constructions for the individuals concerned. We sought to highlight the changes that have taken place in gender and education research, the theoretical shifts underlying such research, and the new theoretical journeys which are being embarked upon. Further, we sought to provide examples of contemporary applied research investigating various issues and facets of identity within the field of gender and education.

Part 1 seeks to 'set the scene'. Jo-Anne Dillabough's chapter outlines the development of research in gender and education since the late 1970s. She discusses in detail the impact of various movements in policy and theory on research in the area, and traces the diverse range of feminist theories which have contributed to this research. She also describes some of the problems which have been raised in feminist theory in the latter part of the twentieth century, and the approaches and concerns of current research on gender and education.

Martyn Hammersley's chapter is intended to raise some of the continuing questions and controversies surrounding the notion of research in gender and education. The majority of contributors to this book are committed feminists, who either foreground gender as a point of analysis in their research, or at least assume that it plays an important part in identity construction alongside other variables. However, Hammersley's work has questioned such assumptions. He maintains that gender should not be elevated over any other factor as a point of analysis, or indeed be assumed to be relevant at all. His criticisms of Linda Measor's (1999) analysis in his chapter here are in keeping with his earlier critiques of research into equal opportunities in education (Foster *et al.* 1996). He maintains that such researchers set out with political assumptions and hence 'find' in their data what supports their political beliefs and assumptions, irrespective of whether or not such factors were actually relevant. Such criticisms may occasionally be valid. However, we would argue that they could surely be applied to all qualitative research, rather than simply to research on gender or other research with emancipatory aims. As feminists have argued, no research is completely objective or free from the values of the researcher (Harding 1990; Stanley and Wise 1993). Feminist research simply intends to make such values transparent from the start. We do not support Hammersley's interpretation of Measor's work, but do see the continuing need for reflection and debate about the validity and practices of 'identity' research.

Part 2 is intended to provide a view of recent theoretical debates impacting on research in gender and education. Here contemporary political and philosophical theories are described and analysed, and their potential contribution to feminist research in education discussed. The various theoretical challenges

raised by postmodernist and poststructuralist theory, and the possible consequences of a focus on diversity and deconstruction rather than solidarity and
reconstruction for emancipatory work, are being increasingly debated (see, for
example, Spretnack 1993; Cealey Harrison and Hood-Williams 1998, 2001;
Francis 1999, 2001; Burgess and Reay 2000; McNay 2000). Carrie Paechter
describes the beneficial contribution of poststructuralist theory for feminist
work, and its application in feminist educational research. Such application
of aspects of postmodern and poststructuralist theory can also be found in a
number of the chapters in Part 3, which describe gender and education
research in relation to particular areas of identity. In Part 2, the chapters by
Wendy Cealey Harrison, Becky Francis and Lynn Raphael Reed examine
some of the tensions and questions raised for feminist educational theory
by the application of postmodern perspectives, and suggest new theoretical
directions which might build from both modern and postmodern positions
and circumvent such dualisms.

The articulation of different aspects of identity in relation to gender and
education is the subject of Part 3. The major areas of identity research
within gender and education research are represented here.[1] The authors
are at the forefront of research in their respective fields, and each attempts
to provide a brief overview of research in that particular field as well as illustrating their explanations with discussion of their own projects and findings.
Dis/ability and gender are explored in relation to education in the chapter by
Sheila Riddell, Stephen Baron and Alastair Wilson. After describing recent
work in this field of study, they discuss findings from their own research
which show how gender impacts on the various educational opportunities
and experiences of people with learning difficulties.

Research on sexuality and gender in education is explored by Mary Jane
Kehily, who describes the hegemonic construction of heterosexuality as
normal and homosexuality as deviant within school culture. She analyses
the ways in which such discourses are maintained, and the consequences
for school pupils.

Anne Phoenix describes developments in research on 'race', gender and
education, focusing on research analysing black experience and perspectives.
She discusses ethnicity, gender and achievement, the subtle way in which
children from ethnic minority groups can be positioned in racial and colonialist discourses by teachers and educationalists, and the consequences of
such positioning.

Conversely, Anoop Nayak's chapter discusses a developing area of 'race'
research, exploring the issue of 'whiteness' in relation to gender and education. His work illustrates the way in which whiteness, ignored as an issue
by educationalists, can be experienced as problematic and contested by
school pupils.

That girls and women also construct their gender identities is a point which
has been occasionally obscured by the focus on masculinity, and Diane Reay's
chapter redresses that imbalance with an examination of femininity. She
discusses the different constructions of femininity that she found portrayed

by the schoolgirls in her study, and the apparent impact of these various constructions on their experience and progress at school.

Christine Skelton describes the rapidly developing field of research on masculinity in education, and presents some of her own work in this area.

The impact of social class and gender is examined in Helen Lucey's chapter, which describes the developments since her seminal study with Valerie Walkerdine of the construction of primary-school girls and their mothers in gendered and classed discourses around democracy and education (Walkerdine and Lucey 1989). As always, Lucey does not just focus on the marginalized class (an approach which risks problematizing and objectifying the working class), but also interrogates the practices of the middle classes.

The final chapter takes a different angle on the discussions appearing elsewhere in the book. It considers how current theories on gender, education and social identity sit in relation to recent educational policy on social justice issues in schooling. The chapter briefly explores how the theories appearing in this book might appear in terms of actual classroom practices for teachers to adopt in working with pupils. We hope that the collection will prove a stimulating read, and one that will encourage readers to pursue further the ideas in the field.

**Note**

1 In terms of representing all facets of identity, it is impossible to provide a completely comprehensive overview in any one book (or indeed, taking up the point made by Cealey Harrison and Hood-Williams 1998, to ever provide a comprehensive analysis of all aspects of identity).

*Part 1* | Gender as a category
in educational research

# 1 | Gender theory and research in education: modernist traditions and emerging contemporary themes

*Jo-Anne Dillabough*

## Introduction

This chapter explores theoretical developments in the study of gender in education. Its primary purpose is to examine such developments over the last two decades, with a particular concentration on the most recent trends in the field. As one element of this task, I also consider some of the changes and continuities which have marked feminist thought and its application to the study of gender in education. In so doing, I argue that gender research in education has moved away from its initial concern with gender socialization patterns, the reproduction of gender inequality in schools and gender equity reforms towards an engagement with social and cultural theory and its analysis of the contested nature of gender identities in schools.

In tracking gender research in education over time, I focus on contemporary gender theory not because it presents a complete picture of feminist educational research or all of its contending positions, but because it characteristically displays, like other fields of humanities research, theoretical conflicts which are apparent in the broader sphere of contemporary social theory. Without an understanding of the relationship between theoretical conflicts in social theory and education as a domain of study, the development of gender analyses in education will remain elusive. It is with the elucidation of this relationship that this chapter is concerned.

I begin with an informal historical sketch of gender research in education followed by a brief reflection on the impetus behind the theoretical shifts in the application of feminist theory to educational research over the last two decades.

## The development of gender in education as a field of study

Some may argue that the field of gender in education has its origins in the theoretical work of Ann Oakley (1972) and education feminists investigating links between gender, school structures and broader social arrangements. Oakley's key argument, for example, was that the social category 'gender' in the study of inequality was preferable to a focus on sex differences, since it perceived gender as a social construction rather than as a fixed biological entity. To put this another way, if gender, as opposed to sex, was ultimately a social construct, then its links to socialization could be understood primarily as an aspect of gender identity formation.

In keeping with this shift, education feminism in the late 1970s and early 80s moved beyond the distinctive concerns of liberal and radical feminists to an analysis of education's role in gender socialization patterns and the reproductive functions of education in shaping gender relations (Dillabough and Arnot, in press). It was in these respects that Oakley's (1972) work provided feminists with the conceptual tools for expanding the boundaries of gender research.

Second-wave feminist concerns influenced the direction in which this kind of gendered analysis of education might go. For example, research documenting the manifestation of sexual discrimination in schools began to emerge (see Wolpe 1976; Byrne 1978; Deem 1978, 1980; Stanworth 1981) alongside studies highlighting the links between the form of girls' education and capitalism (Barrett 1980; MacDonald 1980). In such studies, gender and class differentiation and patriarchal school structures were major concerns, as were the consequent equity issues for education. In following the work of radical feminists, early gender analyses examined the patriarchal language of school subjects and school structures (Mahony 1983, 1985) and exposed what Spender (1980) dubbed the 'patriarchal paradigm of education'. Influenced by a strong Marxist inflection, many education feminists sought to expose the gender and class inequities emerging from sex-segregated schooling, while others identified important links between the aims of educational policy, male domination and a capitalist economy (David 1980; Walker and Barton 1983). By the early 1980s, the most significant motifs were a notion of gender as a theoretical construct, education as a site for the cultivation of gender inequalities (Delamont 1980) and a concentration on the relationship between the state, national policy and the economy in shaping girls' education.

As we will see, the theoretical premises – whether Marxist, structuralist or functionalist – associated with this work emphasized schools as sites for the *potential* democratization of gender relations even though gender socialization was understood to be shaped, above all, by residual patriarchal relations rather than by a dynamic of social *change*. This meant that earlier liberal preoccupations with sex differences and roles began to give ground to deeper concerns about the relation between gender and social structure. Critical forms of gender equity research sought, in part, to challenge those early liberal positions focusing on the psychological characteristics seen as 'intrinsic' to girls and women. In their place came new emphases upon the gendered nature of social structures and the particularity of gender identity formation.

Such concerns contributed to the building of a new theoretical agenda for studying gender in education from a broad social and political perspective to which many education feminists from the late 1970s have remained committed. This was an agenda dedicated to the project of uncovering the gendered nature of school knowledge/curriculum (Bernstein 1978), and revealing its role in shaping girls' and boys' identities and aspirations. It was also an attempt to address the pragmatic problems of gender inequity and feminist pedagogy in schools, drawing upon wider social concerns for, and about, women (Weiner and Arnot 1987; Weiner 1994). In each of these respects, much of the early equity research work represented a sustained attempt to expose sexist school practices, engage in school reform and to challenge what Dale Spender (1980), Bob Connell (1987) and others had identified as patriarchal school structures.

While this early phase of education feminism undoubtedly contributed substantially to the field, its initiatives were not without their difficulties. Indeed, many feminists began to disassociate from mainstream 'equity research' that focused too narrowly on girls' education and issues of discrimination, access and attainment. Such work, it was argued, was entrenched in middle-class values and narrowly defined visions of the category 'female'. As such, it was ill-equipped to address questions about issues of identity, culture and women's differences (Carby 1982; Brah and Minhas 1985). For this reason, the study of identity began to emerge as central to a reconfiguration of the field.

## Gender, educational structures and social reproduction[1]

In this early stage of change, education, as a mediating structure of the economy, was still seen as a major site for the reproduction of class culture rather than as a site for the construction of broader social identities associated with, for example, race and sexuality. Innovative gender research within this tradition was principally concerned with the part played by education in *reproducing* dominant class structures, codes and corresponding classed identities. A theoretical interest in the notion of schools as sites for the cultural reproduction and development of social identities (chiefly relating to class and gender), while distanced from earlier functionalist traditions, therefore continued to emphasize the importance of mapping economic structures onto school structures (Dillabough and Arnot, in press).

Within this framework, significant attention was given to issues of gender politics/inequity in schools (Arnot and Weiner 1987) and to women's education as training a 'hierarchically stratified workforce' for the 'reserve army of labour'. Such work highlighted the role of education in constructing women teachers and female pupils as servants to the state (Steedman 1985). It also revealed the gender hierarchies of educational management and the masculine expectations by which they were framed. In sum, the achievement of such work was to expose the reproductive role of education in maintaining symbolic representations of male rationality and female subservience.

Emphasis on the reproduction of the social and economic order through education led towards a feminist version of *reproduction theory*:

> In 'hard' versions of social reproduction theory (Bowles and Gintis 1976), education was conceptualized as an instrument of capitalism through which the subordination of women and working class girls was reproduced. As might be expected, class culture appeared with great regularity as the social formation which not only pre-figured, but determined, girls' educational experiences, identities and forms of consciousness.
>
> (Dillabough and Arnot, in press: 12)

Later versions of reproduction theory took on somewhat different theoretical inflections, and mark a shift in our understanding of social theory generally, and feminist thinking more specifically. Such accounts of reproduction theory drew widely upon theories of class hegemony (Gramsci 1971), cultural capital (Bourdieu and Passeron 1977) and educational codes (Bernstein 1977, 1978). Of particular significance was the attention which these approaches gave to the role of masculinity and femininity in shaping class relations and gender inequality in schools, with disaffection expressed as a celebration of resistant masculinities (Willis 1977) or a 'cult of femininity' (McRobbie 1978). Here, the cultural reproduction of class and gender positioning in the state emerged as a kind of 'parallelism' (Willis 1977) between young people's resistance to élitist school norms and an apparent class commitment to the construction of traditional gender positions.

As expressed in the now seminal works of Willis (1977) and McRobbie (1978), the emergence of gender inequality in school cultures was not as straightforward as social reproduction theorists such as Bowles and Gintis (1976) had suggested. Male and female youth were also involved in the active construction of their own complex identity positions. Such work revealed the critical importance of diverse school experiences and the cultural identities and social positioning which prefigured them. Cultural identity therefore began to emerge as a much more complex element in the study of male and female youth's lived experiences of schooling.

Cultural reproduction theorists were not without their critics. Their approach tended to devalue women's political agency and the part played by both education and women's movements in the recontextualization of gender and class relations. Nor did they address issues of difference – beyond class – broadly or seriously enough. In particular, the category 'gender' was under reconstruction in some feminist research in this period. Yet cultural reproduction theorists had started gender research on a course which began to resist narrow and overly deterministic understandings of educational processes and school cultures and their role in shaping diverse and resistant identities. Such shifts in educational research were indicative of a larger interest within cultural and social theory of moving beyond 'the charge of essentialism' and challenging what was seen as a conceptually impoverished and reductive way of thinking about identity formation. In the place of cultural reproduction came a broader understanding of gender as a more permeable social construct held together through elements of discourse.

## Transformations in gender theory and educational research

In the light of these broad theoretical shifts, new questions could now be raised about modern feminist theory and its application to the study of gender in education. In looking to these shifts – in effect, the movement from modernist to postmodernist/poststructuralist analyses, or what Francis (1999) has described as a move from a realist to a relativist feminist framework – a number of important theoretical questions have emerged. While still concerned to a degree with gender equity, curriculum and gender reform policies, these newer questions settle their key problematic upon a philosophical concern about the nature of gender identity and the ways in which educational discourses shape the modern individual.

Some of the most salient questions which have arisen about gender in education concern the 'meaning and significance of identity', and 'relationships between identity and difference' (Weir 1997: 1). As a key representative of one side of the debate regarding the formative place of identity in social theory, Judith Butler (1990: 39) writes that the 'heterosexual imperative enables certain sexual identifications and forecloses and/or disavows other identifications'. Butler's words reveal a concern with social difference and notions of female identity 'in which sexuality is the main axis of operation and normative heterosexuality as the main obsession' (Anderson 1998: 8). If we do not wish to repress difference, how, as education feminists, might we theorize it in relation to gender and other social formations 'without making false claims to authority and authorship' (Weir 1997)? These questions have played a substantial role in recasting the debates about gender equity in 'education feminism', though more traditional sociological and pedagogical questions have also maintained much of their force. Gender research has, moreover, continued to shed light on the shifting and constructed nature of curricular knowledge in relation to educational practices over time (Measor and Sikes 1992; Murphy and Gipps 1996; Paechter and Head 1996), as well as on sociological, cultural and historical analyses of women teachers' and teacher educators' working lives (Acker and Feurverger 1997).

Despite the range of topics spanning the field, the argument I now wish to pursue suggests that an emphasis on gender identity rather than equity *per se* has emerged, in part as a response to larger transformations in social theory and the evolution of education within the humanities and social sciences.

Some of the key issues which have emerged as a result of these trans-formations include the viability of the modern democratic education project, the 'death of the female subject' (that is, a uniform notion of female identity), and the question of whether social and cultural theory can serve as grounds for struggle over values inherent in education feminism, such as the goal of gender equity.

At the same time, it is important to remember that there remain education feminists who argue that there is a continuing need to examine the relation-ship between gender identity both as a *category of analysis* and as a coherent narrative which is shaped, in part, through educational *forces*. By contrast, those who are more formally entrenched in assessing the shifting nature of gender identity in schools (for example, poststructuralists) argue that we need to get beyond viewing gender as a core element of selfhood and instead examine the equity implications for education policy of *understanding multiple positions on identity*. Still others argue that equity itself is framed within a liberal humanist or liberal democratic project that honours some female groupings (that is, the middle class) and marginalizes others. There are, then, many diverse positions from which to engage the significance of gender identity for education.

## Emerging themes/theoretical orientations in gender and education

Four major themes mark contemporary theory in *gender in education*. Such themes might be characterized broadly under the following headings: 'Gender, poststructuralism and the "sexed identity"'; 'Gender, ethnicity and social exclusion: the transformative power of black, post-colonial and stand-point feminisms'; 'Gender, markets and educational processes'; and 'New gender identifications and theories of social change'. It is to a consideration of each of these themes, their related research and theory, and their impact on education that I now turn.

### Gender, poststructuralism and the 'sexed identity' in education

The mid- to late 1980s represented a transformative period in the study of gender and education, when it could be suggested, for example, that the cate-gory 'woman' or 'girl' was either illusory or could no longer speak for all women in the name of a straightforward or simplistic notion of social and cultural reproduction. Modernist feminist perspectives in education could therefore be 'seen as rationalistic explanations and master narratives' – which not only identified the causes of gender inequality but had uniformly described the core premises of gender identity formation in modernity' (Dillabough and Arnot, in press). Such explanations, as the work of Willis (1977) and McRobbie (1978) had suggested, bore little relation to the complexity of gender identities and experiences in schools.

In the struggle against essentialism in 'education feminism', a more explicit research interest in the *multiple forms of gender identity* and their manifestations in education began to emerge. Such analyses took a variety of forms, including studies of the part played by the 'sexed identity' (Butler 1990) in school performance (Epstein *et al.* 1998), the role of identity formation in influencing the effectiveness of gender equity policies (Kenway 1997a) or definitions of teacher professionalism and accounts of the lives and experiences of female teachers and teacher educators (Acker 1994).

Within this emergent tradition, one strand of identity research has proliferated in recent years and has addressed the ways in which educational discourses lead to multiple forms of masculinity and femininity in schools. In this section, I highlight how the study of femininity and masculinity – perhaps more than other domains of educational research – is an example of how 'education feminism' has attempted to grapple with changes in social/cultural theory stimulated by poststructural thinking, particularly in relation to shifting gender identities. This shift could be charted as a move away from the 'sociology of women's education' and political and pedagogical concerns with gender equity (as pragmatic issues) towards a broader theoretical concern with the formation of gender identities and novel *gender theories* of education.

One of the most prominent theories drawn upon in recent years to problematize uniform understandings of 'gender' has been feminist poststructuralism. Poststructuralist theorizing within education is now a vast terrain and outlining its nuanced distinctions is beyond the scope of this chapter. In short, however, that which distinguishes poststructuralism from *rational* forms of structuralism or other modernist feminisms is its link to deconstruction as a conceptual tool for critiquing language, and its insistence that gender identity is not a coherent or stable narrative to be known in any ultimate sense.

Several terms favoured by poststructuralists, such as 'discourse', 'deconstruction', 'subjectivity' and 'regimes of truth' have been much drawn upon by education feminists to examine the gendered nature of educational language. The aim here has been to reveal the cultural elements of educational life (for example, peer culture, teachers' talk, school text) as discourses (that is, as embedded in language) rather than rigid social forces, shaping masculinity and femininity. One of the earliest illustrations of this theoretical shift in education was the work of Bronwyn Davies. Davies (1989: 1–2, 13) writes: 'In learning the discursive practices of their society, children learn that they must be socially identifiable as [either male of female]. Positioning oneself as male or female is done through discursive practices and through the subject positionings which are available within those (linguistic) practices'.

While Davies' work was principally concerned educational life in Australia, it drew upon earlier projects on the construction of femininity in the UK. For example, Valerie Walkerdine (1981) and Walkerdine and Lucey (1989), drawing upon both psychoanalytic and poststructural approaches, championed the idea that historical images of women which mirror the private sphere are mobilized within education *discourses* to propogate the subordination of women and girls. Following Foucault, they argued that a 'regime of truth' about gender identity which people understand to be historically continuous and unitary is thus always present in classrooms. In this sense, femininity and masculinity are merely performed in honour of the discourses that construct them. For Walkerdine, dominant understandings of gender identity represent fictional accounts of an old and rather unimaginative reincarnated story about men and women across time and space.

As a further development of this earlier work, the study of masculinity has emerged as central to identity research in education. Often drawing upon aspects of poststructural theory, this research suggests that there is no one form of masculinity in schools; rather, there are many competing and contradictory forms, each of which is contingent on the conditions of gender *regulation* in schools. Examples of this work include studies of the gendered language which is drawn upon by male youth to legitimize various positions on masculinity, a practice which ultimately privileges some dominant 'identity' forms over others – for example, the difference between being a 'swot' or 'wimp'[2] (Mac an Ghaill 1994; Haywood and Mac an Ghaill 1996a; Davies 1997; Kehily and Nayak 1997; Skelton 1997). Other studies address how, for example, homophobia is constructed through the heterosexist language of boys' everyday practices in school cultures (Epstein 1997). Very recent work drawing on poststructuralism has also examined the language forms of educational policy and the media, such as the 'underachieving boy', and the implications such language has for reproducing gender inequity in reactive policy measures such as 'saving' the 'underachieving boy' through educational support offered up by famous footballers (Raphael Reed 1999).

Why has such a sustained focus on masculinity in education taken place in recent years? Even though feminists have explored the lives of girls and women, and described a 'cult of femininity' (McRobbie 1978), they have not until recently fully explored what it meant to study gender (as opposed to sex) in the broadest social sense; to study girls alone cannot address the issue of gender relations. While Willis (1977) entered this territory over 20 years ago, he remained committed to masculinist theories of reproduction to explain masculinity (grounded in notions of class conflict). The contemporary trends in tackling issues of masculinity have attempted to challenge such positions by drawing upon theoretical work which offers new understandings of competing gender discourses and their role in shaping diverse gender identities.

Masculinity research in education also relates directly to the broader preoccupation with identity debates in social and cultural theory. It has exposed novel equity issues associated with a range of masculinities emerging in schools and paved the way for viewing gender as more permeable and changing than in previous periods of educational research. A special concern with the gendered elements of educational discourse has also meant that key issues such as 'failing boys' and 'boys' underachievement' have been examined from a poststructural perspective. Ironically, most poststructuralists were hoping to do away with identity as a category of analysis, but it seems to loom large in most of this work.

There may also be an element of commodification in the study of masculinity. If the state is concerned about 'boys' underachievement' rather than 'girls' success', then doubtless research grants designed to explain and eradicate the problem have fuelled some of this work. Like students and teachers in schools, we, as feminist researchers, are not exempt from the regulative forces of the research culture and the academy in its quest for knowledge. Consequently, we are still left with very practical equity questions unanswered. How far, for example, will this work take us in challenging the difficult problems of gender relations in schools such as 'bullying', 'homophobia', 'school violence', 'critical literacy' and the lack of more open democratic school structures? As Davies (1997) herself has noted, even when teachers encourage students to 'deconstruct' (for example, through critical literacy) uniform and traditional notions of gender, it remains unclear whether gender essentialisms (that is, traditional gender categories) are effectively challenged.

Yet it is clear that this work has been extremely effective in charting the everyday language regulating the lives of male and female pupils and teachers. And in conducting micro-feminist analyses of gender in education and moving beyond liberal, maternal and Marxist accounts, it has achieved much that had seemed beyond the reach of mainstream education feminists.

*Gender, ethnicity and social exclusion: the transformative power of black, post-colonial and standpoint feminisms*

Another example of alternative feminist theorizing which has gained greater prominence over the last decade is 'black feminism' and variants on 'standpoint feminism' (Hill-Collins 1990), some of which are aligned to a greater or lesser extent with 'feminist critical realism' or 'post-colonial feminism' (Brah and Minhas 1985; hooks 1989; Mirza 1993). Key educational ideas which have been central to such analysis can be summarized as follows: (1) women and girls' education is formulated within a colonial narrative where the 'other' emerges as the marginal identity to be gazed upon; (2) colonial models of education reproduce the cross-cultural domination of women and girls through conformity to values and ideals embedded in white narratives of educational success; and (3) educational research fails to recognize the key question of difference – that black and minority ethnic girls' experiences and family life are distinct from the white cultural narrative and therefore cannot be measured in relation to it (Mirza 1992). As I have argued elsewhere (Dillabough and Arnot, in press), much of this research analyses the relationship of black families (Phoenix 1987), communities (Mirza and Reay 2000) and black women and girls to capitalism and imperialism (Hill-Collins 1990). In so doing, the Eurocentric and racist elements of a good deal of earlier feminist theorizing have been exposed (Wright *et al.* 1998).

From its inception, black feminist analysis has revealed the ways in which the liberal democratic education project has constructed stereotypes of the 'black girl and boy' (Phoenix 1987; Blair 1995; Blair and Holland 1995). It also went beyond the school context to explore black family life and its impact on the formation of black students' identities. It therefore challenged traditional and stereotypical notions that black girls suffered from problems of self-esteem against an image of the confident, white, middle-class girl. Instead, it highlighted the positive and subversive power of families in shaping young girls' identities (Mirza 1992). It also castigated liberal and Marxist feminist research for focusing too narrowly on a stereotypical view of black youth that often projected 'black failure'.

Mirza's (1992) work was perhaps the most influential in moving mainstream education accounts of 'black female youth and achievement' studies beyond the schooling context. Her purpose was to critique the liberal emphasis on black female achievement and instead highlight the significance of other contextual, cultural and political issues more broadly linked to identity. Her work therefore exposed the importance of school culture and family as important mediators of girls' racialized identities. Black femininity and masculinity could no longer be solely understood on the basis of what many education feminists had referred to as the 'gender binary' – colonial and class distinctions between male and female or the public and private spheres. Alongside the work of others (for example, Blair 1995; Wright *et al.* 1998), Mirza also exposed the racialized and gendered elements of upward social mobility and illustrated how rationalized strategies of school success served only to reinstate the various educational and labour market constraints that black men and women encountered in the workforce.

In recent years, black feminists have been instrumental in defining a new category of educational research on the 'social exclusion' of black and minority ethnic youth. For example, recent gender/race research conducted by Callander and Wright (2000) has moved beyond a concern with 'girls' and 'women' to an engagement with the ways in which working-class black boys and girls are constructed by exclusionary school processes within 'cycles of confrontation and underachievement' (Wright *et al.* 1998: 85). Such processes include the cultural politics of school sanctions and teacher discipline, and the interactive place of race and gender in the formation of exclusionary school hierarchies.

Perhaps the greatest significance of this important body of work lies neither in the image of black girls resisting power structures nor their compliance in conforming to the achievement standards of an educational system. It rests instead on black feminist emphases on the potentially coercive role of external constructions (the colonial narrative, racism) and exclusions in shaping the gendered and racialized pupil. Gender identity within black feminist perspectives thus emerges as a product of social and cultural experience. It is invoked to highlight the communicative and interactive elements of collective, cultural self-understandings. It is understood as culturally contingent yet indispensable for moving beyond the masculine gaze of an education system premised on colonial practices. In highlighting difference, the question of who benefits from gender equity policies moves to the forefront. As Mirza (1992) suggests, this work should not therefore be viewed as an attempt to accommodate the mainstream. It is an attempt to define what Mirza and Reay (2000) have called the 'third space' – not one which is necessarily embedded in the colonialist tension between the public and private spheres, but one which identifies 'other' worlds. These 'other worlds' represent the value of knowledge claims which emerge from a different cultural standpoint. In charting 'other worlds', both the potential and the limits of purportedly liberating gender school reform policies come sharply into focus.

### Gender, markets and educational processes

Another more recent contemporary theme in gender theory and educational research is feminist analyses of 'marketization', or what is sometimes referred to as post-Fordist analysis. A renewed emphasis on the study of educational markets has been ignited by a return to 'class' issues in ways which move beyond locating class within the individual (for example, 'working-class girls') or viewing class solely as divisive (such as class conflict, social stratification). This return to class is instead concerned with the role of market forces in *regulating* education. While some of this research is grounded in poststructuralist theory (regulation, governance), it also serves as a critique of market theory (for example, Hayek 1976) and its influence over the field of education (Ball *et al.* 1992).

In this model of research, there is a shift away from the study of exclusion as an issue of identity towards a concern with *social inequality* in relation to instituted market policies such as examination performance, school choice, achievement and standards in 'an ostensibly open market' (Brown 1997: 394). Much of this work appears to be concerned with a very particular notion of social inequality that unfolds as an interaction between class positioning and market forces, largely at the expense of a study of race and gender (Carter 1997). The impact of marketization on the formation and regulation of identities positioned differently by race, class and gender is therefore an element of this research that deserves greater attention.

The principal actors in analyses of school markets are consumers (students) and workers (teachers, administrators, policy discourse). It is argued that the interactions between these groups reflect the social and global relations (or language) of production. Key questions therefore arise around notions of identity in market school cultures. Recent work by Ball and Gewirtz (1997), for example, has highlighted the importance of seeing school markets as elements of entrepreneurship which view girls not as students with needs but as commodified 'objects and consumers of the market' (Ball and Gewirtz 1997: 208). In the past, women were constructed as symbolic of the private sphere or objectified as sexualized service providers. In this new school context, governed by market policies, girls and women teachers are presented as consumers and rationalized as a commodity.

Post-Fordist theories have also stimulated feminist research which charts the relationship between family life, education and the market. For example, David *et al.*'s (1994) recent work on mothers and school choice and Reay's (1998) research on mothers' involvement in school markets have exposed the gendered nature of 'school choice' as an element of marketization. They have also highlighted the reproduction of traditional ideals and expectations attached to labels such as 'femininity' and 'motherhood' in schools. Other studies examining the marketization of education focus more directly on educational policy as a form of *regulating* women and girls (see Kenway and Epstein 1996). This work has raised important questions about the regulative role of market discourse (rationality, expediency) and the 'new managerialism' in reconfiguring gender hierarchies in diverse educational contexts (Kenway and Epstein 1996; Blackmore 1997; Mahony and Hextall 1997). Education feminism is also beginning to examine the forces of globalization, and their impact on the way gender is viewed in educational policy under the influence of market cultures (Unterhalter 2000).

In summary, this assembly of work has exposed the gendered nature of market forces in the radical restructuring of schools and their impact on girls and women. It examines how 'education markets' and new right politics undermine gender reforms and create novel forms of gender inequality (Ball and Gewirtz 1997; David 2001). At the same time, such research has exposed the novel forms of male rationality found at the basis of new reform policies, school choice and the like (see Dillabough 1999). As a result, the asymmetry between markets, school cultures and gender equity has come more clearly into view. Feminist post-Fordist critiques of education have effectively demonstrated how neo-liberal educational policies mediate both the economy and gender relations in the interests of the global state.

In analyses of this sort, it can be difficult to discern whether the category of identity sustains any conceptual and theoretical relevance. It is worth noting that researchers such as Ball and Gewirtz (1997) might argue that gender inequality – as one element of social inequality – emerges as more significant in post-Fordist approaches, particularly because market policies, rather than identity, loom large. By contrast, it might also be argued that this work precisely exposes the interaction between school policy and identity (Dillabough 1999). It is, in other words, torn between fixed and more permeable understandings of gender identity in the critique of market ideology.

### New gender identifications and theories of social change

Feminist youth studies and the study of social change – what Madeleine Arnot and I have called '*critical modernization* studies' (Dillabough and Arnot 2001) – are two related and ongoing areas of study in gender education research. This work is firmly rooted in more traditional sociological emphases, since its main concerns are with tracking social change and its impact on male and female youth identities. Broadly speaking, this work is concerned with representing, through the study of youth themselves, both the continuities and transformations in gender identity over time.

Beck's (1992) examination of the 'the risk society' and the 'hidden pressures it places on individuals to engage in a process of "reflexive individualization"' (Dillabough and Arnot 2001: 44) appears to be the point of departure for many gender researchers. In such analyses, feminism is seen as only one of many elements of modernity which have transformed male and female identities. Proponents of this view argue that modernity (as a historical period of social change) has provided a more flexible social context for the construction of gender identity, particularly for girls. However, in a fractured moral society where the benefits of modernity (for example, equal opportunity policies) are only accorded to the privileged few, social theorists such as Beck argue that only particular groups of women and men will benefit from such changes. In the 'risk society', the social world becomes increasingly fractured and gaps between the middle and working classes widen.

Much of the research which falls under the category 'youth, gender and social change' suggests that young girls stand at the intersection of a range of highly contradictory messages deriving, in part, from broad economic and social changes and modern transformations in gender relations (Chilsolm and Du Bois Reymond 1993). Such messages highlight, on the one hand, the significance of new patterns of educational attainment, a more flexible and open workforce (Arnot *et al.* 1999), transformations in gender relations and state commitments to the education of women. On the other hand, such messages coexist alongside reductions in social and educational support for particular groups of female youth, the rise in new right social policies and the escalation in national levels of female poverty. Such tensions are seen as key factors contributing to the increasing levels of school/social exclusion experienced by impoverished female youth and the reconfiguration of youth identities in schools (Holland and Weekes 1995; Hey 1997; Dillabough 2001). Research of this kind therefore tracks the contradictory social changes in education and their *differential* impact on female youth identities (Wilkinson 1996).

At the same time, such research also alludes to changes in class structures and their positive impact on the achievement of girls. For example, Chris Mann's (1996, 1998) work on class and educational attainment highlights the key role of shifting family structures in enhancing working-class girls' chances of educational success. These studies point to the movement of working families into higher level income categories through the educational mobility of parents – what could be identified as the social transformation of, or 'intra-class' changes in, the culture of poverty itself. In these studies, families (largely mothers) who ultimately transcend their own class boundaries are seen to place greater pressure upon schools and teachers to encourage working-class girls to persist with education despite the barriers of class positioning.

Another aspect of this work is the study of gender and performance in schools (Arnot *et al.* 1998a, 1999; Francis 2000a). This work is also concerned with broader debates about gender identity theorizing in social theory, although not explicitly so. Largely through social analyses of changing patterns of male and female achievement, it has brought to centre stage the novel ways in which young people identify with and respond to changes in social, political and educational cultures across time. For example, Arnot *et al.'s* (1999) explanatory account of performance patterns tracks the movement from a Victorian model of women's education to the contemporary moment, revealing key forces of social change in the achievement patterns of girls. It highlights the symbolic power of the feminist movement in shaping female identities, exposes intra-class changes in working-class families, reveals subsequent influences on girls' achievement patterns and highlights the restructuring of equal opportunity policies.

Education feminists have also recently concentrated on clarifying the changing nature of gender hierarchies in schools and higher education, and the changing patterns of women teachers' careers and their experiences of exploitation in the workplace (Acker and Feurverger 1997). Such work has therefore revealed both continuities and changes in the social order, and exposed the enduring stability of the gender order in girls' and women's working lives, despite transformations in contemporary gender relations. Education feminists concerned with social change have thus embraced both the old and the new traditions in gender research in education, viewing them in dialectical relation. No exploration of identity, no analysis of social change can be done without an awareness of the other.

In short, what emerges from this work is new gender knowledge about young people's transitions and the gendered processes of identification at work in social change. Simultaneously, however, it has identified the ways in which 'girls' identities are still mediated by the continuing effects of social reproduction (particularly social class inequalities)' (Dillabough and Arnot 2001: 45). At the level of social analysis, the historicity of women and girls' oppression comes clearly into view as an ongoing force in the processes of social change. As Calhoun (1995: 155) suggests, it also addresses precisely those problems identified in social critiques of postmodernist perspectives on identity:

> They [*postmodernists*] address various changes in media . . . the shift from production oriented consumerism to . . . seduction oriented consumerism but they do not address the empirical question of whether in fact social relations, most basically relations of power, are undergoing fundamental transformations – and whether those transformations affect more the systematic character of indirect [*social*] relations.

## Conclusion

Despite the diversity of thinking in the early stages of education feminism, most feminists remained concerned with women's education, the reproduction of gender inequality in schools, women teachers' work and gender equity policies. Since the mid 1980s, however, education feminism has become more explicitly concerned with issues of gender identity, even though 'gender' has been viewed as a social category since the development of the concept by Ann Oakley (1972). My own argument has focused, in part, on the use by education feminists of 'identity' as a conceptual device for transforming the practice of educational research. I have argued that shifts over time in social theory have influenced the ways in which identity has been taken up as both a critique of education in modernity and as a category of analysis. As a result, identity has been deployed in diverse and contesting ways across the different domains of emerging research traditions over the last two decades. It has also been called upon both to sustain traditional theoretical positions and establish new ones.

At the same time, research traditions in the study of gender and education continue to reflect modernist goals such as class and race analyses. The dual properties of much of this research highlight the importance of understanding that while the development of alternative research approaches represented by poststructuralism may involve a paradigmatic shift, they do not necessarily jettison all aspects of the preceding paradigm. Hence, modernist ideals in education feminism (such as gender equity) will persist to the extent that they drive a relevant research agenda, and are likely to be contested when they undermine shifts in other domains of social theory. The process of change in the progress of education feminism is, like change in other domains, a dialectical one producing a synthesis which is not an abrupt break with the past but moves categorically beyond it.

What then can we make of the diversity of trends in the study of gender in education over the last two decades? How, as feminists and scholars who remain concerned with the positioning of women, should we respond to such trends at the level of theory and practice? These are difficult questions to answer in the short term. However, research which embraces the best of both theoretical worlds – modernist and postmodernist/poststructural theories – will be, in my judgement, the most useful in moving forward. But in so doing, we should avoid consumer-oriented and trendy 'pick and choose' approaches that ultimately possess limited theoretical integrity and analytical cohesion. Educational research needs to wrestle with the tensions in feminist theory and attempt to resolve them. As a form of resistance to recent arguments supporting 'value free' approaches (see Foster *et al.* 1996), we also need to struggle over the values and the potential beneficiaries to whom we wish to commit when setting our research agendas. It may be fashionable – as well as realistic – to accept that we ought to live with contradictions in theory and research. But if these contradictions pose serious problems for the groups in whose name we struggle, then our purposes are merely absorbed into an academic and political culture which is no longer relevant to the people it is meant to serve.

What, then, should be the hopes that we entertain as serious researchers in the field of gender and education? In my view, we ought to come to terms with the impasses that are presented to us in social theory in the name of the political issues still at stake in education feminism. It is time now to get beyond gender 'identity' – both the fluid and the stable – not to repress particularity, but in the true spirit of social analysis in education feminism. We need new terms of reference through which to explore the broad range of exciting research topics which have arisen in recent years. Clearly, identity, as a conceptual tool (if we wish to call it that) cannot be used to situate the range of issues which need exploring, particularly if we wish to sustain an emphasis on gender equity in education.

In light of the collapse of recent gender equity school reforms in Australia and the UK (Arnot *et al.* 1999), a sustained focus on the social and political elements of schooling is important. We need to broaden our theoretical vocabulary in the study of gender and education. In so doing, we may explore unknown territory while remaining committed to the role that feminist educational theory ought to play in our work. Without it, we will be ill-equipped to deal with the challenges which lie ahead and deprived of a clear vision of precisely where we hope to go.

## Acknowledgements

I extend my appreciation to Madeleine Arnot and Phil Gardner for their comments on a previous draft of this chapter.

## Notes

1 Some of the material in this section has been informed by previous work with Madeleine Arnot (See Arnot and Dillabough 1999b); Dillabough and Arnot, in press; Dillabough and Arnot 2001).
2 See Connell (1989). While Connell is not typically viewed as a poststructuralist theorist, his work on masculinity has been drawn upon by many educational researchers with an interest in some aspects of poststructural thought.

# 2

# Obvious, all too obvious? Methodological issues in using sex/gender as a variable in educational research

*Martyn Hammersley*

## Introduction

Until the 1970s, when feminism began to have a sustained impact on research in education, comparatively little attention had been given to sex or gender as variables in educational research.[1] At face value, this is puzzling. After all, gender is an obvious variable in human social life. Indeed, it is so obvious, and was treated as so socially significant, that it was long used in the education system as a key organizing principle. In Britain, up to and including much of the twentieth century, girls and boys were often educated separately; and, even when they were not, differentiation by sex was used formally and informally in schools for both curricular and disciplinary purposes. This differentiation was closely related to the idea that the two sexes were quite different in character, and needed contrasting kinds of education to prepare them for very different future lives (see Purvis 1991). And, in fact, it is precisely this assumption, along with treatment of male-dominated areas of life as the most important, which provides a partial explanation (though no justification or excuse) for the relative neglect of gender in social and educational research before the 1970s. The division of sexual labour, and the status hierarchy associated with it, was largely taken for granted – and thereby rendered largely invisible for research purposes – despite the obviousness of, and great social significance attributed to, gender.

In the 1970s attitudes began to change, and, following the lead of feminist researchers, much more educational research began to focus on, or at least took account of, sex differences in educational outcomes and experiences. A major concern at this time was underachievement by, and discrimination against, girls within the education system. While this concern has continued to stimulate research, in recent years public attention has switched to the issue of whether boys are underachieving, and if so, why.[2]

In this chapter I will argue that the 'obviousness' of gender, along with the welcome increase in the recognition of its significance by educational researchers, nevertheless involves some methodological problems and dangers. To illustrate this, I will look first at the issue of sex differences in educational outcomes, and then at the use of gender in explaining the behaviour of pupils.

## Sex inequalities in educational outcomes

Unlike most other key 'face-sheet' variables, including social class and ethnicity, sex seems to be easily operationalizable. In practice, there is usually little disagreement about the fact that the variable is dichotomous, or about the allocation of individuals to one or the other category. We can assign most people routinely, and without much apparent error, to one category or the other on the basis of their appearance, or on the basis of self-report. This is not true of any other social variable of general significance.[3]

One result of this is that the variable has long been included in official educational statistics. Thus, we have information about sex differences in examination performance, and about changes in these over time. For example, we can document achievement levels in 16+ examinations from the 1970s to the 1990s. And, interestingly, these data tell a different story from the one that seems to be implied in some public discussion of sex inequalities in education. It often tends to be assumed that over this period girls started from a position of underachievement, gradually closed the gap, and then overtook boys. Yet we find that, in terms of general performance, girls were already slightly ahead in the mid-1970s, and that the gap has increased since then, with a sharp increase in the late 1980s (see Figure 2.1).

According to these data for England and Wales, in the initial period boys were underachieving compared to girls by 4 percentage points (on average, 96 boys obtained five or more GCSEs at A*–C for every 100 girls). By 1995, the gap was around 19 percentage points (only 81 boys per 100 girls achieved at this level).

However, as Arnot *et al.* (1996, 1998a), Gorard (2000) and others have pointed out, great care needs to be taken in interpreting information of this kind. One important point is that figures which average across school subjects can hide considerable gender variation in performance between subjects. Thus, in the early 1970s, in terms of qualifications achieved, girls did less well on average than boys in mathematics, physics and chemistry, while doing substantially better in English and languages. What happened over the three decades, in part, is that the differences in performance in mathematics and

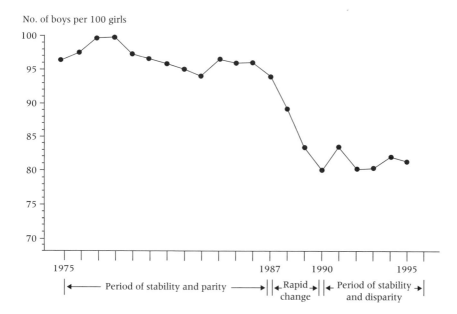

No. of boys per 100 girls

**Figure 2.1** Changing levels of performance at GCE/CSE or GCSE (1975–95): number of boys per 100 girls securing 5+ A*–C grades (England and Wales)

the sciences narrowed substantially, disappeared, or were reversed, while those in English and some other subjects remained stable or increased.

Another respect in which important variation may be hidden concerns different *levels* of achievement. A measure such as securing five or more A*–C grades at GCSE (or SCE Standard Grades 1–3 in Scotland) does not tell us whether the same kind or size of gender gap occurs evenly across all levels of achievement. For example, the data presented in Figure 2.1 would be compatible with more boys than girls getting A* GCSEs; though, in fact, there is no reason to suppose that this is the case.[4]

A third complication is to do with how the numbers of males and females getting particular qualifications are represented. Figure 2.1 used a common metric which separates out the effects of differences between the number of boys and the number of girls taking the examination each year. This is important because the proportions have changed over the period concerned. In the 1970s there were bigger gender gaps in entry at 16+ for particular subjects than in the 1990s. In particular, more boys took mathematics and science GCEs in the earlier period, but the gaps in these subjects have reduced or even been reversed. By contrast, the gap in English literature and modern languages, in favour of girls, has been maintained (see Arnot *et al.* 1996, Ch. 3 and Appendix A on the problems of measuring entry).

Of course, any difference between the sexes in the numbers *entered* for an examination may be of interest in itself, perhaps being treated as inequitable.

**Table 2.1**   Sex differences in performance at GCSE and GCE A level among students taking these examinations at the typical age, 1990/1 and 1997/8 in the UK (figures in thousands)

|  | 1990/1 | | 1997/98 | |
| --- | --- | --- | --- | --- |
|  | *Females* | *Males* | *Females* | *Males* |
| 5 or more GCSEs or equivalent grades A*–C (1–3 in Scotland) | 51 | 49 | 179 | 149 |
| GCE A level, 2 or more passes or equivalent | 76 | 72 | 138 | 116 |

*Source:* DfEE (1999, Table 4.1)

Today, this is an especially significant issue in relation to subjects at A level.[5] Here, we need to measure any entry gap between the sexes as well as any achievement gap. Or, alternatively, we might want to compare the proportion of the relevant age group of girls and boys who obtained a particular qualification, combining entry and achievement gaps, on the grounds that this differential may affect gender patterns in future recruitment to high level occupational positions.

There is another important problem involved in documenting trends in the relative educational performance of the sexes over time, to do with changes in the number of pupils of *both* sexes entering an examination or achieving at a particular level (see Gorard *et al.* 1999). In order to illustrate this I want to examine some recent trend data for achievement at 16+ and 18+ in the UK (see Table 2.1).

Looking at this table, it is not difficult to see that there was an achievement gap at both levels in 1990/1, with females scoring higher. Furthermore, the gap seems to have increased over the course of the 1990s. In 1990/1 11,000 more girls than boys got five or more GCSEs at level C (Scottish equivalent, Level 3) or above; and 4000 more girls got two or more A level passes or equivalent. In 1997/8 the figures were 30,000 more girls and 22,000 more girls, respectively. In other words, the gender gap grew by 19,000 pupils at GCSE and by 18,000 pupils at A level.

However, we need to take account of the fact that the overall number of young people entered for and succeeding in examinations at these levels has changed considerably over the period concerned. Indeed, in the case of GCSE, the numbers of pupils achieving at the level measured has more than tripled; and there has also been a substantial increase at A level. This fact has important implications for measuring the gender gap. Some of the change here – calculated in terms of *numbers* of boys and girls succeeding at the two levels – simply reflects this overall growth, rather than any change in the *relative* performance of boys and girls.[6]

**Table 2.2** Sex differences (as percentages) in performance at GCSE and GCE A level among students taking these examinations at the typical age, 1990/1 and 1997/8 in the UK (data derived from Table 2.1)

|  | 1990/1 | | | 1997/8 | | |
|---|---|---|---|---|---|---|
|  | *Females* | *Males* | *Gap* | *Females* | *Males* | *Gap* |
| 5 or more GCSEs or equivalent grades A*–C (1–3 in Scotland) | 56 | 44 | +12 | 55 | 45 | +10 |
| GCE A level, 2 or more passes or equivalent | 51 | 49 | +2 | 54 | 46 | +8 |

One way of eliminating this factor is by calculating the gap between girls and boys relative to the overall numbers who achieved at the relevant level in each year. Doing this, we get Table 2.2.

Controlling for the increases in the overall number of pupils succeeding at each level, we now find that the gender gap at GCSE/standard grade in 1990/1 was 12 per cent, whereas in 1997/8 it was 10 per cent. In other words, it has actually narrowed. By contrast, at A level/higher grade it was 2 per cent in 1990/1 but was 8 per cent in 1997/8. So, on this measure, the gap between boys and girls has reduced in the first case, but has widened in the second.

One final technical point. There is a danger that we will misunderstand the nature of these changes unless we distinguish between percentage point gaps and percentage changes in these gaps. Thus, what has happened at the GCSE/standard grade level is not a 2 per cent but a 17 per cent reduction in the gender gap.[7] And in the case of A level/higher grade the difference of 6 percentage points between 1990/1 and 1997/8 represents a 300 per cent increase. (Of course, despite these differences in the direction and size of change, the gender gap is still bigger at the GCSE/standard grade level, in percentage point terms.)

As if all this were not enough, there are several further cautions that need to be observed in interpreting data about gender gaps; this time not about how these are calculated but about more substantive issues. The first issue concerns what is actually measured by examination achievement. It is tempting to assume that this represents the quality of the education that pupils have 'received'.[8] However, while there may be a relation between the two, they are not the same. After all, if you ask people what they see as the priority in a good education, you are likely to find considerable variation in response. And while examination performance may measure *some* of these priorities reasonably well, it will not measure them all. For example, we might argue that the most important function of education is to prepare children to be good citizens. Performance in 16+ and 18+ examinations does not seem likely to be an effective measure of how well pupils are being educated in this sense. Indeed, even if there were an examination in citizenship, it is not clear that performance in this would measure good citizenship, since an important element of citizenship is attitudinal and behavioural, and the examination is unlikely to measure this well. Moreover, there are different views about what 'good citizenship' entails.

Sometimes, what examination results are taken to measure is life chances: the chances of obtaining high income, high social status and perhaps 'high powered' jobs. But this is not necessarily the same as getting a 'good education'. Furthermore, the relationship between examination success and occupational destination is not a simple and strong one (see Foster *et al.* 1996: 156–9). Indeed, in the face of current public concern over male underachievement in education, some feminists have pointed out that females' relatively high level of educational success does not seem to have translated into a similarly high level of success in occupational recruitment (see, for example, Epstein *et al.* 1998: 10).

Another point is that aggregate figures about the achievement levels of females and males hide variation within each category, and the considerable overlap that exists between the two distributions. Moreover, some of the internal variation will be associated with other causal factors, such as social class and ethnicity. While it is tempting to focus on single variable contrasts in educational outcomes, and for some purposes this may be sufficient, the multi-variable complexity of reality must never be forgotten.

The final point to be made is that differences among the sexes in educational outcomes are not *in themselves* inequitable. A difference is a matter of fact; an inequity is a matter of value. Yet, in the education literature, the term 'inequality' is often used in ways that automatically imply inequity (Foster *et al.* 2000). This is one effect, it seems to me, of the fact that most researchers in this area are strongly committed to the reduction or elimination of 'inequalities', tending to assume that *any* differences are obviously inequitable, and thereby ignoring the need to make clear the value assumptions on which their judgements are based. For example, it is often assumed that a lower number of girls achieving qualifications in mathematics and science at 18+ represents an inequity. Yet, while this is true on the basis of *some* conceptions of social justice, it is not in terms of *others*.[9] Furthermore, part of this inequality is an entry gap resulting from choices made by pupils themselves; and while these choices are open to evaluation, criticism of them needs to be made explicit and justified if the value judgement is to be convincing.

Furthermore, value assumptions are often closely related to what is and is not taken into account in discussions of sex differences in educational outcomes. Thus, whether the difference in numbers of boys and girls obtaining A levels in mathematics and science is an inequity depends, partly, on whether or not one assumes that there are systematic (albeit probabilistic) differences across the sexes in abilities relevant to these subjects, and whether these differences should be allowed for in judging equity. This issue arises in other areas too. Girls usually perform better than boys on reading tests,

and this may reflect inherent differences – for example, in speed of matura-
tion. Again, we might argue that such differences, if they exist, should be
taken into account when judging whether the education system is treating
the sexes equitably; or, alternatively, we could argue that the education
system needs to compensate for these differences, or that it should change
the mode of assessment to eliminate their effect. However, such arguments
need supporting justification.

In summary, then, any broad generalization about 'the gender gap in educational achievement' is likely to be misleading. This is not to suggest that
there is no problem with boys' achievement levels, or that there are not continuing problems with girls' educational achievement. Rather, the point is
that in any analysis careful specification is required of what is being compared,
for what purpose, and in relation to what value standard. As a result of
research in this field, we now know quite a lot about the pitfalls involved in
interpreting data about sex differences in educational outcome.

## Explaining pupil experience and behaviour in terms of gender

The second area I want to look at is the use of sex as a variable in explaining
what is going on in educational settings, and especially in explaining pupil
behaviour. In the 1950s and 60s much study of the education system was pre-
occupied with social class differences. Not only were class differences in
*outcomes* the main focus, but, in examining the structure and process of the
education system, social class was often taken to be the key variable. In the
case of pupils' behaviour in schools, as feminists have pointed out, researchers
tended to study male pupils, even while presenting claims as if these applied
across the sexes. In other words, gender was largely ignored.[10] Since then, as I
noted earlier, a great deal of work has been done which *does* make sex a focal
variable, and this includes study of pupils' experience in schools. At the same
time, interest in other variables, especially social class and ethnicity, has not
been abandoned. Indeed, there has been some consideration of how their
effects are interrelated with those of gender, one key area being the experience of African-Caribbean girls (see Fuller 1980; Mirza 1992, 1995a) (see also
Chapter 9). Nevertheless, there are some serious methodological problems
in identifying the role of gender (and of other variables) in generating pupil
behaviour.

To illustrate this, I will look at a brief extract from an important article by
Measor (1999), in which she looked back at research she did in the 1980s
on the movement of pupils from middle school to high school (Measor and
Woods 1984). In this article Measor examines the data collected about the
behaviour of boys in the classroom and elsewhere, applying some of the
results of feminist theorizing about masculinity. Here is an extract from her
discussion:

> Other joking behaviour we witnessed seemed to be intended to bid for
> control over a classroom setting:

A teacher explained a mathematical theory. She explained it very thoroughly and it meant she occupied the centre stage for a long time. She finished brightly:

*Teacher:* So you could go on doing the square of numbers for ever and ever and ever.
*David:* Amen

His timing was perfect and the class collapsed into sustained laughter, after which it was difficult for the teacher to restore the situation. (Measor and Woods 1984, p. 112)

The boy shouted the joke loudly in the classroom, and it was sufficiently amusing to the rest of the class that the teacher's control of the pace of teaching was disturbed and she could not carry on with what she wanted to say. Research like that of Hargreaves (1967) and Willis (1977) has suggested that disorganizing classroom processes is one of the objectives which at least some boys have in the classroom. Their research was more directly concerned with social class than with masculinity, but their data can be reinterpreted to offer insight into gender issues too. Arnot suggests that proving masculinity, 'may require frequent rehearsals of toughness, the exploitation of women and quick aggressive responses' (1984: 46). Much of the boys' behaviour fits this blueprint, and can be understood as the public performance of masculine themes.

(Measor 1999: 181)

Measor (1999: 181–2) notes how some previous researchers have tended to valorize this kind of disruptive behaviour on the part of boys, treating it as representing working-class resistance to social class oppression:

A feminist approach throws a more negative light on what is going on, and indicates that we need to ask searching questions about the processes by which masculine identities develop and their implications for the construction of male power and patriarchy. These no doubt interweave with social class in complex patterns.

There is a great deal to be said for Measor's argument here. There was a tendency on the part of many researchers in the past to interpret the behaviour of pupils almost entirely in terms of social class differences. And, in many cases, there was a valorization of disruptive behaviour as 'resistance' (on this tendency, see Hargreaves 1982). Measor's discussion provides an important corrective to this. But it seems to me that the main problem with earlier explanations, in terms of social class, was that they were often speculative: they were not systematically tested. And there may be a danger of simply replacing them with a similarly speculative approach based on gender. Indeed, what I referred to earlier as the obviousness of sex may encourage this. Thus, indicating that the pupil who said 'Amen' was a boy (and providing no other information about him), and indicating that the teacher was female (and providing no other information about her) may itself encourage us to jump to the conclusion that sex is the key variable in this incident.[11] Yet these two people had many other unmentioned identities and characteristics, some of which could be relevant to explaining the incident.

Indeed, looking closely at this example, a couple of points can be made. First, what David says is not *obviously* intended as a challenge to the teacher's authority. While it takes off from something she says, it does not reflect negatively on this, at least not in any straightforward way. Nor, second, is the humour directed at her identity as a woman.[12] So, it is not clear *from its content* that this utterance is either challenging or gender based; though, of course, it may nevertheless have had these characteristics.

One obvious way of trying to assess the extent to which gender is the cause of particular types of classroom action is to categorize these in ways that aim to capture their nature but do not pre-judge their explanation, and then to look at their relative frequency across the sexes. If there were systematic sex differences in key types of classroom disruption, as there may well be, we would have more grounds for concluding that gender is a key factor, especially if there does not seem to be similar variation across other competing explanatory categories.

However, even if we found a correlation, we would still need to be cautious. The fact that in aggregate terms boys engage in disruptive actions more frequently than girls would not establish that gender is the prime cause.[13] We would need to examine the proportions of boys and girls who engage in these actions. It may be that it is a *minority* of boys rather than the majority who do this, and that some girls engage in these activities as well. If so, then we need to consider whether there is some third factor, or set of factors, which is the cause – such as levels of confidence in public contexts, levels of aggressiveness, interaction between gender, social class, and forms of pedagogy etc. We could also look at the targets of disruptive acts in terms of gender, not just at their sources. Is cross-sex disruption (especially boys against female teachers) more common than same-sex disruption? In short, before we can be sure about the validity of Measor's explanation, as presented in the brief extract I quoted, we need to find ways of judging it in relation to competing hypotheses.[14]

Moreover, these analytic strategies lead us to more fundamental questions about the conceptualization of sex/gender: How far does any explanation of pupils' classroom behaviour in terms of gender rely on an essentialist conception of that variable? If we are appealing to how children have been 'gendered' through socialization, or even to how they construct gender identities through social interaction, can this be separated from biological differences? And are those differences to be treated as given, at least for the purposes of social analysis; or should they themselves be seen as discursive constructions?[15]

There are also difficult questions about the relationship between sex/gender and other variables. For example, some male pupils may react antagonistically to particular male teachers, labelling them as effeminate. Here, perhaps, we have gender operating as a variable through different versions of masculinity, ones that are structured as hegemonic and subordinate (Connell 1987). Equally, though, we might see such antagonism, even if expressed in gender terms, as reflecting a particular view of power, which treats it as only properly exercised by those who have authoritative personal character- istics, rather than merely occupying formal office.[16] More specifically, for some pupils, perhaps especially for some working-class pupils, it may be that teachers are only to be respected if they can demonstrate the kind of 'personality' that would give them high status in the pupils' peer group or in the local community culture (see Dubberley 1988). This might lead to some gender difference overall in terms of the prevalence of disruption, as regards both source and target; but, even if it did, the result is unlikely to be clear- cut. Moreover, we might argue that gender is not central to the causal process involved, even though it is implicated in it. My point, however, is simply that much depends on how we are conceptualizing this variable and its relations with others.

In summary, there is no doubt that sex/gender is an important factor affect- ing pupils' behaviour. But we must be careful not to allow its obviousness to lead us into exaggerating its role; to overlook the problems involved in pro- viding convincing evidence for explanations employing it; or to forget the difficult issues surrounding its conceptualization.

## Conclusion

In this chapter I have outlined some methodological problems involved in investigating gender as a factor in educational outcomes and processes. In relation to outcomes, I discussed the various complexities we face in identify- ing gender gaps in performance, and in evaluating these as inequities. In the second section of the chapter I looked at the use of gender in explaining the behaviour of pupils in school, arguing that there are some difficult issues to be tackled in drawing sound conclusions about this.

Right at the beginning I acknowledged how the largely unconscious assumptions of predominantly male educational researchers in the past had shaped the research they carried out, leading to a relative neglect of sex and gender as a variable. I want to end by emphasizing that it is still possible today to be led astray by our assumptions and commitments. One example may be the rush, on the part of some commentators, to declare that there is a major crisis of male underachievement in schools, and to produce specula- tive explanations for it. Another could be the reaction of those, including some feminists, who down-play the issue of male underachievement by label- ling it as the product of a 'moral panic', or explain it in ways that they would not countenance in the case of girls.[17] In this field of inquiry, as in all others, unbiased attention to methodological issues is required – even though it may be difficult for any of us to achieve this, and impossible for us to know with certainty that we have done so.

## Acknowledgements

I am grateful to Madeleine Arnot, Sara Delamont, Stephen Gorard, Lynda Measor, Chris Skelton and Peter Woods for comments on an earlier draft of this chapter.

## Notes

1 I will use the terms 'sex' and 'gender' interchangeably throughout most of the chapter. On the neglect of sex and gender in educational research before feminist work in the 1970s, see for instance Acker (1981).
2 For discussions of how the issue of boys' underachievement arose, see Mahony (1997) and Delamont (1999).
3 This is not to say that there are no conceptual problems involved in sex/gender as a variable, or to deny that these raise doubts about its easy operationalization. See Kessler and McKenna (1978), Davies (1989) and Hood-Williams (1996). See also Chapter 4.
4 The detailed data presented for Wales by Gorard *et al.* (1999) show that this is not the case there: that girls outperform boys at the highest levels.
5 Arnot *et al.* (1998a: 15–16) show that substantial sex differences remain in choice of A-level subject in England and Wales, and that these have increased in the case of male-dominated subjects.
6 This factor was also eliminated by the metric deployed by Arnot *et al.* (1998a) used in Figure 2.1.
7 Calculated as 2 per cent divided by 12 per cent, multiplied by 100, and rounded up. For the significance of the distinction between percentage points and percentage changes in this context, see Gorard (1999, 2000).
8 I have put quotation marks around 'received' because the very idea that education is a good which can be distributed or delivered is questionable.
9 On diverse interpretations of equity, see Hammersley (1996).
10 There were exceptions, of course. One is the work of Lambart (1976, 1982, 1997).
11 In their 1984 book, Measor and Woods' analysis places explanatory emphasis on the other identity-pair indicated in the extract: teacher and pupil.
12 We can contrast this example with a widely cited one in Walkerdine (1981), where nursery-age boys challenge a teacher using language which can be read as positioning her as a woman, through references to underwear. For a useful critical discussion of this example, see Mackinnon (1984).
13 Just as the fact that, in aggregate terms, they may get more attention does not show that gender is the key factor producing this. See Hammersley (1990).
14 Note that the points I have made here about what would be required to show the effect of gender on pupil behaviour apply to the use of any other causal factor, including social class. Also, I must emphasize that other examples are discussed in Measor's article – I have concentrated on one example here simply for the purpose of illustrating the problem; a problem which faces all researchers working in this area.
15 For example, Hood-Williams (1996) treats the obviousness of sex differences as a cultural-historical product, and challenges the conventional distinction between sex and gender, arguing that we are dealing with a single phenomenon which cannot be separated out into cultural and biological elements. Moreover, with

Cealey Harrison, he argues that sex differences are discursively constructed, and made relevant, differentially across contexts (see Cealey Harrison and Hood-Williams 1998).

16  This is one possible interpretation of the attitude of Willis' (1977) 'lads' to authority.

17  For example, by using explanations that are open to the charge of blaming the victim. For a study which shows signs of both these tendencies, see Kenway and Willis (1998). At one point they comment: ' "Strutting and fretting" at the centre of the gender reform stage in the mid-1990s is the "under-achieving boy" ' (p. 47).

*Part 2* | Recent developments in gender theory

# 3

# Using poststructuralist ideas in gender theory and research

*Carrie Paechter*

## Introduction

In recent years, poststructuralist ideas have become increasingly important to researchers and scholars working in the field of gender and education. They have had a wide influence, particularly in terms of ways of interpreting and theorizing about gender research, with a lesser impact on data collection foci and methods. In this chapter I want to explore some of the reasons that I use poststructuralist approaches, and how they have influenced my thinking about the nature of gender.

## What is poststructuralism?

I will start by examining what is meant by 'poststructuralism'. There is a wide range of poststructuralisms in the same way as there are a variety of feminisms, but they do have a number of features in common. First, there is the importance given, within the social sciences at least, to the concept of discourse. A discourse is a way of speaking, thinking or writing that presents particular relationships as self-evidently true. Because such 'truths' are presented as unchallengeable, this means that, within a particular discourse, only certain things can be said or thought; to challenge these assumptions is to step outside the discourse. Another way of putting this is to see discourses as 'socially organized frameworks of meaning that define categories and specify domains of what can be said and done' (Burman 1994: 2).

Discourses are important because they structure the ways in which we can think about things. Because they are treated as, and appear to be, self-evidently a reflection of 'reality', they can remain unchallenged, prescribing for us what is 'normal' or 'natural' behaviour, and penalizing those who attempt to challenge or step outside them:

> It is not enough to say that science is a set of procedures by which propositions may be falsified, errors demonstrated, myths demystified, etc. Science also exercises power: it is, literally, a power that forces you to say certain things, if you are not to be disqualified not only as being wrong, but, more seriously than that, as being a charlatan.
>
> (Foucault 1988: 107)

The centrality of discourse to poststructuralist thinking brings with it an emphasis on the role of language 'It is in language that our subjectivity as well as social organizations are defined, contested and constructed' (Weiner 1994: 99). However, this comes with two caveats. First, the location of the meaning of any statement has moved away from simply reflecting the intentions of the author. Meaning is constructed, instead, in the relations between the originator of a statement, the language in which it is expressed, the discourse of which it forms a part, and the understandings of those who read/ hear and interpret it. Thus when reading a text, for example, it is the contextual interpretation that is key, not the intention of the author. This can of course be somewhat scary for authors (myself included) but it is potentially very empowering for readers, who are thus enabled to take from a text what is useful and important to them, even if this is not central to the author's focus or intentions.

Second, the effects of language range far beyond the purely linguistic; the discourses in which we operate affect how we behave at a very visceral and physical level. Discourses, for example, can be inscribed on the body – that is to say, the ways in which bodies are used reflect the discourses in which that use takes place (Shilling 1993). For example, the discourse of the good quiet girl, instantiated for example in the widely held belief that girls are less boisterous than boys from birth, actively constrains the ways in which young girls are able to use their bodies. The discourse contains within it a view of the 'normal' girl child which controls the way the child uses her body by drawing attention to instances of deviance – and this happens through language. Expressions of surprise at a girl's adventurousness, or the use of descriptions like 'tomboy', position as 'abnormal' those young girls who use their bodies actively; in order to be seen as 'normal' a girl has to act in conformity with the assumptions of the discourse (thus reinforcing the taken for granted assumption that these gender differences are 'natural'). These constraints on bodily use in themselves shape both the young female body itself (it becomes comparatively less fit and strong) and also the range of movement available to that body within the normalizing discourse of gender difference.

Furthermore, discourses are intimately involved with power relations; one is not free simply to choose which discourse one wishes to operate in. Some discourses are more powerful than others. This is partly a historical phenomenon. For example, from the period of the Enlightenment in the eighteenth century to the middle of the twentieth century and beyond, discourses of reason and rationality have dominated western thought to the extent that other ways of seeing the world have taken on pejorative connotations that have an almost moral force. Positioned as self-evidently positive by Enlightenment discourses, they have as their opposites a pair of terms which carry the marks of chaos and disorder: unreason and irrationality. To question the power of reason thus becomes an act of moral degeneracy, not dispassionate (another loaded Enlightenment word) debate.

In arguing that discourses are intimately bound up with power relations, I am treating power itself in a particular manner. Following Foucault, I see power as relational, as operating in a network-like fashion throughout the social world, inscribed in our social formations, the language we use and the ways we move. Power in this formulation does not emanate from one source, and cannot be held by any one individual or group. It is everywhere, in our institutions, our ways of being and the spaces we inhabit: 'Power is not something that is acquired, seized, or shared, something that one holds on to or allows to slip away; power is exercised from innumerable points, in the interplay of nonegalitarian and mobile relations' (Foucault 1978: 94).

Furthermore, it is in the action of discourse to constrain what can be regarded as 'true' that power and knowledge are inextricably bound together (Foucault 1978). Different forms of discourse result in the prioritizing of different forms of knowledge; change the power relations between discourses and the knowledge relations associated with them will change as well. Consequently, both particular power/knowledge relations and particular discourses have to be seen as constantly shifting and contested.

A key aspect of power seen in this way is that it is conceived of as coming from below, from the small local interactions between individuals and groups, within, and in opposition to, dominant discourses. At the same time, resistance is seen as being inseparable from power; wherever there are power relations, there are also relations of resistance: 'These points of resistance are present everywhere in the power network. Hence there is no single locus of great Refusal, no soul of Revolt, source of all rebellions, or pure law of the revolutionary. Instead there is a plurality of resistances, each one of them a special case' (Foucault 1978: 95–6).

This constant interaction of power and resistance is a particularly important but sometimes ignored aspect of Foucault's thinking about power. His work has sometimes been read as suggesting that our analyses of powerful discourses should be dispassionate and neutral (Said 1986; Fraser 1989; Hartsock 1990; Soper 1993a), and it is the case that his own writing often comes across in this way. However, the salience of resistance in Foucault's conceptualization of power allows us both to retain a place for human agency with respect to power relations, and to see how the deconstruction of discourses is an important aspect of and precursor to the construction of resistant counterdiscourses:

> We can never be ensnared by power; we can always modify its grip in determinate conditions and with a precise strategy.
>
> (Foucault 1988a: 123)

> The resistant subject is one that refuses to be scripted by the dominant discourse and turns instead to subjugated knowledges to fashion alternative discourses of subjectivity.
>
> (Hekman 1995: 84)

This view of power and resistance as inseparable, locally acting and constantly shifting, has fairly direct implications – for example, for how we see feminist action. It means on the one hand that there is no real possibility of a wholesale gender revolution in which the present order will be turned upside down and women will be, if not in the ascendancy, at least treated equally with men in social and political arenas. On the other hand it means that the small local resistances practised by many feminists – such as bringing up our sons to be more gentle than their fathers, challenging male dominance in our personal and workplace relationships, complaining about advertising posters that exploit women – do have importance in working towards changes in gender relations in society as a whole. Although change is slow, it does happen, and we can all take part in supporting it, wherever and whoever we may be.

Poststructuralism has a further key feature, which it shares with its cousin postmodernism: a stance of 'incredulity towards metanarratives' (Lyotard 1979: xxiv). Metanarratives are the all-embracing explanatory concepts favoured by Enlightenment thought and associated with the perception of power as located in particular structures, groups or individuals; examples include capitalism, patriarchy and reason. These metanarratives tell big, explanatory stories about the world as a whole. Poststructuralism, by contrast, is focused on small, local stories about specific discourses and power relations. The distrust of metanarratives can be problematic (some poststructuralist feminists have regrets – for example, about the loss of patriarchy as an explanatory concept) but it brings with it the benefits of challenging what are extremely powerful discourses that structure many of the common-sense ways we think about the world. In particular, the resistance to meta-narratives makes possible a challenge to dominant discourses of reason and rationality, which privilege ways of thinking and behaving traditionally associated with masculinity over those traditionally regarded as inhabiting the realm of the feminine (Paechter 1998a, 2000).

Finally, and related to this challenging of traditional masculine/feminine divisions, is the emphasis that Foucault-derived poststructuralism places on the body, embodiment and discourses of bodily uses and forms. Traditional Enlightenment thought has largely ignored the body; indeed, the mind/ body distinction stretches back as far as Descartes, one of its main founding fathers. By challenging the dominance of discourses of reason over those of emotion, poststructuralist thinkers have made a space for the discussion of the physical, visceral and emotional as important factors both in power/

knowledge relations and in our thinking about the world more generally. For me this is a particularly important feature of poststructuralist thought and one on which I will focus for most of the remainder of this chapter.

### Why use poststructuralist ideas in gender research?

Taking a poststructuralist approach to research concerned with gender brings with it a number of implications, some of which are more beneficial than others. An initial issue is the centrality of the text to poststructuralist thought. This can mean a number of things for gender and education research. One important effect is that it focuses attention on the ways in which curriculum texts are produced, used and interpreted. Hawkes (1977) points out that a text can be treated as either 'readerly' or 'writerly'. When a reader treats a text as 'readerly', she or he remains passively oriented towards it, reads the text 'straight' and does not make any attempt to interpret it. Treating a text as 'writerly', by contrast, involves creative interpretation, making the text one's own and relating it to other experiences. Clearly, whether a teacher or group of teachers treat a curriculum text in a 'readerly' or 'writerly' fashion can be very important for what actually takes place in the classroom and whether official curriculum documents are seen as a strait-jacket or a flexible basis for planning (Bowe *et al.* 1992). Approaching teachers' responses to curriculum texts in this way in my own research has enabled me to see how creative interpretations of texts, presented as if they were pure readerly accounts, have been used in gendered debates between teachers about curriculum content and form (Paechter 1993).

The focus on text does, however, have its problems. Poststructuralism has its origins in literary theory, so it is not surprising that the text and textuality are so important to the initial formulations of the approach. When applied elsewhere, though, it is not clear why textuality should be so central. Do we have to see a body as a text, for example – as something that is simply created by discourse (Shilling 1993)? While it does seem to me to be the case that how we experience our bodies is fundamentally affected by the discourses that surround the physical aspects of gender, it remains the case that gender is attributed to others on the basis of physical forms and signs, and lived, at least in part, through one's particular embodiment. Similarly, it may be stretching the idea of the text to treat physical space as a text within a discourse, and we may instead want to find other ways of treating space, time and our relationship to these.

Centrally important to the ways in which I use poststructuralist ideas is the Foucauldian approach to power and the power/knowledge relation. This is because once power is seen as distributed, inhering in relations between people and groups, it becomes clear that there is no knowledge that lies outside power relations. This in turn has implications for the way we regard areas of knowledge for which, and through which, power has been claimed, because of their purported abstract nature. Once we have drawn attention to the contingent nature of the power associated with, for example, mathematical knowledge or particular forms of moral thought, we are then able to consider what would be the case if we did not treat these forms as powerful, and what the alternatives might mean for gender relations. What this has meant in my own work is that I have looked at the historical origins of the primacy of certain forms of knowledge such as mathematics, both within the education system and in society more generally, and at the gendered power/knowledge relations with which they are associated. This has allowed me to challenge both the primacy of decontextualized knowledge within education systems and the concomitant association of these forms of knowledge with hegemonic masculinity (Connell 1995). This in turn has led me to look at curriculum history in ways which take into account prevailing power/knowledge relations in wider society and the ways in which these have been used to prevent girls and young women from taking full advantage of educational opportunities (Paechter 1998a, 2000).

Foucauldian poststructuralism, because of its emphasis on the distributed and resisted nature of power, also forces us to focus on the ways in which power operates, and in particular on the ways in which we are ourselves seduced into accepting what are in some respects oppressive power relations. Power is not simply oppressive; we are caught in its networks precisely because some aspects of the exercise and experience of power are profoundly pleasurable (Foucault 1980). Power is bound up with our desire – the desire to know and to understand: 'Power is pleasurable. It is the triumph of reason over emotion, the fictional power over the practices of everyday life' (Walkerdine 1988: 186).

This way of looking at power can clearly be very illuminating when we come to consider gendered power relations. It can help us to see why some aspects of gendered behaviour persist despite their otherwise disempowering nature. For example, teenage girls have a tendency to reject physical education as part of an assertion of femininity, something that is clearly prejudicial to their health and well-being. However, from the girls' point of view, there are benefits in the assertion of femininity through this means – not least that their bodies will remain more stereotypically feminine in shape and their heterosexual orientation will be (however mistakenly) taken for granted, in contrast to common (and equally as often mistaken) assumptions about the lesbianism of female athletes (Lenskyj 1987; Coles 1994–5).[1]

Emphasis on the distributed nature of power also makes it clear that institutions and practices may be simultaneously repressive and liberating in their operation. Foucault (1997) illustrates this most clearly by tracing the development of the prison, from an institution whose prime function was to punish, and which was therefore extremely brutal, into one with a much greater emphasis on prisoner reform and rehabilitation. While this seems a clearly beneficial change, in as much as it has meant that prisoners' lives have become generally pleasanter and punishments less painful, it has brought with it increased intrusion into the inner workings of the prisoner's minds. The punishment view of imprisonment set a tariff; once the offender had paid the price that was all there was to the situation. As the emphasis changed towards ideas of reform, prisoners were increasingly kept under surveillance, with a view to gauging the length of the sentence according to whether the prisoner was deemed to have repented and reformed. This approach to prisoner release dates remains part of the UK system for those offenders who have been sent to special hospitals; they are only released when deemed 'cured'. In a parallel way, the distributive nature of power leads us to look at educational innovations in terms both of their obvious benefits and of their less visible 'disbenefits'. For example, moves by some schools to give value to aspects of students' out-of-school lives by including them in Records of Achievement are used very positively to build bridges between school and non-school achievement. At the same time, however, such developments mean that an increased amount of a student's private life is subject to the disciplinary gaze of the school, something that can be to the detriment of individuals, particularly those whose pastimes do not conform to school expectations (Paechter 2000). Furthermore, it is by examining some of these comparatively small aspects of educational practice and change that the dominant discourses in education are uncovered. Foucauldian poststructuralism gives us a way of approaching discourses that have so thoroughly entered our 'thinking-as-usual' (Schutz 1964) that they are not only unchallenged but unseen. It enables us to uncover the hidden workings of gendered power/knowledge relations, and therefore to challenge them.

## Embodiment and the performance of gender

In the rest of this chapter I want to focus in more detail on how this approach to discourses helps us to interrogate gender, and particularly gender identity and gender role behaviour.

There is a long-standing distinction, which I use here for convenience, between sex, gender assignment, gender identity and gender role (Kessler and McKenna 1978). *Sex* refers to matters of biology. Although how we understand these is culturally constructed, a person's sex is usually taken to be a matter of biological fact, and manifested in particular hormonal configurations, bodily forms etc. *Gender assignment*, at its most salient and forceful, occurs at birth and is based on perceived physical characteristics. However, we all assign gender, all the time, to the people we meet; we do this so unconsciously that we only notice ourselves doing it when we make a 'mistake' or when someone presents themselves to us sufficiently ambiguously for us to have to weigh up the probabilities. Gender assignment is usually, though not always, aligned with (some definition of) biological sex. *Gender identity* refers to a person's own feelings about their gender – whether they are male, female, both or neither. This may be different to their assigned gender. It is something privately experienced; the only way to establish someone's gender identity is to ask them (Money and Ehrhardt 1972; Kessler and McKenna 1978). Finally, *gender role* refers to a set of behavioural prescriptions or proscriptions for individuals who have a particular assigned gender. These will vary between cultures (Money and Ehrhardt 1972; Kessler and McKenna

1978; Whitehead 1981; Nicholson 1994). In order to distinguish gender role from the other three, I will talk about masculinity and femininity in this context – though this should not be taken to mean that I hold any sort of essentialist notions about these concepts.

If we take a poststructuralist view of gender, we can see that masculinity and femininity are discourses which are imbued with power/knowledge relations and act upon individuals within particular societies. What this means is that how individual males and females behave involves an enactment of their gender roles, as interpreted by them in their social context and as constrained by their experiences of their bodies. What we need then to consider is how discourses of masculinity and femininity are constructed and maintained, and how they support and are supported by power/knowledge relations.

The distinctions between masculinity and femininity that are current today have their roots, like so much else, in Enlightenment thought. They are built around a series of parallel dualisms that were seen as particularly important in the eighteenth and nineteenth centuries but whose effects remain today. These dualisms are deeply implicated in gendered power/knowledge relations, aligning themselves with and underpinning the distinction between masculinity and femininity. They include participation in civil society versus rootedness in hearth and home, hardness versus softness, activity versus passivity, reason versus emotion and transcendence versus embodiment. They are summed up in a passage from Tennyson's poem *The Princess,* published in 1847:

> . . . but this is fixt
> As are the roots of earth and base of all;
> Man for the field and woman for the hearth:
> Man for the sword and for the needle she:
> Man with the head and woman with the heart:
> Man to command and woman to obey:
> All else confusion.

Although we do not consciously believe these sentiments, and indeed may well find some of them somewhat ridiculous, they still underpin the way we perceive, act out and encourage the take-up of gender identities and roles. In saying this I am not just recognizing that many men do believe that they should command and their wives obey, although this unfortunately remains the case. The influences of these roles linger on very concretely in the ways in which male and female babies and children are treated. Smith and Lloyd (1978), for example, studied how a baby's perceived gender affected how he or she was treated by adults. Thirty-two mothers of babies between 5 and 10 months old were given an unknown 6-month old baby to play with for ten minutes. The babies (both males and females) were presented by their own mothers and given a name that reflected the clothing they were wearing but not necessarily their biological sex. It was found that the mothers interacted with 'boys' and 'girls' differently. For example, 'boys' were given more encouragement to crawl, walk or engage in other large-scale physical action than were 'girls', and gross motor behaviour[2] of the infant was responded to with whole body stimulation more often with perceived boys than with perceived girls. This suggests not only that a child's gender assignment leads parents and others to modify their behaviour in particular ways and from a very early age, but also that these differences in the ways in which boys and girls are treated reflect some of the supposedly defunct Enlightenment distinctions between masculinity and femininity, such as the idea that males are more active than females.

The salience of these dichotomies in underpinning discourses of gender role can also be demonstrated when we look at manifestations of masculinity and femininity that are transgressive in some way, and particularly at those in which transgression cuts across dominant gendered distributions of power. Female bodybuilders, for example, clearly do not conform to the stereotypical soft, gentle and weak feminine bodily presentation. Their bodies are hard, their muscles developed, their postures far from girly. The transgressiveness of this, however, is treated as problematic even within the practices of body-building itself, where there are clear attempts to make the self-presentation of female bodybuilders non-threatening: 'In the media, at women's body-building championships, and in gyms, the "How much is too much muscle" debate rages again for women – but not for men. Even in sports magazines, female muscles are often hidden through "soft" poses and occasionally even airbrushed away' (Nelson 1996: 24).

Coles (1994–5) further points out that women are expected to compete in heavy make-up, with bouffant hair, and that competitions are often judged using conventional ideas of female attractiveness rather than just muscle size. This attempt to undercut the transgressiveness of the female bodybuilder even extends to pressure on top competitors to preserve some of their feminine presentation by having breast implants to replace breast tissue lost as a result of exercise (Johnston 1996).

This pressure to provide indications of gender role conformity, acting on those whose public gender role behaviour transgresses stereotypical discourses of masculinity and femininity, also points up the performative aspects of gender (Butler 1990). What this means is that we cannot take gender as simply given; we have constantly to 'perform' our gender and to interpret the performances of others. Gender identity, as I said earlier, is a private matter; we demonstrate our gender identity, by and large, by the playing out of gender roles, and these roles are learned – usually unconsciously, and usually in early childhood and in adolescence. That gender role behaviour is not simply a matter of gender identity being played out in 'natural' ways of behaving is clear from the changes that transsexuals, particularly male-to-female transsexuals, have to make not just to their appearance but to their gross and subtle ways of behaving. Male-to-female transsexuals have to unlearn, for example, masculine ways of walking that have been taken up and become ingrained despite the inner conviction of being female, and learn other, more feminine movements. Feeling female, then, clearly does not mean that one automatically walks in a feminine way; it is a learned performance that is both part of feminine gender role behaviour and serves to demonstrate the actor's femininity to the world at large. Furthermore, I would argue that this performance is not just for those we encounter, but for ourselves; we create and reinforce our gender identity by the performances we put on. Even dissonant performances are used as confirmatory of the desired gender. Male-to-female transsexuals, for example, before opting for gender reassignment, may attempt to make their gender identity conform to their gender assignment by joining the army or becoming lorry drivers; trying to feel more male by performing stereotypically masculine roles.

The increasing focus on the body among poststructuralist feminists, however, also reminds us that, while gender has an important performative aspect, the material body cannot be ignored completely. The body is not just constructed by discourse; we experience the world and perform our genders with the bodies we happen to have, even if we have these surgically altered, better to make them to conform to our perceptions of ourselves. So our experience of gender identity and role is partly an acting out of gendered discourses and counter-discourses and partly a discourse-mediated experience of our own bodies, with these two reflexively feeding into each other. If I am a tall broad-shouldered female sailing instructor I may find it difficult to perform a stereotypical femininity because my body simply does not look the part – it is too strong and powerful. On the other hand, it may have become that way partly because of my refusal to conform to these stereotypes and thus my feeling able to engage in activities that developed this strong and powerful physique. The two intersect and interact.

This understanding of gender identity and role, both as performative and as mediated by the experience of the material body, is particularly useful for those of us working in educational research. It allows us to see not only how gendered behaviour is constructed by dominant discourses, but why children at particular ages demonstrate extreme gender stereotyped behaviour and how we may intervene in this. In adolescence, for example, young people are trying to define themselves as adults, and, as their bodies change, as adult men and women. Particularly when their bodies do not mature at the rate of their aspirations, they go to great lengths to perform what they perceive as being adult masculinity or femininity. In a situation in which gender attribution is comparatively precarious, because the bodies concerned are not fully developed and so remain somewhat androgynous, while at the same time gender difference is experienced as particularly salient, the exaggerated performance of gender is the easiest way for the adolescent to avoid the humiliation of mistaken gender attributions from others. Girls become less active and adopt more feminine or sexually inviting forms of dress. Boys take on masculine postures, exaggeratedly sexist attitudes and a rejection of what are seen as feminine pursuits such as reading or other activities which require control over bodily movement.

Seeing the surge of stereotypical behaviour in terms of gender role performance at the juncture between childhood and adulthood, rather than as resulting from a surge of hormones, allows us to consider the possibility of intervention and subversion. It means that we have the possibility of fore-stalling the extremes of gender stereotypical behaviour by providing a much wider range of examples of adult masculinity and femininity. By presenting to them secure adult masculine or feminine performances that do not involve stereotypical stances, bodily uses or behavioural restrictions, it may then be possible to reduce the frequency of extremes of masculine or feminine perfor-mance in young people.

Foucault-derived poststructuralist ideas can, therefore, be of both theoreti-cal and practical importance in feminist work on gender and education. They allow us to undercut many taken-for-granted assumptions about both gender and schooling, and show ways in which we may work to subvert the domi-nant gender order. My own work reflects the wide-ranging flexibility and applicability of these ideas. I have used them to deconstruct dominant assumptions about gender and to look at how and why girls and young women are positioned as Other in the schooling system (Paechter 1998a). In my writing about educational research I have interrogated some of the power/knowledge relations implicit in particular practices and approaches in the conduct and writing up of research (Paechter 1996, 1998b). In my work on curriculum innovation, I have used Foucault's ideas to examine gendered power/knowledge relations and how these affect the negotiation of curriculum, both inside and outside classrooms (Paechter 1993, 1995, 2000; Paechter and Head 1995, 1996). This flexibility in Foucault's ideas in terms of their applicability to a wide variety of sites, ideas and instances is one of poststructuralism's most fundamentally important aspects, and reflects Foucault's own stance in encouraging a writerly approach to his work, as is encapsulated in the following injunction, with which I end this chapter: 'All my books . . . are, if you like, little tool-boxes. If people want to open them, or to use this sentence or that idea as a screwdriver or spanner to short-circuit, discredit or smash systems of power, including eventually those from which my books have emerged . . . so much the better (Foucault 1975, quoted in Patton 1979: 115).

## Notes

1 I do not want to imply by this that I support compulsory heterosexuality. However, given the homophobic atmosphere of many secondary schools, being perceived as lesbian can be very problematic for adolescent girls.

2 'Gross motor behaviour' refers to large movements of whole limbs, for example (in this context), waving the arms, stretching out or attempting to crawl – as opposed to smaller movements involved in fine motor skills, such as the finger-thumb pincer grip.

# 4 | Truth is slippery stuff

*Wendy Cealey Harrison*

## Introduction

Most of us feel reasonably confident that, in discussing questions of equity in education, one of the first things we have to do is to establish the truth of the situation. It therefore comes as something of a surprise that Valerie Walkerdine of the 'Girls and Mathematics Unit' begins her chapter on 'The Truth about Girls' in *Counting Girls Out* (Walkerdine 1989) by querying the whole idea of the truth:

> This may seem a strange way to begin, but we do not think that finding the truth about girls and mathematics is possible. There are scientific 'facts', of course, but we shall demonstrate that these are open to serious question. We should, however, state straight away that we do not want to argue that current work on girls and mathematics is a false or pseudoscience and that what is needed is a feminist science, which will unproblematically tell the unbiased and undistorted truth.
>
> (Walkerdine 1989: 6)

It looks, then, as if Walkerdine is suggesting that it is not possible to arrive at 'the truth' – whatever we take it to be. This chapter is about why it is that a refusal of the conventional idea of 'truth' – a refusal which looks as if it might be disabling to the very claims Walkerdine is making – is actually the very thing that allows her to produce both a stringent critique of existing work on girls and mathematics and a powerful and compelling alternative account. What I intend to do is to explore themes and questions which were innovatively presented in that project and remain pertinent today.

There are two related reasons for wanting to return to the work of the Girls and Mathematics Unit. One is that, since *Counting Girls Out* was published, it has come to be seen as part of a broader intellectual movement, usually now referred to as 'postmodernism', which is seen by many as a deeply problematical approach. Under the broad postmodernist umbrella huddles an ill-assorted collection, which ranges from the work of someone like Judith Butler (1990, 1993), who combines an eclectic mix of theoretical approaches, to the work of the historian Denise Riley (1988) or, indeed, what the Girls and Mathematics Unit itself describes as its 'poststructuralist' account. What all of these forms of analysis have in common, though, is that they throw a broad range of fundamental issues into question and force us to think through them more carefully.

Work described as 'postmodernist' is often interpreted as potentially threatening to feminism by, for example, questioning the very possibility of reliable knowledge and unbiased truth – indeed, truth of any kind. I intend to argue in this chapter that, in relation to one such piece of work, precisely the opposite is the case. What I hope to demonstrate is that not only is very useful and perfectly reliable knowledge produced within this body of work but also that what is produced by way of knowledge is perfectly in keeping with a feminist agenda; indeed, it serves it rather better than many conventional approaches described as 'modernist'.

The second reason has to do with the recent concern about the performance not of girls but of boys at school. Might the sort of analysis that the Girls and Mathematics Unit were pioneering over a decade ago have something to tell us about the debate we are having now? My suggestion would be that it might. This work implies that, in scrutinizing the evidence in any debate about the relative successes or failures of boys or girls in education, we need to do far more than establish whether or not it is well founded. Similarly, scrutinizing the evidence involves more than simply debating causes.

**What are little girls made of?**

In exploring the claims and counter-claims about girls and mathematics, Walkerdine (1989) noticed that the debate was premised on a single, shared and unexplored assumption: that of female failure. In other words, whether or not it was assumed that girls *could* be as successful as boys in mathematics, it was widely accepted that they were failing to succeed and the issue raised centred on explaining this failure. Participants to the debate distributed themselves between two forms of explanation: 'nature' versus 'nurture'. For some of them, girls were simply constitutionally different from boys and therefore showed less facility for mathematics. For others, girls were socialized in such a way as to think of mathematics as a 'boys' subject, or were discouraged from doing science or maths courses. What was missing from all of this, though, was a systematic exploration of the question of whether or not girls really *were* failing in mathematics.

That is not to say that statistics on this were lacking: plenty of data were presented to suggest the relative lack of success of girls in mathematics.

Traditionally, then, we might have expected Walkerdine and her collabora-
tors to do no more than to mount a critique of these data – of the way they
were compiled, the interpretations they were given and the conclusions
drawn from them. This is certainly something that she did do. However, as
the quotation at the beginning of this chapter demonstrates, she also makes
it quite clear that she is not setting out simply to *falsify* the current work on
girls and mathematics. How should we make sense of this apparent paradox?

There are two ways of reading the statement that Walkerdine is not setting
out simply to falsify the work on girls and mathematics. One way is to suggest
that she does not deny the value of the evidence presented. The other is to
suggest that she is trying to do something different from falsifying a given
point of view. I would argue that both interpretations are correct. First, she
does not deny the reliability of the evidence so much as the case that is
built upon it. Second, she is engaged in something other than the production
of a contrary case: she wants to locate that point of view in a particular social
context and, in so doing, open up a different set of questions.

The key to this argument about truth lies in the starting point, which
involves another surprising claim: 'Our starting point is that there is no
simple category "woman" which can be revealed by feminist research, but
that as feminists we can examine how facts, fictions and fantasies have
been constituted and how these have affected the ways in which we have
been positioned, understood and led to understand ourselves' (Walkerdine
1989: 7).

Our commonsensical assumptions about truth tend to assume a world of
objects whose character is, broadly speaking, stable. Tables, frogs or fossils
are definable objects, on which a series of forces can be said to act. These
objects may undergo changes (a frog has not always been a frog; it used to
be a tadpole), but they have a distinct identity, which allows us to expect
that any truths we establish about them will hold good from now on (for
example, frogs are amphibians and, as long as frogs are frogs, they will
always be amphibians). Walkerdine's (1989) argument here is essentially
that 'women' do not constitute objects of this kind for feminism. But why
not? It would seem self-evident to most of us that the terms 'women',
'men', 'girls' and 'boys' clearly identify something specific. The question we
need to ask ourselves is: 'On the basis of what criteria do they constitute
apparently identifiable and stable objects?' What exactly are we referring to
when we refer to 'women' or 'men', 'girls' or 'boys'? The answer, of course,
is that when we assume the identifiability and stability of these categories
of human being, it is on the basis of biological criteria. But feminism has
always concerned itself with 'women' as a *social* grouping. Leaving aside the
question of whether or not biology really does supply us with such a clear-
cut means of identifying human beings (and there are arguments that suggest
that the picture is much more complicated than that),[1] we have to ask
whether or not we can attribute this degree of consistency to the social groupings we label 'women' and 'men'. Should we simply take it for granted that
because sexed groupings appear to be coherent and to show a degree of

consistency, we should attribute the *same* degree of consistency and coherence to the social groupings? Are we right simply to suggest that gender follows directly from what we nowadays define as 'sex'?

The issue here is whether we might be making a *presumption* of coherence and consistency for a social grouping on non-social (i.e. biological) grounds. After all, we know that it means rather different things in different societies and different social settings, within different cultures and at different historical periods, to be what is designated, in those societies, settings, cultures and periods, a 'woman' or a 'man', a 'girl' or a 'boy'. Certainly, all of these designations ultimately refer to something that *we* would now identify as a reproductive difference, but even ways of understanding and making sense of this reproductive difference will vary. We only have to go back to the Renaissance in Europe to identify a very different way of seeing bodies and the differences between them (Laqueur 1990). From antiquity onwards, women's bodies had been seen as built on the same basic ground plan as men's but as lacking in 'vital heat', which was believed to make them less perfect and to lead to their sexual organs being retained inside their bodies. There was no idea of women as an 'opposite' sex, which might have a set of characteristics complementary to those of men. Indeed, some of the character-istics that women were deemed to have – 'lustfulness' for example – are those we might nowadays associate with men. The idea, for instance, that men want sex while women want relationships is precisely the reverse of beliefs about men and women in Europe before the Enlightenment.[2] If we take the past (and indeed other cultures) seriously, then we have to allow for the fact that: 'The past is a foreign country. They do things differently there' (Hartley 1953: 7). This means that the ways in which human beings are seen and treated are many and various, *even* when it comes to something as apparently stable as sex.

If, however, we assume that 'sex' means the same thing wherever we go, then we will inevitably tend to assume that 'women' and 'men', 'girls' and 'boys' constitute unproblematic categories simply because they share common biologies. But that really tells us nothing about the ways in which they are treated. This was the point behind the idea of 'gender'.[3] 'Gender', as a concept, evolved to point out that a distinction needed to be drawn between what women were as a consequence of their biology and what they were as a consequence of the societies within which they lived and the ways in which they were treated (Oakley 1972).[4]

The Girls and Mathematics Unit do not discuss the idea of 'sex', but they clearly want to allow for the variability and complexity of the ways in which the social categories of 'women' and 'men', 'boys' and 'girls' are iden-tified, and regard this as central to their analysis. Their starting point is that 'woman' and 'girl' (and, indeed, 'man' and 'boy') must be seen, intrinsically, as mutable objects which shift and change as a function of the social worlds they inhabit and of how they are defined and identified in those worlds. Furthermore, they identify the task for feminism as one of examining how facts, fictions and fantasies have been constituted and how these have affected not only how women have been positioned and understood, but also how they have been led to understand themselves.

Walkerdine (1989) derived this way of seeing the social world and the human beings within it from a perspective she identifies as 'poststructuralism', a term which, in the intervening years has come to mean many things (not all of them complimentary!), but their main source for this account was the work of the French philosopher, Michel Foucault. Foucault's contention was that major changes take place in the social worlds we inhabit because of shifts in the configurations of knowledges and powers (by means of which we act upon those knowledges) – what Foucault referred to as 'discourses'.[5] The truths we construct for ourselves, rather than being things that hold for all time, are going to be closely associated with the social worlds within which they are produced. This does not necessarily mean to say that they are going to be 'relative' – in other words, only partially true because they are restricted to a particular standpoint – but that the *kind* of truth they represent and the social purposes that truth is keyed into needs to be established. Within that context, Foucault saw the task of the intellectual as seeing if it was possible to think differently, because he felt that there were more potential freedoms and more ways of being out there than we normally allow ourselves to imagine. If we are unhappy with the world we live in, the first task we have is that of establishing what has shaped that world, which is why, according to Foucault, we need to develop an awareness of from where our current thinking derives. By understanding where and when and how we began to think in the ways that we nowadays take for granted, we open up the possibility of reshaping things along different lines. Of course, political action – and successful political action at that – does not depend upon these different ways of thinking, but to ignore such a task is to remain bounded within existing terms of reference.

The Girls and Mathematics Unit therefore felt that just to accept the categories and terms within which this debate was constructed was to remain restricted within its current terms of reference and to fail to explore important issues about how gender operates. If we simply accept a given set of definitions and the current ways of framing a debate, we shall be trapped within what Walkerdine (1989) calls 'empiricism' (broadly speaking, taking for granted what seems superficially to be the case) and be compelled to respond defensively towards our political opponents. For a radical politics such as feminism it is important therefore to question the very frameworks of debate. These frameworks, however, are responsible for shaping much more than academic disputation, for they have produced the character of our world and of ourselves as creatures within it – as Walkerdine (1989: 7) insists, 'the ways in which we have been positioned, understood and led to understand ourselves'. Discourses define the way things are for us, although within this we do have the possibility of reframing things, of producing a different understanding and beginning the task of reshaping the world we live in.

This way of looking at knowledge and truth produces a very different account of the task of the social science which is assumed to inform feminism.

It sees truths as contextual and as bound up with the processes by means of which we create and sustain social forms; as the Girls and Mathematics Unit say, 'different concerns at different historical moments have themselves helped to produce different definitions of – and solutions to – the "problem"' (Walkerdine 1989: 6–7). We cannot, then, restrict ourselves to establishing whether or not something is 'true' in the limited sense of whether or not it obeys appropriate methodological principles or canons of scientificity – although we may need to do that too – because 'issues of truth, scientificity and method are more complex' (Walkerdine 1989: 6). Equally, the human beings who are at the heart of this cannot be thought of as comprising – or automatically belonging to – simple and straightforward social categories, for those social categories are continually in play. In looking at issues of gender in education, we have to take on board the fact that the social categories we are referring to do not constitute something clear-cut, stable and unproblematic to which we can appeal. Instead we have to investigate how they are being constituted, and what is being appealed to and why. The process by means of which the social categories are defined and constituted is of a piece with a particular sociopolitical and historical landscape.

## Knowledge and truth

If 'issues of truth, scientificity and method are *more complex*' (Walkerdine 1989: 6, emphasis added), what we are *not* talking about is relativizing truth, but rather expanding how we investigate the truth of something. The methodological principles or canons of scientificity that are supposed to govern social science research are not being rejected so much as amplified by a further set of considerations. Of course, any methodological critique worth its salt will enquire into the theoretical presuppositions that have informed a piece of research. What is different here is how far that theoretical investigation extends, since, in a classically Foucauldian sense, it seeks to uncover the whole process by means of which a complex set of social forms is being constructed and the ways in which the production of evidence is used to support parts of that process. According to the Girls and Mathematics Unit, evidence about the relative success or failure of girls in mathematics cannot be divorced from the way in which mathematics education is conceptualized and practised.

In a subsequent chapter of her book, Walkerdine (1989) opens up the issue of how mathematical success is construed in terms of what is deemed to count as 'real understanding' in mathematics. This, in its turn, is related to the role that mathematics education plays in the production of the rational citizen, who is both capable of reasoning and reasonable. Enmeshed in both of these things in quite intricate ways are conceptions of gender which, for example, associate 'real understanding' with activity, and activity with boys, and read the success of girls at certain mathematical tasks as evidence of 'rote learning' rather than 'real understanding'. The capacity to reason, which mathematics is assumed to develop in the child, has to deal with the active, dynamic and enquiring (for which read 'potentially unruly') child, who is typically read as male. Male and female children therefore constitute different kinds of problem in respect of mathematics education. Girls are assumed to be compliant and unproblematic pupils, whose very compliance is also an indicator of the fact that they are doing the 'wrong kind' of learning – passive rote learning. Where they are demonstrably successful, their success is re-read in these terms. Boys, on the other hand, whose activity (which may encompass naughtiness and rule-breaking) is assumed to show a capacity to develop 'real understanding' have to be made tractable while not losing the independence of mind that is believed to be the key to reasoning and mathematical understanding. Pedagogical practices designed to achieve this will mobilize a set of fantasies of absolute control for the child, fantasies that belie the real situation in which the child finds itself (Walkerdine 1989).

The statistical evidence that is produced about the relative success or failure of boys or girls cannot therefore simply be taken for granted. Our examination of the issue also cannot just be a matter of adjudicating (by means of an inquiry into the data) as to whether or not girls actually do achieve 'real understanding' or whether or not boys fail to do so. The Girls and Mathematics Unit's analysis of the statistics that have informed the debate on girls and mathematics is perfectly conventional in social science terms: they look in detail at the statistical basis on which many of the arguments about the alleged failure of girls are mounted and suggest that, on that basis, many of the claims made are unwarranted. This is not to say that there are no differences evident in the data, nor is it to say that they fail to acknowledge these differences. But the data are not their prime concern. Instead the data provide a stepping-stone into opening up much more interesting but also more complex and potentially problematical issues.

## The nature of 'the problem'

One such issue concerns the way in which particular social and political contexts frame what look like conventional empirical problems. Here Walkerdine (1989) focuses on uncovering the context within which a particular debate about equity in education is framed. Concern was first expressed, in the 'Great Debate' on education under the government of James Callaghan in Britain in 1976, about the 'wastage of talent' which was leading young women not to enter careers requiring scientific and mathematical training. Walkerdine (1989) points out that concern about education in Britain since the Second World War had focused first on working-class boys and subsequently, by the 1970s, on girls. However, the issue was never really about *all* girls, but only about those who might be likely to do GCE A levels and, perhaps, go on to a university degree – a very small percentage of the group overall. Nevertheless, the assumption was made that the problem was a general one. Presumably, if the 'best' girls were failing then *all* girls, implicitly, must be failing. The difficulty for the politicians, in other words, was quite specific:

how to get a particular group of girls into high-level careers based on science and mathematics.

However, given the general political concern with inequalities between women and men, it seemed 'obvious' that any group of girls would be typical of their sex. No one felt the need to enquire as to whether or not this particular group of girls was typical of all girls or whether or not what was allegedly happening had anything to do with the 'girl-ness' of the girls. Whatever 'being a girl' might mean, it seemed 'natural' to presume that it was in some way implicated in the cause of the problem. There are already two questions being begged here by the definition of the 'problem': one is whether or not there really *was* a problem of girls failing; the other is whether or not, if a problem existed, it was girl-specific or related to something else.

**Explaining 'the problem'**

A variety of approaches were used to come to terms with this presumed wastage, from American social psychology to a British social democratic interest in aptitude and ability, and how they could be discovered and fostered. Two sorts of explanation tended to be produced, however: those that appealed to differences between the sexes and those that appealed to gender-specific experiences or discrimination. Needless to say, those approaches that were most contentious were those that made some appeal to differences between the sexes, such as the arguments about superior male spatial ability, whether this was given an environmental or a genetic formulation. (Alternative approaches, by contrast, tended to stress the question of whether or not girls were being discouraged from taking courses in science and mathematics.)

> The genetic lobby would link the work to differences in verbal and non-verbal intelligence and with research on brain lateralization. The environmentalists use ideas of sex-role stereotyping to suggest that girls and boys have different play and developmental experiences. There is scant definition, however, of the precise link between performance on visuo-spatial tests and school mathematics.
>
> (Walkerdine 1989: 8)

Walkerdine's analysis of the way in which explanation of the problem came to be constructed reveals a series of such gaps and deficits in reasoning, and this applies as much to the approaches that show an environmental leaning as to those that do not. There is, for example, a literature of 'fear of success' which suggests that it is girls who show an orientation towards traditional femininity who take flight from mathematics, and a literature that talks of maths phobia and anxiety in women. Yet, to talk of maths phobia and anxiety in women, they argue, is to ignore evidence that suggests it is not necessarily that men are *not* anxious or phobic about maths, but that they are socialized into *not displaying it openly*. The issue is potentially much more complex than that of a simple difference between women and men: 'In our view . . . anxiety cannot be separated from complex social processes nor from the involvement in mathematics of fantasies of masculinity and femininity' (Walkerdine 1989: 9). One cannot therefore take data at face value, nor presume *prima facie* that differences exist.

Because gender is naturalistically assumed to overlap and coincide with sex, the spontaneous assumption tends to be that such differences exist. What they consist of, what their extent is and what causes them may be at issue but their existence goes largely unchallenged. Feminism – because it emerged to counter inequities between women and men – finds itself caught up in tussles over extents and causes. What the detractors of the capabilities of women had attributed to 'sex', feminism attributed to 'gender'. So, Walkerdine argues for a different kind of feminism, one which gets *behind* the 'obviousness' of differences between women and men to ask, not so much about how the differences come about, as how the construction of the *problem* of their difference comes about. We might therefore say of research into the differences between the genders/sexes that it tells us more about the social, political and intellectual concerns that animate it than about the difference between boys and girls or women and men. That is not say that such differences might not be perfectly real and recordable ones, but there are more options available to us than attributing them to the 'nature' of boys and girls, whether we say that this nature is socially constructed or that it is biologically given.

Both in its more 'progressive' incarnations and in those that are regarded as less so, much of the research into the 'failure' of girls in respect of mathematics and science has necessarily neglected disconfirming evidence and overstated the significance of what it finds, because of the very formulation of its research question. This is because its orientation is towards a narrative of female failure. Walkerdine (1989) makes the case, for example, that the 'learned helplessness' literature, which suggests that girls develop a feminine passivity, is not borne out by the fact that the very sex differences it is allegedly meant to explain 'are neither as consistent nor as strong as has been postulated' (1989: 10). For example, the literature that suggests that boys and girls attribute their successes and failures differently, with boys tending to give stable causes (such as ability) as reasons for their success and external, unstable ones (such as lack of effort) for their failures, and girls reversing the pattern, shows only *slight* differences where it affects maths. Girls rate ability as *a little* more significant when accounting for their failures than boys do for theirs (Walkerdine 1989: 10).

More to the point, however intuitively and commonsensically plausible such accounts may sound, what cannot be avoided is the fact that 'girls' mean scores are roughly equivalent to those of boys, even in secondary school' (Walkerdine 1989: 11) – in short, the very effect the research is allegedly set up to explain is simply not there. We could quibble over how 'rough' the equivalence has to be before we say that there is something there to be investigated, and, indeed, statistical tests of significance carried out on small scale samples can be used to allow us to make just this kind of judgement. What is interesting here is the gap between the alleged size of the difference that is being detected and the arguments about difference it is being used to support.

The Girls and Mathematics Unit mention that their investigation of the six major Assessment of Performance Unit (APU) surveys of 1980–2 only show differences in performance in the top 25 and 15 per cent of children in secondary school – certainly those children about whom anxiety is being expressed, but not girls as a whole. They also propose (although they do not explore) a possible counter-argument. Many of these children, but not all, will be middle class. Insofar as not all of them are middle class, however, and as working-class girls experience stronger pressures towards sex-typed occupations than do middle-class girls, 'there seems to be an important and interesting phenomenon relating to the differential performance, attitudes and experience of middle and working-class girls' (Walkerdine 1989: 11). This is a much more specific effect than many of the studies would suggest, which is bound to be overlooked when the predominant concern is with accounting for the alleged failure of girls *per se*. This is not to say, of course, that we should simply accept the social categories of 'working class' and 'middle class' without qualm. The concept of 'class' is itself recognized to be deeply problematical, and, at the very least, we would need to open up issues around 'class' in just the same way as those around 'gender' have been opened.

**How girls 'fail'**

Another problematic issue is the way in which statistical data is open to a variety of interpretations (see Chapter 2). Walkerdine (1989) examines two APU primary mathematics surveys for 1978 (APU 1980) and the 1979 Schools Council study (Ward 1979), in relation to the studies that were based upon them (all cited in Walkerdine 1989). The surveys themselves tend to be quite circumspect about their results, but the studies based upon them are less so. The first APU study, for example, states that: 'the data on sex differences show a slight, and generally non significant, advantage in boys in most sub-categories, but girls perform significantly better statistically in computation (whole numbers and decimals)' (APU 1980, cited in Walkerdine 1989: 14). All three give little emphasis to an *overall* sex difference (although they *are* comparing the categories of boy to girl on each of a series of sub-categories of tasks), and where statistical significance is mentioned (sometimes it is not), they stress caution in interpreting it.

However, later studies based on these statistics tended to consider the population along a single line of cleavage, that of boy to girl: 'the reification of the category "girl" and "boy" produces explanations which favour sex-specific characteristics, so that more complex analyses of masculinity and femininity are impossible' (Walkerdine 1989: 13). This means that non-differences become non-results: 'similarities are usually treated in terms of their failure to show significant differences' (Walkerdine 1989: 13).

The small differences across some of the subcategories in the surveys, which the Unit estimate to amount to between 1.25 and 3 IQ points ('a trivially small difference by any reckoning') are thus taken by others to indicate that boys perform substantially better than girls (Walkerdine 1989: 15). For example, based on these surveys, Shuard (1981, 1982) is quite happy to speak of boys and girls as two distinct groups with markedly different levels of success. Also, the subcategories of mathematical performance were to play a crucial role in the argument about female failure, for even though what was being noted in the studies as a *success* on the part of the girls in some of the subcategories, was re-read as female failure. Bound up in the discussions about mathematical ability, according to Walkerdine (1989: 24) is a tacit differentiation between skills that are deemed to be a matter of 'rule-following' and those which are deemed to indicate 'understanding':

> Mathematics teaching will be approached differently depending upon whether its aims stress one side of the distinction or the other. Which side is stressed may depend upon what the educator thinks mathematics education is for: what use the pupils will make of it. Those who stress teaching children ultimately to take money and give change in shops, to count components on a production line, to measure up rooms to lay carpets, tend to stress the 'procedural'. Those, on the other hand, teaching budding computer programmers, mathematicians and physicists stress the 'propositional'. However, this distinction is not simply of theoretical value. Ever since the inception of compulsory schooling there has been a debate about what kind of mathematics was to be taught to different pupils. The distinctions are, of course, class-, gender- and race-specific, and naturalistic arguments are brought in easily to show that some pupils are simply more naturally suited to the menial rather than the intellectual.

The assumption is that it is possible to follow rules without understanding them, an assumption which is being applied to those successes the girls are acknowledged to have, since they are deemed only to be *capable of* 'rule-following'. Behind the statistics, then, lies an educational discourse about mathematics within which a distinction is being made between someone who can successfully complete a practical task through the application of a procedure, without understanding the reasons for doing so or grasping why the procedure is effective, and someone who has a deeper comprehension of the meaning of what they are doing and why the rules work (Walkerdine 1989).

One troubling issue about the status given to the differences between boys and girls is the way in which other issues are obscured. Differences that are much larger in absolute terms, but which either do not have the same political significance or are regarded as politically far *more* troubling, such as class differences or geographical differences, disappear behind the creation of categorical differences between boys and girls:

> The differences between boys and girls ranged from 1 or 2 per cent to about 8 per cent. They were considerably smaller than the differences

between pupils living in metropolitan areas and those in non-metropolitan areas, and were totally swamped by differences between the regions of the United Kingdom or between schools having high or low percentages of free school meals.

(Walkerdine 1989: 17)

## The truth about girls

What the work of the Girls and Mathematics Unit sought to achieve was to open up a different set of questions which might otherwise have gone unnoticed in the preoccupation with the relative fates of boys and girls. This inevitably alters the frame of reference surrounding the research results and reveals some of the deficits in the ways in which they have been interpreted. Doing what Michel Foucault described as 'the history of the present', Walkerdine (1989: 29) identified the conditions which 'produced our taken-for-granted practices so that they come to seem obvious and unchallenged facts'. The Unit were concerned with 'the way in which certain observations made about girls in relation to their classroom performance and to results of mathematical tests are presented as "hard evidence" to service a particular sort of debate when neither the evidence presented, nor the conclusions drawn, are as strong as they are presumed to be' (Walkerdine 1989: 20).

Truths, then, are contextual and contested. What we can discover about the social purposes that surround these truths can illuminate for us why it is, for example, that there may be missing links in some of the argumentation, or why some evidence gets neglected and some forms of investigation are not pursued. However, any claims that finding the truth about girls and mathematics (or boys and literacy, and so on) is impossible are, I would argue, over-stating the case. Much more appropriate is the idea that truth is slippery stuff, made up of many more things than we might at first suspect, such as 'fantasies and fictions which have been made to operate as fact' Walkerdine 1989: 19). The idea of 'fantasy' and 'fiction' *operating* as 'fact' inevitably means that 'truth', like 'fact', is possible.

What Walkerdine's work allows us to do is to take a closer look at the way in which our underlying assumption that truth is independent of context can skew our approach to (and our interpretation of) social research. Post-modernist work of the kind exemplified by Walkerdine has drawn attention to the way in which this assumption can also lead to the reification of concepts like 'sex' or 'gender' into taken-for-granted social categories, at the expense of other issues (Cealey Harrison and Hood-Williams 1998). This demonstrates the need for us to consider complex questions such as these in research on gender and education.

## Notes

1 The classics in this field are Kessler and McKenna's *Gender: An Ethnomethodological Approach* (1978) and the more recent work of biologists such as Anne Fausto-

Sterling and Nelly Oudshoorn. See for example, Fausto-Sterling's (1989) work on the attempt by geneticists to locate the origin of sex differences on a portion of the Y chromosome, 'Life in the XY Corral', and Nelly Oudshoorn's history of the hormonal body *Beyond the Natural Body* (1994).

2 For a detailed account of this, see Thomas Laqueur's brilliant book, *Making Sex: Body and Gender from the Greeks to Freud* (1990).

3  This has led some feminist theorists like Christine Delphy to complain that, as she puts it, 'gender has not taken wing' – in other words that its full potential has not been explored because it remains tethered to the idea of 'sex' (1984: 24). Far from seeing sex as an unproblematic categorization for human beings, Delphy sees it as a discriminatory marker which identifies oppressor and oppressed. In other words, 'sex' as a category is the result of 'gender', rather than the other way round.

4 Ann Oakley (1972) was really the pioneer here, although the conceptual distinction between what we now call 'sex' and 'gender' was being drawn before she came along, at least implicitly. See, for example, the opening chapter of Simone de Beauvoir's *The Second Sex* (1972).

5 For an example of this, see Michel Foucault's *Discipline and Punish* (1977).

# Beyond postmodernism: feminist agency in educational research

*Becky Francis*

## Introduction

Postmodernist and poststructuralist theories[1] have had a profound impact on feminism. They have compounded, and have helped to theorize, the timely crises in identity politics, and have left us with new ways of looking at the world. But postmodernist and poststructuralist positions incorporate a relativism[2] which make them unwieldy for use in an emancipatory endeavour. They can be used effectively to deconstruct masculinist assumptions, but go further and deconstruct our own assumptions about right and wrong, justice and injustice. And if our moral arguments are deconstructed or positioned as invalid, political movements founded on such arguments are also problematized. For this reason it has been argued that relativist postmodern theories can also cause political paralysis and a narcissistic turn to the academy at the expense of challenging the inequalities which continue to persist in the world at large (Hartsock 1990; Spretnack 1993; Eagleton 1996; Francis 1999, forthcoming). Some feminist researchers have, therefore, become dissatisfied with postmodernist accounts of the world, and are seeking new ways to theorize social relations. This chapter will consider some of the key issues in the debate, and possible ways forward.

## Identity politics and sex-role theories: the crisis of feminist theory in the late twentieth century

As we saw in Chapter 1, the 'second-wave' feminism precipitated by the Women's Liberation Movement in the late 1960s was by no means a unitary school. It incorporated a variety of different outlooks, from the 'radical' to the 'liberal'. However, across these various schools a common theme could be found where women were perceived as sisters in struggle, united by their femaleness and the consequent oppression by patriarchy. The suggested methods with which to challenge male domination differed between feminist schools, but the assumption of womanhood as the founding subject of feminism, and the emancipatory intentions, remained unifying themes (Assiter 1996).

In order to explain why women and men behave in different ways, many feminist researchers applied socialization theory to sex difference, showing how norms of behaviour for men and women are reproduced through society's institutions. In education some feminists drew on Marxist concepts of a 'hidden curriculum' to explain how a male-dominated schooling system reproduces stereotypical gender roles in pupils. Women's lack of power in society was taken as a given, and explained by a process of socialization, beginning in the family and reinforced by schools and other institutions.

But by the late 1970s and early 1980s the feminist founding subject 'woman/girl' was being problematized. Black, working-class, lesbian and disabled feminists questioned the assumption of women's equality of oppression under patriarchy, pointing to the ways in which other forms of discrimination interact with gender discrimination, with various consequences for different groups of women. They argued that feminist theory and practices used a white, heterosexual, middle-class and able-bodied model of womanhood as a norm, and marginalized the experiences of 'other' women. These women drew attention to the ways in which white, middle-class, heterosexual feminists have discriminated against 'other' women in the past and present, demonstrating that power relations and inequalities exist between women, as well as between women and men. The assumption that feminists could speak to and for all women on the basis of their shared womanhood and oppression was consequently exploded (Mirza 1997).

Parallel to these developments in the feminist movement at large was the emergence of a growing criticism of the notion of a 'reproduction of roles' in the social sciences and education. In his influential study of working-class groups of boys in secondary schools, Willis (1977) showed that the societal roles of working-class schoolboys were not reproduced by the school in a uniform way, but rather were actively negotiated by the boys, often in resistance to the guidance of the school. Likewise, feminist studies in education began to demonstrate that girls and boys take up gender roles in ways which are multiple and contradictory, simultaneously accommodating and resisting them.

In short, feminist researchers were realizing that the generalizations and 'truths' about gender and power relations which had previously seemed to many to be clear and secure were not actually so stable (or even 'right'). Society, the people constituting it and the power relations between them were more complex and diverse than had often been assumed. But how to theorize this difference and diversity? To some feminists, poststructuralist theory appeared to provide an answer.

## The contribution of poststructuralism

Poststructuralism originally developed in response to the structuralist move-ment in literary criticism. Poststructuralists such as Barthes (1990) and Derrida (1976) refuted the structuralist belief in a 'scientific' approach to language, pointing out that we are all immersed in language or 'text', and that text can be interpreted in many different ways, allowing the possibility for dominant storylines to be 'deconstructed'. Foucault's concept of discursive power was particularly influential within the social sciences (see, for example, Foucault 1980). He maintained that the self is not fixed, but is rather posi-tioned in discourse. Discourses wield power by constructing objects in differ-ent ways, and it is for this reason that individuals can simultaneously undergo and exercise power, and be positioned in different ways at different times depending on the discursive environment.

Elsewhere I have discussed in detail the benefits (and disadvantages) of poststructuralist theory for feminism (Francis 1999). I argued that poststruc-turalist ideas appealed to some feminists (including myself) for a number of reasons. The poststructuralist articulation of destability and complexity was appealing to those frustrated with the oversimplistic binaries of identity poli-tics. Foucault's concept of discourse provided a new theoretical tool with which to view gender relations. It could also explain how power is constituted in multiple ways between women (and between men) as well as between men and women. The poststructuralist rejection of the coherent self also decon-structs gender as something fixed, a perspective which appealed to, or fitted with the theories of, some feminists. If gender was simply just another dis-course, this could explain why gender 'roles' appeared to be simultaneously accommodated and resisted.

There also appeared to be some common ground between poststructuralism and feminism, as poststructuralists shared the feminist scepticism of the Enlightenment discourses which take a 'rational' approach to the world and suggest a possible objectivity (which, feminist researchers had revealed, disguised a masculinist world view which was far from value free).

As such, poststructuralist theory has often aided feminist work, and pro-vided the tools with which to analyse the complexity of human interaction around issues of identity and power. Discourse analysis has proved an effec-tive method with which to reveal the gendered assumptions and motivations underlying people's talk, and the impact of such discourses on people's power positions.

## Implications of poststructuralism for emancipatory intentions

On the other hand, when poststructuralist ideas are taken to their natural conclusion the consequences can be seen as threatening to feminism. The key areas of tension concern agency and value. I have asserted elsewhere that 'pure' poststructuralism and feminism are actually incompatible (Francis

1999, forthcoming).[3] This argument is based on a particular view of feminism (and, indeed, of poststructuralism); one that some feminists might not support. 'Feminism' is an umbrella term which admittedly incorporates a great many different, often opposing, schools of thought. Yet I maintain that there remain unifying themes central to all feminist perspectives. These are: a concern with gender; a perception of women as generally disadvantaged in gender relations (while often viewing men as requiring liberation too); a perception of this gender inequity as wrong; and consequently an aim to change things for the better. As Assiter (1996) observes, the latter is an emancipatory aim, and feminism is an emancipatory movement.

From a poststructuralist perspective, feminism's emancipatory narrative can be seen as a modernist 'grand narrative', based on moral truth claims. Poststructuralist theory is a relativist one, which seeks to deconstruct such truth narratives. Feminists have always argued that what counts for knowledge and 'truth' in our society is a male version of knowledge and truth, yet feminism also draws on humanist values of justice and human rights in order to argue for gender equity. To many poststructuralists, truth discourses or 'grand narratives' exercise a power relationship (as they make totalitarian claims to 'right'), and consequently require deconstruction. So although poststructuralist work does not instruct people to abandon work to end oppression, it does deconstruct the foundational conceptions of morality, justice and truth on which many such movements are based (Francis, forthcoming).

The assumption of human agency evoked in the notion of emancipatory endeavour (our ability to make decisions and to act on the world in order to change it) is also questioned by poststructuralism. Jones (1997) observes that such notions of agency are based on the humanist (modernist) concept of a self which is an already existing individual. To poststructuralists we are simply vessels positioned and repositioned in relations of power through discourses: we do not actively choose which discourses we take up and use. The belief that we have our own coherent, meaning-making personalities is simply due to our positioning within discourses of liberal, humanist individualism (Jones 1997). And of course, this 'death of the self' perspective also deconstructs the very notion of sex/gender (which has been so central to feminist thought in the past). There are no women or men, only selves positioned in gender discourses.

## Selfhood, agency and power

However, it has been argued that this concept (and poststructuralist thought generally) ignores the issue of structural power. Soper (1990) notes Derrida's (1976) argument that we should abandon the category 'woman' in order to break down the gender dichotomy (if we cease to speak it, it will cease to be). She maintains that Derrida's argument illustrates the extent to which poststructuralism is divorced from social reality. Soper points out that a woman may still fear a man when walking down a street alone at night, whether or not she agrees theoretically that we should reject the categories 'male' and 'female'.[4] Of course, as McNay (2000) points out, many post-structuralists recognize the embodiment of binary divisions inscribed by gender discourses. But they criticize the reification of the (to them, fictional) notion 'woman' (see, for example, Butler 1990). This, again, undermines the political use of the term, and arguably undermines the use of gender as a point of analysis.

Foucault's vision of power as exercised through a 'net-like organization' (Foucault 1980: 98) and constituted via discourse has been invaluable for explaining our multiple power positionings. It has helped us to see that power does not simply 'belong' to oppressors at the expense of the oppressed. Rather, one may be positioned as powerful via gender discourse in one inter-active moment, and as powerless via social class discourse in the next. But this vision can end in relativism, because the import or strength of one discourse cannot be weighed against another (Burman and Parker 1993). To give an example, if a white person and a black person in western society are victims of racist abuse they are both positioned in racist discourse. From a post-structuralist perspective there can be no recognition of the different conse-quences for the recipient in terms of power depending on their ethnicity. Some writers have attempted to circumvent this problem by reinserting value, weighing different discourses as 'dominant', 'hegemonic' and so forth. Yet as Jones (1997) and Hood-Williams (1998) point out, such value judge-ments are inconsistent with the poststructuralist deconstructive position.

Although power relations are multiple and specific to local interactive environments, inequalities according to ethnicity, gender, social class and so on continue to exist at a macro level. These general differences may be less straightforward than we have previously supposed, but this does not mean that they do not exist.

The poststructuralist concept of the self as lacking coherence and agency also holds consequences for the feminist project: struggles for emancipation are rendered pointless if we actually have no control of our lives. Elsewhere I have observed that few of us, poststructuralist or otherwise, actually experi-ence ourselves as non-coherent or lacking all agency (Francis, forthcoming). In our daily lives most, if not all of us, go about our activities feeling that we are unique individuals with our own particular personality. To actually begin to feel that we do not have a coherent personality and freedom of choice would be devastating, with arguably terrifying consequences in terms of the meaningfulness of our lives and our attempts at political improvement. Some poststructuralist writers do see the self as having some limited agency, but this agency as being prescribed by the discursive possibilities open to it. Any agency is bounded by the discursive environment (reflecting the structuralist notion of 'the prison house of language').

As we have seen, poststructuralist work acknowledges that we feel our-selves coherent, meaning-making selves, but explains such feelings as an illusion caused by our positioning in Enlightenment, individualist discourse (see Jones 1997). In comparison with this poststructuralist position, the traditional feminist position can be seen as a modernist one (Balbus 1987), with the emancipatory aims often reflecting a humanist stance and conception of self (Soper 1990, 1993b; Raphael Reed 1996). After all, if feminists did not believe in the value of human life, in human agency, and in morality and justice, they simply would not have become feminists (Francis, forthcoming). The feminist tradition of valuing personal experience also reflects a humanist perspective, because of the view of such experience as valid and authentic.

So, regarding issues of value, agency and the construction of the self, humanist feminism and poststructuralism appear to stand in opposition. Both perspectives on these issues appear limited. A humanist feminist position has been revealed as often oversimplistic and unitary, with an inadequate recognition and explanation of the complexity of power relations. A poststructuralist position, on the other hand, cannot address trends of inequality, and potentially deconstructs the very notions of value and agency on which feminism is based. These complex theoretical tensions mean that many writers in the field of gender and education appear to have come to a theoretical impasse, where emancipatory aims and concerns incongruously rub shoulders with postmodernist relativism (Spretnack 1993; Francis, forthcoming). The following section aims to reappraise issues of selfhood in an attempt to move the discussion forward.

## Identifying identity

It is not my intention to return us to the humanist model of the unitary self. It is evident that we are not born with a complete, fixed personality which remains constant over time and in all social situations. As Billig *et al.* (1988) observed, people articulate different views depending on whom they are with and where they are. My own work with primary- and secondary-school pupils has shown how their constructions of gender often differ depending on the interactive environment (see, for example, Francis 1998; 2000a). And likewise, our power positions also fluctuate depending on the discursive environment. It is possible to reflect on some of these processes in our own lives. For example, we can all recognize the way in which we frame our opinions differently depending on the perspective of the listener. We can also identify the way in which aspects of identity such as gender, race and social class can impact on us differently at different times depending on our interactive environment. Applying these observations to research, they support the argument of Putnam *et al.* (1998) that the researcher should not assume that a respondent's construction in one environment is more or less valid than their different construction in another.

But must these acknowledgements necessarily lead to the conclusion that there is no coherence to our 'personhood', and that our lives are determined by discursive forces? I would question this. It seems to me that, rather than being born an essential personality, we are shaped by, and draw on, experiences and influences around us, and we continue learning. In this sense our 'personality' develops and changes throughout our lives (Francis, forthcoming). However, there are certain things about us which appear to remain fairly constant to our 'personality', albeit that they may develop over time. Hence those who 'know' us intimately may be able to predict our behaviour and responses to events quite accurately. Just as it is evidently true that our positioning and presentation of ourselves differs in various interactive contexts, it is also the case that, for most of us, some aspects of our beliefs and/ or our presentation of self remain the same in many contexts. So, for example, although I may articulate arguments against gender discrimination differently depending on my listener, and although my own constructions of gender may be non-unitary and problematic, I still hold the maxim that gender discrimination is wrong, and try to argue that point whenever I encounter other views. As I observe elsewhere (Francis, forthcoming), this continuation of belief and construction of ourselves can be illustrated by the discomfort we often experience if in some conversation we feel we have not been 'true to our beliefs', or have presented a 'false picture' of ourselves.[5]

So if we apply these points to the validity of our respondents' various constructions in our research, one of the main reasons we cannot judge the extent of the 'truth' of one response against another is that as researchers we usually do not 'know' the respondent concerned. Therefore we cannot make judgements about the extent to which their responses are 'representative' of their usual behaviour. But their close friends, or even their teacher, might. Of course, one could never be confident about such judgements because, as I have noted, we *do* present ourselves differently in different environments, and a pupil may be, say, far more assertive and confident at home than they are at school. Nevertheless, even when we do not know respondents well, we can spot continuations as well as differences in their presentations of self in different environments. Indeed, some pupil respondents in my research articulated the same opinions, and presented themselves with great consistency, irrespective of the interactive environment (Francis 1998).

What further complicates this mixed picture of consistency and inconsistency is the way in which our constructions of self clearly depend on other people as well as ourselves. This social construction of self has always been recognized by social constructionists (for example, Berger and Luckman 1966; Shotter 1989). Just as we temper our speech depending on our perception of the views of those with whom we interact, so too their perceptions of us and their responses to us inform our constructions of self. Hence, for example, my construction of myself as assertive has been built by comparing my actions to those of others, and by the responses of other people to my behaviour.

So the self incorporates both contradiction and consistency, and is constructed by ourselves and by others. That this is a complex picture seems to me to be hardly surprising, given the complexity of human behaviour and social interaction. And it seems plausible to assume that human power relations might be equally complex and contradictory. To think, for example, that while power relations are exceedingly complex at a micro level, and power is not a 'possession', certain factors such as wealth, social class, gender, ethnicity and so on are also likely to impact on groups of people in particular ways, either limiting or aiding access to power and financial security.

## Diversity and similarity

This acknowledgement of the complexity of human power relations, and of the impact of material factors on our power positions, leads us to a further question. Is there sufficient similarity of identification on which to build emancipatory movements around factors such as gender, ethnicity and so on? Or are such movements based on false and totalizing constructions of sameness (for example, shared womanhood)?

Writers such as Mirza (1997) credit postmodernism with providing the theoretical tools to reveal the exclusions of the totalizing theories articulated by white, middle-class feminists. I reiterate that the adoption of the unitary approaches to political theory which Mirza criticizes is indeed unhelpful and potentially unjust. An acknowledgement of the limitations of our 'grand narratives' must be retained and maintained in feminist research. However, it seems depressing that recourse to postmodernism was necessary in order for us to recognize power differences among women. Reflection on our personal, micro lives and relationships (a traditional feminist method used to inform macro theory) reveals plainly that experience is diverse, that we are not all positioned in the same ways in gender discourse and that other factors apart from gender impact on our power positions.

We speak from our various subject positions, which depend on the material reality of our lives (for example, whether we have male or female genitalia, black or white skin, ready money, and so on), and on our consequent positioning in discourse. So, for example, someone with a penis is positioned as a boy from birth, and this will impact on his view of the world, with the result that he has to work hard to see the world from other perspectives. Similarly, as a white, middle-class woman my experience and perception will be skewed in a particular way. It is impossible that I will experience, say, the issue of racism in the same way as a black woman. Even when I experience racism, I do so from a completely different perspective due to the historical colonialist context and (in Britain) to being a member of the ethnic majority group. It follows, then, that because I am not a black woman, I cannot (or should not) speak of how it feels to be a black woman. It is this materialist rationale which leads some men to call themselves 'pro-feminists'. These men believe that they cannot experience what it is like to be a woman, and therefore cannot speak for or with women. Instead they show their solidarity and respect for a feminist position by calling themselves 'pro-feminists'.

However, these conclusions are problematic for a number of reasons. The very concept of 'personal' reflection on experience is based upon the humanist notion of 'authentic' selfhood. It assumes that one can 'know oneself' in a relatively consistent and unitary way, and that consequences necessarily follow from material factors such as sex or skin colour. This position, then, potentially returns us both to humanism and to biological essentialism. Yet conversely, the conclusion that material differences mean that we cannot share experiences holds significant, destabilizing consequences for emancipatory movements. For example, if women all experience life differently depending on their ethnicity, social class and a myriad of other important factors, is the creation of a movement based on the 'sameness' of one aspect of their identity (gender) a fallacy? Could such a movement ever have relevance for the diverse experiences of all women? As has been observed above, many black feminists have been critical of white feminists' generalizations about 'all women'. Yet sometimes they in turn have been accused of making generalizations about all black women, or subsuming all minority experience under the heading 'black', when in fact experience differs between ethnic minority women depending on ethnic group, religion, class and all the other factors alluded to above (Mirza 1995b; Ahmed 1997). Hence the full acknowledgement of difference destabilizes and threatens to fragment *all* emancipatory allegiances concerning gender, 'race' and so on (Archer *et al.* 2000).

Indeed, some have argued that the various structural factors affecting identity are so complex that it becomes impossible to analyse them all. Cealey Harrison and Hood-Williams (1998) criticize notions of the 'intersection' of aspects of identity such as gender. They assert that such factors do not merely intersect: rather, a multitude of different factors are inseparably intermeshed. Cealey Harrison and Hood-Williams conclude, therefore, that it becomes meaningless to attempt to analyse one factor of identity (such as gender) at the expense of others, but also that so many factors impact on dentity in such multiple ways that attempts to analyse them all are futile.

Hence we arrive at another theoretical conundrum. On the one hand, our experiences are to some extent determined by material factors; yet on the other hand we cannot assume that others similarly positioned will necessarily share our perspectives and experiences. At which conclusion, one might as well abandon all political movements based on alliances and shared values!

Yet thankfully, we are not without agency. We can choose to talk to, form relationships with, and read about the experiences of people with different material characteristics. In this way we are able to learn about and to imagine what it is like to experience life from their perspective. (Or conversely – for example in the cases of white middle-class feminist assertions to men in the 1970s and black, working-class and lesbian feminist assertions to white middle-class feminists in the 1980s – we can choose to insist that others recognize our different experiences.) It is this learning process which has resulted in many white, middle-class feminist researchers in education endeavouring to acknowledge the impact of ethnicity, social class and so on upon interaction besides gender (realizing that simply because we cannot speak 'for' all women we must not marginalize others by speaking as though ours is the only experience). On the other hand, it remains inevitable that this endeavour will always be limited and incomplete. It seems clear to me that we have to acknowledge our human fallibility in our work, and maintain an openness to constructive criticism and information from those from material backgrounds different from ours. Variously positioned as we are, we ought to make clear that all our statements concerning power, equity, inequality and so on are generalizations, and consequently limited.

Yet this recognition does not prevent the generalizations from remaining important, where they can be made convincingly and appear to hold material consequences for particular social groups. Humans *can* form political movements, alliances and strategies with which to act on the world. The results of such strategies may be unpredictable and limited, yet the potential to improve human life remains. We need to maintain idealism as a mode of self-motivation in a far from ideal world.

## Ways forward? Epistemic and interpretive communities

Faced with the dilemmas caused by the relativism of postmodern theory, a number of feminist researchers in education and other fields are attempting to find new ways of conceptualizing solidarity as well as difference, so that work for social justice may be progressed (see, for example, Yuval-Davis 1994; Assiter 1996; Francis 1999, forthcoming; Hey 1999; McNay 2000; and Chapter 6). As Hey (1999: 17) explains, the emergence of these attempts reflects concerns to 'reinstate the possibility of collective or at least collaborative or co-operative "action" in contrast to a withdrawal from taking any responsibility for anybody on the postmodern grounds that nobody can claim to speak for anybody about anything'.

Hey admits that the concepts of 'empathy' and 'rapport' (implying that we can 'know' one another) are steeped in humanism. However, she maintains that the development of 'dynamic partiality of rapport' in some areas does not necessitate the negation of difference, or a return to a traditional humanist position. Despite our non-fixed subject positions, points of affinity can be found and maintained between people in order to form rapport and beneficial social movements. Such a position is arguably more convincing if we accept the argument made above that there is *some* coherence in people's selfhood, allowing agency and strategy.

Cealey Harrison and Hood-Williams (2001) suggest that Mills' analysis of social relations offers an alternative to the binaries of humanist and anti-humanist positions. Mills' account (cited in Cealey Harrison and Hood-Williams 2001) is also particularly appealing to me because it retains discourse analysis (which I have found to be an invaluable theoretical tool), while reintroducing agency. Mills maintains that discourse is the vehicle through which social relations are conducted, rather than being all powerful in itself (as suggested in Foucault's conceptualization). While people are positioned in discourse, Mills maintains that this positioning is conducted by other human beings (in their deployment of discourse) rather than by discourses themselves (see Cealey Harrison and Hood-Williams 2001). The suggestion that people actually choose the discourses which they draw on in order to deliberately position others runs counter to poststructuralist positions (see

Jones 1997; Hood-Williams 1998). Jones interprets such ideas as reflecting a humanist belief in a coherent subject, yet it does not necessarily follow that, just because people can choose which discourses to draw on, they do so in any completely consistent or coherent way (Francis, forthcoming). Again, it is our ability to choose different discourses which enables us to go beyond our personal material realities and envisage the world from other perspectives, enabling sympathy and rapport.

I suggest that reader-response criticism offers some potentially useful concepts with which we might negotiate a path between relativist and realist approaches to difference, similarity and the notion of emancipation (Francis, forthcoming). An example is provided by Fish's (1987) concept of interpretive communities. Given the premise that meaning is not fixed, but rather all readers read texts differently, Fish sought to explain why any two readers ever agree about a text's meaning (in the context of this chapter the question would be why different individuals with multiple subject positions ever hold shared views on the world). Fish argued that there exist various 'interpretive communities': groups of readers with shared values, who will apply a particular perspective to a text and therefore construct the same (or similar) meaning from it. This is similar to Assiter's (1996) concept of 'epistemic community', again formed around shared values, though containing an (often eclectic) mix of individuals and their experiences. Both Fish and Assiter postulate that one individual can be the member of a number of different epistemic/interpretive communities, presumably according to their subject positions and chosen perspectives. (So, for example, one might belong to an antiracist community as well as to a postmodernist one, and so on.)

Feminism, then, is one example of an interpretive community. If we reject biological determinism, and also accept that all women (and men) are different and variously positioned in discourse, it might be argued that sharing a feminist intention and ideological position necessarily makes one a feminist, irrespective of one's sex. Indeed, this is a position I support. I consider that sex is socially constructed (see Davies 1989; Butler 1990), and that feminism is simply a political position, rather than a reflection of biology.

## Conclusion

This chapter has summarized the problematic implications of poststructuralist positions for feminist research. It has discussed some of the points of concern, examining concepts of identity, difference and the tensions between humanist and relativist positions. Some alternative ways of looking at these issues have been explored. Finally, the emergence of a movement towards a new feminist position free from the relativist/realist and humanist/anti-humanist dualisms has been traced. This analysis suggests that the evolution of such an account will require the development of theory in two main areas. The first is discourse analysis: continuing analysis of the various gender discourses is required, in order to provide greater understanding of the ways in which we use them, their impacts on our lives, and potentially how we might resist or reconfigure them. We also need to explore and develop our understanding of consistency and agency in human subjects as well as diversity in subject positioning and presentation. Finally, in order to maintain our feminist 'epistemic' or 'interpretive' community, we need to maintain and develop our openness to, and respect of, the accounts of 'others' within that community.[6]

## Notes

1 The terms 'postmodernism' and 'poststructuralism' have sometimes been used interchangeably in the literature. In this chapter, 'postmodernism' refers to the body of work which revels in the deconstruction and fragmentation of modernist narratives and claims to scientific truth. Poststructuralism, on the other hand, refers to that movement emanating from, and reacting to, the structuralist movement in literary criticism. Where postmodern writers often argue that identity has *become* fragmented by consumerism, globalization etc., a poststructuralist position maintains that the self was never unitary but has always been positioned in discourse.

2 By 'relativism', I mean the sceptical outlook which questions whether there can be any certainty over issues of truth, morality and so on. All values vary from person to person and from culture to culture, and therefore may be seen to be relative. These questions can be applied to all notions of certainty, including that of the coherent individual or 'true self'.

3 In my discussion of the full implications of poststructuralism for feminist positions I differentiate between a 'pure' poststructuralist position and one which appears 'contaminated' by humanist assumptions (Francis 1999). However, I recognize the irony in the notion of a 'pure' poststructuralism, when the poststructuralist position rejects all claims to truth and certainty.

4 Soper (1990) also points out that Derrida's (1976) argument is self-subverting, in that he must allude to the category 'woman' in order to urge us to reject its use.

5 Although of course some poststructuralists might acknowledge such feelings, interpreting them as the self's fanciful quest for authenticity.

6 We are all 'other' from one another in some respect (for example, a working-class lesbian mother occupies a different subject position from a working-class heterosexual primary-school girl, despite sharing their gender and social class). Yet while acknowledging diversity, we need to retain analysis and acknowledgment of the potential impact of these various material factors on our lives and power positions.

# 6

'Re-searching, re-finding,
re-making': exploring
the unconscious as a
pedagogic and research
practice

*Lynn Raphael Reed*

## Introduction

In this chapter I explore a range of tensions within a number of dominant discursive positions on power and method, and voice some uncertainties, intuitions and possible insights in relation to the research act and researcher identity. In particular I question paradoxical certainties within certain postmodernist, poststructuralist and feminist perspectives, challenge persistent attempts to fragment our identities through the lens of social and intellectual critique and untidy some current conceptions of autobiography, voice and identity by asking about the 'unconscious'. I conclude by describing ways in which I have tried to integrate and act upon the ideas expressed here in my own work as a teacher and researcher, specifically in relation to my work on masculinity and schooling, and articulate some wider implications for our pedagogic and research practices.

> *I had a dream last night. In it, I was working in the margins of a gloomy and dusty vestibule in a university; the place where people came to pick up their mail. Congregating here were a number of eminent and published feminist academics. One of them I had wrapped and bound in long strips of parchment linen, and lain down next to her on the ground. In my dream I knew that I was wondering whether she could be my mummy. It was only on rising that the significance of the ambiguity of that term became open to my conscious exploration.*

I am indeed looking for female guides to other wisdoms; 'mothers' to validate and resonate with my search for new ways of seeing the world, breaking out from phallocentric and logocentric knowledge and its attempt to place, marginalize and own me (Luke and Gore: 1992). I have felt comforted to read:

> we can understand the Logos, and the pedagogical production of 'rational argument' itself, as an historically specific phenomenon. The investment of reason in the sexed body, as the foundation of modern scientific rationality, not only locates self control in rational argument, but also places it at the centre of an omnipotent fantasy of control over the workings of the universe. Mastery and control of the 'real' are centrally located in claims to truth and therefore to possess knowledge. In this sense mastery, control and bourgeois masculinity are cojoined in that uncertain pursuit of truth . . . In this the fraudulence of the Logos is that it holds masculinity not in an assurance of control but in a desperate terror of its loss. It is important, then, that we as women should not also be caught in an attempt to master the Logos, to take it as our guarantee and arbiter of truth, and of the possibility of change and transformation . . . its very production and reproduction depends upon a denial of desire and a displacement of the irrational on to women.
>
> (Walkerdine 1985: 234–6)

At the same time, I have strong feelings of ambivalence about many of the female sources I find in the places and spaces I look: the postmodernist and poststructuralist feminist enquiries of the mind; the clever and engaging deconstructions of arguments and epistemologies in words playing through discourses of challenge and empowerment. I recognize that such women work hard and are committed to important academic and political agendas in many and various ways and yet, why is it that I feel at the end of the day that I am not fully animated by their tune; that I do not fully desire them?

At times I am seduced by their embroidery of intellectual cloth, and in some senses shamed by my feeling that I have retreated from political struggle inside and outside of the academy in an easily recognizable activist form. I long for their senses of certainty and community. However, in my heart I still feel that I am being asked to conform to a set of meanings, of symbolizations of how life is, that cannot fully sustain me on my own ground; that cannot support me in a journey towards individuation and the delineation of an authentic self (Jung 1957). Somehow there is still a risk of death in lying down with that body, trickster style – pretending to accept fluidity, diversity, difference; claiming to unknot the grand narratives and rationalist epistemologies, while holding on with integrity to social justice; yet something, somehow, still telling me that this is how it is: this is how it ought to be. I am left feeling that some important part of the 'patchwork' (Griffiths 1995a) is missing. (Perhaps we need to look a little more closely at how these particular discourses themselves construct a set of solid meanings and oppositions; how they become themselves regimes of truth, and what remains in the domain of exclusion.)

Any attempt to explore aspects of 'power' in relation to research method and outcomes immediately raises contextualizing issues of beliefs, values and purposes (Gitlin 1994). Undoubtedly, the juxtapositioning of the two terms 'power' and 'method' itself situates the discussion within a particular discourse: one which assumes that all forms of knowledge are socially constituted and constitutive; that knowledge itself is imbued with 'power' – power to define, demonstrate, disrupt and desire certain social/psychological relations, formations and experiences. At the same time, knowledge (including that advanced in this chapter) is contingent; historically and culturally situated: issues of social import cannot be understood outside their own historical and cultural contexts, any more than they can be comprehended apart from the discursive mechanisms which frame them' (Ledger *et al.* 1994: 7).

In my endeavour to explore and voice my uncertainties about issues of power and method in research I feel both vulnerable and risqué; relatively nude but curiously embodied; eroticized by such visibility and transgression (McWilliam 1996; Rudberg 1996); moved by something other than simply the force of critical analysis (Yates 1992). I can feel/imagine the gaze of authoritative discourse (Bakhtin 1981) on my shoulder in disapproval of the venture, and I am reminded to be cautious about revelation. As Paechter (1996: 81) has said, 'The act of confession is the enactment of a power relation; it confers on the listener the power that accompanies the acquiring of privileged knowledge, in silence. Through the knowledge of the speaker's heart and mind, the confessor is thus enabled both to interpret and to judge.'

Yet rebelliousness still rises as I return continually to the questions: What is it that I feel, yet cannot feel safe to say? What kind of 'knowing' is it that we still cannot talk about, that we still feel uncertain about bringing to the table of our enquiry? What sense of 'self' is it deemed appropriate to reveal (and revere), and which remains shadowy (and troublesome)? What is it that I'm doing in trying to walk this way? Is there power in this method, and if so, what is the method of this power? And what are the implications of all this for how we might research, create future knowledges and dream new ways to be (Griffiths 1995a: 191)?

### 'Power' in a postmodern world: fishing for a slippery eel on an unstable sea

A persuasive and powerful discourse which pervades current discussions of power and method in educational practices is that inscribed by versions of postmodernism, and I therefore feel the need to place myself in some way in relation to this. At the same time I feel ill-equipped to grapple with the body of meaning identified by that term – although that in itself feels like something inherent in its nature as much as my own ineptitude at reeling it in. I also feel myself drowning in a sea of complex interpretations, which I somehow feel I have to have mastered in order to open my mouth. Cixous

(1981: 51) describes this feeling well when she observes: 'the moment women open their mouth – women more often than men – they are immediately asked whose name and from what theoretical standpoint they are speaking, who is their master and where they are coming from: they have, in short, to salute . . . and to show their identity chapters'.

Indeed, Griffiths (1995b) usefully reminds us that postmodernism, as feminism, has multiple versions, and that how these are articulated and utilized can often be confusing and incoherent. As Luke and Gore (1992: 4–5) point out, we walk through landscapes of meaning which do not necessarily take us where we want to go, and the struggle to define our own path is both difficult and potentially misleading:

> Our identity chapters are dog-eared passports, marked by entry and exit stamps among foreign discourses and languages in which we have travelled as tourists. We speak here at a moment in history, in a language and textual terrain not of our own making . . . These treks have taught us that there are no finite answers, no certainties in any one position . . . Trajectories of difference cannot be subsumed under a generalized other.

At the risk of oversimplification, my understanding of the issues and practices, shaped by postmodernist ideas, includes as central the call to abandon essentialist and humanist versions of 'reality', and to see that all versions of the world are partial, fluid and multiple, inscribed with and enacted through power, constituted primarily through language and relationality (in the way that language, situated in specific historical and cultural moments, fragments yet contains 'reality' in oppositional and binary carvings of space and meaning). Postmodernism centralizes an interest in 'self' and 'other' and in the significances of the boundary between.

In some senses it appears a profoundly micro theory – engaging us in close attention to diversity, difference and the performance of subjectivity in specific contexts. On the other hand, it has a macro quality in its insistence that the centre cannot hold, that the grand narratives are no more than fables of explanatory unity, from which the concept of 'discourse', unicorn like, can carry us away. Jane Kenway (1995a: 52), in her materialist feminist critique of postmodernism, calls it 'a new and sneaky disciplinary technology which, by handing around the tools of its own dismantling, reasserts its discipline'.

While postmodernism itself may be ambivalently situated in relation to emancipatory intention, its flexibility and prising open of spaces appears to have energized a number social change theorists across potentially antagonistic positions. As Apple (1996: 141) concludes:

> A good deal of the postmodern and poststructural emphases now emerging in 'critical educational studies' has had a positive effect. It has increased the number of 'voices' that need to be made public. It has helped legitimate and/or generate a welcome return to the concrete analysis of particular ideological or discursive formations, as well as the

multiple sites of their elaboration and legitimation in policy documents, social movements, and institutions (Hall 1992: 537). This focus on the concrete historical instance, without always having to search for 'hidden' sets of determinations, in part does free us to understand the complexities of 'the local' and contingent.

Indeed, the centrality of 'voice' is significant in a number of current writings on power and method. Despite some of the problems identified with it (which I will come on to later) I find the concept of 'voice' very attractive, precisely because of its discursive fluidity; its ability to conjure material and immaterial images; its reference to both socially constituted effects and, at the same time, its embodiment across mental and emotional spheres; its combination of socialism, spirituality and sexuality (it makes me think simultaneously of militantly shouting slogans on demonstrations, mediums speaking in tongues, and Eartha Kitt); and for the idea that I too might speak out and answer back.

The appropriation of 'voice' by social change theorists rests upon another touchstone of our times: 'research as empowerment'. This again has multiple and contradictory uses in the literature, mapped out and critiqued succinctly by Troyna (1994). In some cases, the notion of empowerment of marginalized voices in the research process (as much as the pedagogic process) rests upon participatory and dialogic visions of the encounter, claiming 'catalytic validity' through both changed understandings (of researcher and researched) and observable, transformative effects (Lather 1986). In others, the meaning appears to imply that the very act of recovering, renaming and rehearsing in speech or text (particularly through autobiography) is a radical and empowering act; the reclaiming and restitution of lives lived in the straitjackets of 'race', class', 'gender', 'heterosexuality' and a whole host of 'normalization' discourses (Steedman 1986; hooks 1989). The feminist 'tradition' of claiming the personal as also political, and building between women shared and new namings of (and engagements with) experience, bridges elements of the individual/collective divide (Griffiths 1995a). Magda Gere Lewis (1993: 5) writes: 'With Adrienne Rich I believe that: "only the willingness to share private and sometimes painful experience can enable women to create a collective description of the world that is truly ours"' (Rich 1986: 16).

Of course, the 'project' of 'voice' as 'empowerment' has its limitations. First, there is the danger in a postmodernist application which slips into the proposition that 'anything goes' and that even while telling the tale there are no authentic authorings of a historically and socially situated reality (identities are endlessly fluid). A number of feminists have pointed out the convenience of such an expression for those who might want to deny the significance of gender in power positioning: 'Why is it that just at the moment when so many of us who have been silenced begin to demand the right to name ourselves, to act as subjects rather than as objects of history, then just then the concept of subjecthood becomes problematic?' (Hartstock 1990: 163)

This last point is shared by a number of leftist theorists (Troyna 1994; Apple 1996; Bradley 1996), concerned that the emphasis on identity work as an issue primarily of expression (an epistemic project) leaves unaddressed the need to engage in political struggle over the material and structural conditions of people's existence, and to have 'theories' which are up to that task:

> It would be nice if the social world were no more than a contestation of meanings, so that merely by renaming the world, we could change it . . . [However] our everyday engagement with the process of defining the world takes place within relationships of power which involve differential control of and access to a range of resources, material, political, cultural and symbolic, including the utilization of force and violence. Power relationships put constraints on our ability to remake the world . . .
>
> (Bradley 1996: 9)

For some feminists struggling to articulate together the meanings associated with both 'structure' and 'agency', the solution adopted appears to be to draw on both 'standpoint epistemology' and 'poststructuralist feminism', while recognizing the inherent theoretical tensions that this involves (Harding 1987; Weedon 1987; Luke and Gore 1992; Weiner 1994; Eliot *et al.* 1996). Together these approaches acknowledge the power and effect of discourse; that 'knowledge' is standpoint-specific to where one is located in relation to the dominant discourses; and that only through a politicized and active reappropriation of perspective and identity, on a foundation that respects difference, can we know and engage with the world more productively and transformatively in changing structures and practices. Such a political purpose itself may require the pragmatic utilization of perspectives which cross the modernist/postmodernist boundary:

> We need to be conscious that any research is likely to incorporate elements from both modernism and postmodernism. The view here is that concepts and structures such as imperialism, capitalism and patriarchy will still continue to be explored: the point to make is that a single explanation (or even several) is unlikely to provide the complete (or even a complete) picture.
>
> (Paechter and Weiner 1996: 270)

At some point you have to step off the 'sea of postmodernist theoretical indeterminacy' (Luke and Gore 1992: 7) – not to stake out some kind of permanent territory, but to check that your compass is true to your purpose. The problem returns to one of values, and for feminists an underlying 'moral/ political stance which upholds freedom, justice and solidarity for women' (Griffiths 1995a: 231).

Second, the interest in 'giving voice' as an emancipatory action, for pedagogues and researchers alike, may easily become naive, patronizing or controlling. This is explored successfully in a number of critiques of 'critical pedagogy' (Luke and Gore 1992; Gore 1993; Lewis 1993; Gitlin 1994; Singh 1995). Can such an action in and of itself truly confer power? How does 'giving voice' work strategically in the process of leading to certain outcomes?

How do we identify who are the 'disempowered' and the 'silenced' and how do we know that their presentation of themselves in certain contexts and encounters really represents disempowerment and silence? Is forcing people to break their silence in certain contexts itself oppressive? Who, in any case, is 'Us' and who are 'Others'? What 'totalizing fallacies' are at work when we begin to construct collective identities through structural characteristics? And how do we begin to really get to grips with the complexities of circulatory power in social interactions between people who may be empowered and disempowered in different ways at different moments?

If our interests and our agendas are framed around social action in the interests of social justice then the criticisms and concerns outlined above of the conceptualization of 'voice' as a mechanism of 'empowerment' are all ones to take seriously. The implications of these particular debates around power and knowledge in a postmodern world seem to point out some profoundly uncomfortable epistemological and political tensions, which pull us in different directions. I am left feeling intellectually seasick, not at all sure what I've caught in my net, or that I've got on the right boat. Time to check my compass.

### A different vision of the 'self': the 'unconscious', the psyche and the transpersonal

I started out by saying that I had a feeling of searching for something that I could not quite name or find, and that my readings of writers referenced here did not quite fulfil my needs. This is definitely not an 'either/or' scenario, but more of an 'and also' position. This discussion remains very tentative, since I feel myself moving into a landscape that is not so familiar to me, and for which I do not yet have easily accessible reference points by which to find my way. It is also, I am aware, potentially a mirage.

I want to return to some conceptualizations of the 'self' in these writings, and to consider what we might be missing. I wonder whether there are not some differently empowering ways of 'knowing' about and 'enquiring' about our existence if we took greater risks when stepping outside our logocentric ways of looking at the world. I am using the term 'logocentric' to apply also to much of the feminist writing I have been referring to here, since it seems to me that these women are using a voice that privileges rationality and intellect over emotion and intuition, and also that there is a strong tendency in poststructuralist and materialist feminist writing to insist that a social goal can be achieved by naming it and striving for it in collective actions, without sufficiently envisioning, clearly or creatively, what world space, what senses of 'selves' we wish to unlock: 'resisting oppression means more than just reacting to one's oppressors, it means envisioning new habits of being, different ways to live in the world' (hooks 1991: 218).

I remain interested in the concept of 'voice' (despite the limitations and dangers expressed above) as a mirror into the inner worlds we all inhabit, as much as a strategy for change. My proposition is that we need better to understand the unconscious at work in ourselves as teachers, learners and researchers, so as to move forward to visionary futures. No attempt to discipline, harness and shape the unconscious by our ideological commitments will remove its power over us and between us. At the same time I am suggesting that our cultural tendency, as intellectuals within this historical moment, to ridicule and dismiss the spiritual, transcendental or transpersonal in our search for new futures, is disempowering and moreover out of step with some powerfully transformative elements in cultural expressions around us. Furthermore, our 'ways of knowing' are profoundly ethnocentric and western. Can we 'know' with our hearts? What place does 'intuition' have in our perspective on, and relationship to, the world? What way of knowing, for example, arises from meditation rather than scholarship (Donaldson 1992)? It may be that I am trying to articulate the need for a 'new-age social theory of education' (Wexler 1995), but one that does not leave our socialist and feminist understandings behind.

There is a tremendous anxiety in our postmodern/poststructuralist context about being seen as 'essentialist' or 'humanist' in any way. I understand the importance of resisting any attempt to inscribe particular social formations with naturalistic rationalizations: essentialism can justify discrimination (for example, 'Of course girls can't go to university; their brains aren't up to it'). I would argue that there are essentially human qualities, and that, moreover, many people would articulate their journey in life as being about finding their 'true selves' – a sense of being born into the world with some essence (not a blank page) that then unfolds, damaged or nurtured in a thousand and one ways by a life lived among others. I would also argue that humanism, as a quest to integrate the affective and cognitive in the self-realization project (Rogers 1983) carries an important expression of this quality. This is not to say that there is ever a way of retrieving a romantic notion of the pure self or that our ways of strengthening our sense of authenticity, groundedness or fulfilment do not depend on us understanding and exploring the effects of socially constituted discourses, practices and structures on the unconscious and conscious elements of our identities (see also Francis, Chapter 5).

I am using the term 'self' here in a Jungian sense:

> The self is a quality that is superordinate to the conscious ego. It embraces not only the conscious but also the unconscious psyche . . . There is little hope of our ever being able to reach even approximate consciousness of the self, since however much we may make conscious, there will always exist an indeterminate and indeterminable amount of unconscious material which belongs to the totality of the self . . . The self is our life's goal.
>
> (Jung 1957)

This Jungian interpretation of self has many aspects. The self is an unknowable essence that lies within us; the central archetype; the mosaic that underlies the pattern of the psyche; the transcendence of opposites including the 'anima' and 'animus' within us all; visions of wholeness; and the inner

guide. Representations of this meaningfulness of the self are found in symbolizations like the mandala. The concepts of anima and animus may be
important to our attempts to understand and transform gender relations.
As Connell (1987: 209) says:

> Jung, in his essay 'Anima and Animus' . . . suggests that sexual character
> is systematically layered in the sense that the public face of femininity
> and masculinity, compatible with the conventional social role, is
> always constructed by a repression of their opposites. A kind of un-
> conscious personality (the 'anima' for men, the 'animus' for women)
> develops as a negative of the socially acceptable one, and their incom-
> patible demands underlie many of the tortured emotional dynamics of
> marriages . . . Jung's argument dramatizes . . . that femininity and
> masculinity can co-exist in the same personality . . . The evidence for
> layering is convincing, and requires us to see the tension between the
> different layers or tendencies in personality as a constitutive force in
> gender relations.

This has some similarities with the call to bridge binary oppositions as a
means of liberation, to 'trace the other in self' (Spivak 1990: 326), but it is
also a method of overcoming the subject–object dualism by theorizing the
dialectic between them in the human psyche. It also provides a handle for getting a grip on the 'masculine' within us all; when I respond to the world I am
bringing to that encounter my own masculinity or animus, constituted in and
by the unconscious, yet powerfully shaping my responses in the conscious
world. The idea of the anima and animus carries social and psychological
dimensions combined – female and male principles inscribed in interactions
between women and men, and a symbolic theory of what our internal
world of sexualized identity is. That is to say, *how* we carry the opposite
within us. One of the most problematic aspects of researching into boys and
masculinity in schools (Raphael Reed 1999) is that we haven't begun to
find an adequate way to talk about power, identity, sexuality and the unconscious; to get at the quality, the texture and the textuality of this in our lives in
a way that can take us further forward; to understand the masculinity within
us (Redman and Mac an Ghaill 1996).

Dreams are just one way of making contact with the complexity of the self
within. Karen Signell (1990: 39–40), in her book *Wisdom of the Heart: Working
with Women's Dreams*, asks 'how can you experience the self?':

> You know you are in its presence when you feel tremendous energy and
> emotion, for the Self has numinosity, an aura of wonder and mystery.
> It is the source of the life-force, creativity, love and healing. You can
> experience this special energy as the buoyancy of the playful spirit, a
> feeling of certainty in yourself, the excitement of creativity, the warmth,
> tenderness and passion of love, the feelings of grace and harmony that
> can come from the transcendent power of healing. The pure energy-
> force of the Self, and the primal feelings that flow from it, are sometimes

too powerful to encounter as forces and too fluid to comprehend; they often take form as images, which we can understand and handle more easily.

Such feelings and experiences are widely felt and are not solely explainable by having achieved an 'emancipatory' political position or collective harmony with others. Awareness of such potentiality may partially explain why increasing numbers of people in our society are turning to eastern meditative spiritual practices, including physical forms like yoga and t'ai chi, forms of psychotherapy (transpersonal psychotherapy, core process psychotherapy and psychosynthesis) and alternative medical practices (homoeopathy, acupuncture, shiatsu etc.) which are predicated on ideas of 'intangible nature', individual wholeness (mind/body/soul) and energy exchanges that cross individual boundaries and unite us across space and time.

People consciously engaged in this particular sense of a journey point to the material effects of these practices. This is not to say that this is any kind of 'proof', but it is to point out that there are other dimensions to experience and 'knowingness' being mapped out here, which the terror expressed of anything 'essential' in currently influential discourses on 'empowerment' may well be blocking. It may be that what is being described here is partially captured by the idea of 'empathy' – i.e. connectedness across frontiers, even without a rational sense of shared subject positions: 'people, not belief systems, have dialogues' (Sellar 1994: 246). These are unfashionable thoughts in the context of the academy, so I am reassured to find some articulation of the same issues elsewhere (hooks 1991; Donaldson 1992; Wexler 1995). As hooks (1991: 218–19) puts it:

> I have been most interested in the mystical dimension of religious experience. And that concern has not been experienced as being in conflict with political concerns, but more as in harmony with them. They are integrated for me, part of a whole . . . There is such perfect union between the spiritual quest for awareness, enlightenment, self-realization, and the struggle of oppressed people, colonised people to change our circumstance, to resist – to move from object to subject; much of what has to be restored in us before we can make meaningful organized protest is an integrity of being. In a society such as ours it is in spiritual experience that one finds a ready place to establish such integrity.

What this speaks of is the importance of identity work as a mental health issue, the possibility of *combining* spirituality with a radical political position, and the need to find a means of integrating the different parts of our identities – to seek and find some harmony, as a means of empowerment.

This notion of finding 'integrity of being' contrasts starkly with the fragmentation and fluidity of identity and subject positions proposed by the postmodernist ethic. It is closer in a sense to feminist attempts to cohere female identity around a politicized purpose, recognizing that there is a need to reappraise and articulate together different senses of one's self, different elements of experience and different subject positions, using introspection, community and 'critical autobiography' (Griffiths 1995a).

A distinguishing feature for me in responding to such writings, is the degree to which theoretical articulations of social categories ('gender', 'class', 'race') intrude upon and determine the stories we are told, and the extent to which centripetal forces (rather than centrifugal) shape the account (Rosen 1993). I remain dissatisfied with critical auto/biographical accounts (of which there are many) which tidy away the disruptiveness and the insight of the unconscious, where the emotional and intuitive domains are kept firmly within the control of the intellect, and where the proposition that we can make ourselves more whole by a politicized retelling of our lives so obviously ignores certain aspects (particularly problematic and shadowy aspects) of our identities. I find more satisfying accounts in the writings of those who dig a little deeper (Walker 1984; Miller 1987; Milner 1987; hooks 1989; Le Guin 1989) and respect deeply those able to acknowledge that their sense-making of the world is profoundly shaped by that which we can hardly name:

> we all bring almost unnameable information from childhood. We are unable to shuffle off that particular mortal coil. If we are lucky, we make transitions, and don't live in that time of pain and rejection and loneliness and desolation. But there will understandably be bits of it which adhere to us and will not be pulled off by love nor money.
>
> (Angelou 1988: 6)

## Telling the stories we feel we can't tell/accessing the unconscious to empower our voice

In this section I want to describe some of the ways in which I have tried to integrate and act upon some of the ideas expressed here in my own work as a teacher and researcher, and to illustrate some of the effects. I engage in life history and autobiography work with the students I work with (trainee and qualified teachers, mainly women), often in conjunction with a programme on feminist methodology and life history methodology. I do this within an explicit context that stresses the discursive marginality of narrating experience in our education system and acknowledges that in telling such tales we are reordering and selecting for specific purposes, not all of which we will be conscious of. Life stories:

> should be seen not as blurred experience, as disorderly masses of fragments, but as shaped accounts in which some incidents were dramatised, others contextualised, yet others passed over in silence through the process of narrative shaping in which both conscious and unconscious, myth and reality, played significant parts.
>
> (Samuel and Thompson 1990, quoted in Rosen 1993: 9)

I demonstrate the notion of explaining ourselves and our practices with different 'voices' by unpacking my own work, currently concerned with 'working with boys', illustrating the difficulty we have in accessing and articulating certain layers of identity which are being projected onto, and sustained by, what we are doing as researchers in certain contexts. This illustrates a number of important points. First, that researcher identity, like teacher identity, is not static or fixed, and individuals have multiple subject positions from which to make sense of their world (Norquay 1990). Second, that issues of power and method profoundly affect that which may influence us as researchers but will not be easily owned up to or discussed as a valid research issue. Finally, that we can productively use the idea of 'voice' from different layers of the psyche, rather than from different subject standpoint positions alone.

The first 'voice' I use is that of an academic feminist sociologist in a new university department of education, interested in exploring and theorizing the issues around the dominant discourses on boys and schooling (see Raphael Reed 1995a, 1997). The second 'voice' is that of a radical inner-city teacher, experienced at working with boys in many challenging contexts, and angry and militant at the manipulation and undermining of teachers committed to and struggling with the issues in classroom spaces (see Raphael Reed 1995b). The third 'voice' is that of a mother of sons, closely and personally interested and implicated in their growth into manhood (I have two sons aged 19 and 8, fathered by two different partners, one dead and one alive, which suggests an understanding of presence and loss – perhaps another 'voice' to know?). The fourth 'voice' is the hardest to own in a public space, and yet possibly the one that has most significance in terms of why I am doing this work at all – what I bring to it, what I see in it, what I make from it for others and myself. It is a voice from my unconscious, found by my own processes of introspection and discovery through a theraputic process using multiple ways of accessing the unconscious: dreams, guided imagery, painting, narration and meditation. It is a voice that understands and feels the damage caused by being the daughter of parents who wanted me to be a son; the daughter of a father whose own psychic pain caused him to project onto me the necessity to reflect back to him that he was 'all right' when he most obviously wasn't – to heal his wounds by endless attention to his ego. I was a daughter of a mother and a female lineage where female power, particularly through female sexuality, was denied (afeared of). Having finally been found and given permission to speak, this voice has given me a certain freedom from an endless repetition of the same dynamic with 'boys' in my life (boys I teach, boys I research, boys I live with, boys I work with). It is a voice reconnected to the self, with a powerful surfacing of my anima through dreams and images of the psyche; a voice I find expression for through particular forms of language, writing and art. Such profoundly personal and individual insights may also be seen as a recognizable feature of the psychic effects of patriarchy, identified so well by Walkerdine and others. But knowing this intellectually, and exploring it in the unconscious by the use of therapeutic and spiritual devices, are two very different things. The second, I would claim, has far more transformative value.

The response from the teachers to the session I teach on exploring the unconscious through spirituality and therapeutic devices is often incredibly powerful and positive. They report feeling tremendously energized and empowered by hearing me explore these elements across the conscious/unconscious divide. They take from it a realization of the richness of understanding and insight which they too might gain by researching their inner worlds in this way, and by refusing to keep the inner world and the outer world separate. Many of them see the possibility of using autobiographical work to explore some elements of the unconscious for themselves, in tune with hooks' (1991: 6) description: 'Often I felt as though . . . the shape of a particular memory was decided not by my conscious mind but by all that was dark and deep within me, unconscious but present. It was the act of making it present, bringing it out into the open, so to speak, that was liberating'.

In encouraging my students in this direction there are pieces of women's writing that I use as triggers, and objects which spark off memories. I have used art materials, encouraging people to use marks and symbols to represent their life story to themselves and others; I have encouraged people to make unedited and private tapes of their own reminiscing, and to keep dream diaries. I have used templates to enquire into the constitution of our own teaching and research perspectives, identifying significance from a number of different standpoints and layers: 'personal', 'professional', 'past', 'present', 'thoughts' and 'feelings'. The philosophy of my practice stresses that: 'by keeping to the foreground the rich emotionality of our own and others' personal narratives, we can find ways of resisting the encroachments and confinements of oppressive institutional structures and political ideologies' (Middleton 1995: 98).

Not all of these strategies are appropriate in all contexts; in particular, they require trust and willingness to explore identities in this way, and undoubtedly there is much personal material which it is not safe to explore in certain public contexts. I am not pretending to offer therapy. In addition, I do not have a simplistic notion of the forms of expression that will arise in such contexts. For a start there are the performative effects of any kind of memory work in a group – things being said for a particular audience and within a particular context. Mary Kehily, reporting on the work of the Gender and Sexuality Group at Birmingham University identifies this clearly:

> [My] stories were indeed social acts, points of public negotiation between self and others. They can also be read as my desire to shape an individual identity which would have resonance with what I perceived to be the more collective identity of the group – a way of saying, 'This is me and I'm also one of you, want to be one of you'.
>
> (Kehily 1995: 28)

However, I would suggest that this way of working casts some doubt both on Volosinov's (1973) claim that all communication is social and Bruner's notion that there are only two ways of knowing: paradigmatic and narrative (Bruner 1986). I think that some of these ways of listening in, knowing and expressing, present an alternative concept of the 'human mind', one that can operate in 'point' mode as well as 'line' mode (Donaldson 1992), closer in some ways perhaps to the Buddhist concept of 'primordial clarity of mind'.

## Relandscaping 'research'

Finally, there are a few things to say about the implications of all this for us as researchers. I am not saying that researchers should operate in the field as therapists for others, which would be entirely unethical, although without a doubt there is often a sense of unburdening which operates in certain situations, often between women, or where the researcher is projecting and employing active and empathetic listening skills (Oakley 1981; Brannen 1988). However, I do think that we need to acknowledge two dimensions to the research experience: one is that we bring with us to our enquiry a set of issues, ways of looking and stories of sense-making which are profoundly affected by 'knowledge' and significances we carry in our unconscious; the second is that if this is true for us as researchers, it is also true for us and others as teachers and learners. This is a domain of influence most certainly affected by discursive practices and political structures, but also potentially a window into our psyche that connects us and influences us beyond social determination (i.e. through the transpersonal and the spiritual). My suggestion is that we bring all of this into play in our performative expressions (actions and words), yet this is not an arena fully researchable through empirical observation or conventional interpretive devices, nor is it usually recognized as a research effect. I have tentatively suggested in this chapter some ways of exploring the unconscious in and through research and would welcome further discussion.

It is also my claim that we can utilize exploration of our unconscious as researchers to enrich and deepen our engagements with the world through the research act. This can happen in three ways: first, by allowing us an added layer of 'meanings' and positionings from which to understand what we are seeing, how we are interpreting what we see and how we are interacting with those around us; second, to sensitize us to the multiplicity of layers of meaning-making going on among those we are researching; and third to see the research effect upon ourselves as an internal dialogue of creation. By this I mean that research is potentially a fertile medium for exploring and transformation our own identities, weaving new wisdoms through re-searching, re-finding and re-making.

*Part 3* | Identity constructions revisited

# 7 Gender and the post-school experiences of women and men with learning difficulties

*Sheila Riddell, Stephen Baron and Alastair Wilson*

## Introduction

It is often possible to learn a great deal about a field by looking not at the well-trodden ground, but at the gaps, the absences and the silences. Until relatively recently, the sociology of disability has been a very underdeveloped area (Barton 1994), a fact that has implications for studies of educational settings. As a broad field of study, education draws on a wide range of disciplines and it is not accidental that in some areas (for example, special educational needs) the ideas and methods of psychology are often used, while in other areas (for example, youth culture) the ideas and methods of sociology are adopted. This chapter begins by looking at three distinct areas which have remained in relatively watertight compartments, but which could provide new and interesting insights if brought together. These three areas are the sociology of education, the sociology of disability and feminist social research. It is argued that the reason for the separate development of these fields is far from accidental and betrays a limitation in their fundamental vision and concerns. Subsequently, an example is given of a piece of research which attempts to draw creatively on each of these fields. This research explores individuals' experience of learning disability in the context of lifelong learning, drawing out gender and class differences. While identifying social barriers, the researchers wished to understand the different ways in which these are experienced by women and men in particular situations. Although there is a burgeoning literature on lifelong learning, very little has been written about the experiences of people with learning difficulties within the learning society. Finally in this chapter, we indicate future research routes which might be pursued in the school and postschool context.

## The sociology of education

The sociology of education developed in the postwar period with a focus on the charting of social class inequalities in the selective education system. Subsequently, interest developed in the sociology of youth cultures and studies such as Paul Willis' *Learning to Labour* (1977) provided insight into the production of masculine identity. As has been observed in previous chapters, by the late 1970s, interest was growing in gender and 'race' both in terms of achievement and the management of identity. However, apart from a small number of texts such as Tomlinson's *A Sociology of Special Education* (1984), special educational needs remained the territory of psychologists, who still retain a strong presence and focus on teaching and learning in relation to the individual child. There are glaring gender differences in this area (see Daniels *et al.* 1994; Riddell 1996).

For example, three quarters of children with a Statement (England) or Record of Needs (Scotland) are boys. In the post-16 arena, most students on special needs further education courses or on government training programmes are male. In certain non-normative categories such as emotional and behavioural difficulties the gender imbalance is particularly marked, with boys accounting for 80 per cent of such pupils. Pharmaceutical solutions are increasingly sought to deal with the problems such pupils pose to schools' endeavours to improve their attainment levels. While boys' greater susceptibility to genetic disorders, early illness and accidents explains some of the gender disparity in the field of special educational needs, major cultural factors are also at play. However, we still lack an effective ethnography of the experiences of pupils with special educational needs. The research discussed later on in this chapter applies ethnographic methods to the study of adult learners.

## The sociology of disability

This seam of study has been opened up relatively recently by writers such as Oliver (1990), Barnes (1991) and Barton (1994). Drawing on Marxist theory, these writers seek to identify the economic causes and effects of disabled people's oppression. The major organizing concept here is the social model of disability, based on the premise that disability is the product not of individual impairment, but of the social, economic, cultural and political context in which impairment is experienced. Writers like Oliver and Barnes have questioned the validity of qualitative methods and rejected individualized accounts which, they say, simply reinforce the notion that disability is a personal tragedy rather than a social product. Writers in disability studies have begun to question this outlawing of personal accounts. Carol Thomas (1999), for instance, points to a key lesson of feminism – that understanding and critiquing personal experiences may fuel political struggles. Shakespeare *et al.* (1996) provide accounts of disabled people's sexuality to counteract the absence of any discussion of sex and love, even in books on disabled people and marriage (Parker 1993). Shakespeare *et al.*'s book had a very mixed reception, with one eminent reviewer suggesting that some of the accounts were 'perverse'. Clearly, then, there exists a tension between the focus on identity and experience of much recent sociology and the determination of some sociologists of disability to shift away from discussion of the personal towards structural accounts.

## Feminist social research

A further lack of *rapprochement* has existed between feminist scholarship and the work of disabled feminists. Jenny Morris (1993), for example, criticizes much feminist work for being rooted in the concerns of middle-class, white and non-disabled women. She is particularly critical of some feminist work on community care (for example, Finch and Groves 1983) which suggests that moving disabled people out of long-stay institutions is likely to create an additional burden for women. Similarly, Morris is critical of much work in the 'young carers' research movement, which again pitches the interests of disabled people against those of children, instead of recognizing reciprocity in relationships and that the real problem is the lack of funding for adequate services. While some of these issues have been addressed, it is clear that major gaps exist between the work of mainstream feminist scholars and disabled feminists. Some research which deals with the construction of identity forgets that disability may be of central importance to many women, particularly as they get older. Similarly, research which seeks to return to a focus on structural factors (for example Skeggs 1997) foregrounds gender and social class, and ignores disability.

The insularity of the broad fields described above may well be to do with unresolved power differentials between particular social factions. However, as noted earlier, our central argument is that there is much to be gained from breaking down these barriers which are both theoretical and methodological. Below, we draw from a study which took as its starting point some key concerns in the sociology of post-16 education. The central concern of the study was to understand the ways in which the learning society was being played out in the lives of a group at the margins of that society – people with learning difficulties. The study sought to understand the way in which a constellation of factors, including disability, gender, social class and age, interacted to shape the social conditions in which people experienced lifelong learning (see Riddell *et al.* 2001b for a full account of the research). While we drew extensively on ethnographic methods, we also conducted an extensive interview survey with service providers and rooted our account in an analysis of official statistics on the education, training and employment experiences of people with learning difficulties in Scotland.

## A brief account of the research

The Economic and Social Research Council project '*The Meaning of the Learning Society for Adults with Learning Difficulties*' (Riddell *et al.* 1997, 1998, 1999, 2001a, 2001b; Baron *et al.* 1999), from which the summary case studies are drawn, used a range of methods to explore the lifelong learning opportunities available to people with learning difficulties. In Phase 1 of the research, carried out between September 1996 and August 1997, we undertook 100 interviews with a range of key informants throughout Scotland in order to map lifelong learning opportunities and explore discourses of disability embedded in the nature of services and their mode of delivery. Representatives of education and social work departments in the 32 Scottish local authorities were interviewed, along with training managers in 22 Local Enterprise Companies (the Scottish equivalent of the English Technical Enterprise Councils). Further interviews were conducted with key informants in voluntary organizations, user groups, the Employment Service and careers companies, as well as with senior civil servants. Official documents on lifelong learning and community care were also reviewed. Phase 2 of the research, carried out between September 1997 and September 1999, consisted of 30 ethnographic case studies of women and men with learning difficulties. Each individual was visited about ten times over a six-month period in a range of settings such as their workplace, a social setting or their home. Interviews were also conducted with significant others and these were particularly important in relation to people with little or no speech.

A number of theoretically informed criteria were used in the selection of case studies. More men than women were chosen, reflecting the fact that men outnumber women in this group by about 2: 1. Half of our case studies were in a rural area where services were sparsely distributed and half were in an urban area where services were perceived as relatively well-developed. With regard to age, individuals were selected from three groups, the post school group (16–24), the post-transition group (25–39) and the middle to older age group (40+). We had hoped to include some individuals from minority ethnic families but managed to identify only one individual from a South Asian background to participate. Professionals felt that people with learning difficulties from minority ethnic backgrounds are often not included in opportunities for further education and training.

We deliberately avoided a clinical definition of learning difficulties, although a range of surveys conducted from a health perspective (see Espie *et al.* 1999 for review) suggest that about 4 per cent of the population has a learning disability and the proportion may be growing at about 1 per cent per annum. Rather, we adopted an operational definition so that our focus was on people identified by services as having a learning difficulty. It was evident that the category of learning difficulties covered a very wide range of people, from those with little or no speech to those who had little cognitive impairment but experienced extreme social disadvantage. Tables 7.1 and 7.2 summarize key characteristics of case study individuals. In writing about the case studies, we emphasize that each is unique. At the same time, reading across the case studies, a number of recurring themes emerge concerning the social forces shaping individual identities and life courses. Both the particularities and commonalities of the case studies are referred to in the discussion section. The particular cases selected for discussion in this chapter exemplify recurrent themes in the education and training of males and females emerging from the ethnography. Both their typicality and particularity are discussed.

In exploring post-school experiences, we were particularly interested in the ways in which social capital (networks based on mutual trust and reciprocity) was used by women and men (see Riddell *et al.* 1999; Blaxter and Hughes 2000 for further discussion of social capital). We were particularly interested in exploring the ideas of Putnam (2000) that there are two essentially different types of social capital. *Bridging social capital*, characterized by loose ties, helps people escape from their existing social position by making links with others. *Bonding social capital* links people to others in the same social world, thus helping people to 'get by' rather than 'get on'. Bridging social capital is described by Putnam as a 'sociological WD-40', whereas bonding social capital is described as a 'sociological superglue'. In the following sections we demonstrate how we have applied social capital theory to the lives of men and women with learning difficulties, drawing particularly on the notion of bonding and bridging social capital. At the same time, we have attempted to infuse our analysis with an awareness of the ways in which gender structures people's relationship to social capital. We begin with a broad analysis of the types of social capital experienced by the 32 case studies of people with learning difficulties, drawing out gendered dimensions of their experience. Subsequently, we present two case studies of a man and a woman with learning difficulties to illustrate how social capital is experienced in particular lives.

## Broad themes in the post-16 experiences of women and men with learning difficulties

Tables 7.1 and 7.2 summarize key aspects of the lives of the 30 case study individuals. A key feature of these lives is the extent to which the status of being a person with learning difficulties dominates the nature and quality of accessible social capital. For example, most individuals attend special school, where they are unlikely to acquire the social capital likely to be of use to them in opening up employment opportunities. From special school their lives continue along a 'special' trajectory, moving into special Further Education (FE) courses and training programmes, with little access to mainstream opportunities. The post-school transition period is often followed by placement in a day centre, where short periods of supported employment alternate with intermittent short-term courses in further education. This finding from our case studies is supported by Scottish Executive statistics, which show that 93 per cent of people going to day centres do not have paid work; only 20 per cent of activity in day centres takes the form of education and employment; while 28 per cent involves leisure and recreation. Only 25 per cent of

**Table 7.1** Case studies from urban area

| Pseudo-nym | Age | Gender | Nature of impairment | Domestic circumstances | Primary responsible organization | Main daytime placement | Primary context studied | Interviews conducted with significant others | Major issues |
|---|---|---|---|---|---|---|---|---|---|
| Fred | 17 | M | Communication disabilities | Home: mother | FE | FE college | FE class | Mother, course tutor, key worker, observation of FE class | Mother withdrew permission for case study to continue. Whole FE class researched while studying Open University module 'Equal People' |
| Roger | 17 | M | Heart complaint and non-specific mild learning difficulties | Home: mother, partner & brother | Local voluntary organization specialist training provider | LEC skillseekers specialist training provider | Work placement | Voluntary organization training manager, placement employer | Health problems and difficulties finding employment |
| Dean | 17 | M | Autistic spectrum | Home: parents, brother | FE | FE class | FE class, outdoor activities class | College tutors, parents | Need to find niche in which to use considerable IT skills |

| Name | Age | Sex | | Home | Local voluntary organization specialist training provider | LEC skillseekers specialist training provider | Work placement | Voluntary organization | |
|---|---|---|---|---|---|---|---|---|---|
| Reggie | 18 | M | Non-specific learning difficulties, scarring as a result of an accident | Home: mother, 3 siblings | Local voluntary organization specialist training provider | LEC skillseekers specialist training provider | Work placement | Voluntary organization training manager, placement employer | Continual training, difficulties in finding employment, viewed as suitable for marginal employment only |
| Kelly | 19 | F | Muscular dystrophy – non-specific mild learning difficulties | Home: mother, brother, sister | FE | FE class | Home, FE class | Mother, father, course tutor | Serious debilitating health problems limit engagement with education and work |
| Martin | 23 | M | Down's syndrome – moderate learning difficulties | Home: parents and sister | Social work & FE | Adult resource centre/classes at college | FE class, adult resource centre | Mother, key worker | Difficulties in becoming independent from home and day care |
| Mick | 33 | M | Down's syndrome – moderate learning difficulties | Home: elderly mother | Social work | Adult resource centre | Adult resource centre, FE class, dance class | Mother, key worker | Over full timetable with only 2 hours work, benefits problems |

**Table 7.1** continued

| Pseudo-nym | Age | Gender | Nature of impairment | Domestic circumstances | Primary responsible organization | Main daytime placement | Primary context studied | Interviews conducted with significant others | Major issues |
|---|---|---|---|---|---|---|---|---|---|
| Bobby | 39 | M | Non-specific moderate learning difficulties | Supported in own home by housing association | Social work & housing association | Adult resource centre & P/T work via supported employment with job coaching. | Adult resource centre, home, work | Keyworker, employer – voluntary organization manager | Benefits difficulties permitting only 2 hours work per week and supported living difficulties, problems surrounding development of intimate relationships |
| Clare | 43 | F | Down's syndrome – moderate learning difficulties | Supported in own home by housing association | Social work | Adult resource centre with P/T work at weekends | Adult resource centre, home, FE classes, dance class, camera class | Social worker, key worker, home support worker | Issues around legal status of *incapax* preventing increased independence and work, value of employment to increasing social contacts |

| Name | Age | Sex | Disability | Home situation | Agencies | Services | Settings | People involved | Issues |
|---|---|---|---|---|---|---|---|---|---|
| Ronald | 44 | M | Non-specific mild learning difficulties | Home: elderly mother | ES | Supported employment, ES wage subsidy scheme | Work | Employer, union representative, manager of specialist voluntary organization providing ES supported employment place | Rationalization by employer leading to threat of disciplinary action and certification as disabled with ES intervention |
| Liam | 47 | M | Non-specific moderate learning difficulties | Home: brother, brother's family | Social work and voluntary organization | Adult resource centre/voluntary organization specialist training provider work programme | Work, adult resource centre, FE class, voluntary organization recreation club | Keyworker, brother, voluntary organization training manager | Failure of specialist training provider to cope with challenging behaviour |
| Fiona | 49 | F | Non-specific moderate learning difficulties | Supported in own flat (weekly visit) | Social work & voluntary organization providing supported living | Adult resource centre/looking for employment with assistance of voluntary organization | Adult resource centre, home, FE class | Social worker, support worker | Previously worked F/T now restricted by benefits problems to P/T, social life structured around activities of now deceased mother, need for new social opportunities |

**Table 7.1** continued

| Pseudonym | Age | Gender | Nature of impairment | Domestic circumstances | Primary responsible organization | Main daytime placement | Primary context studied | Interviews conducted with significant others | Major issues |
|---|---|---|---|---|---|---|---|---|---|
| Basil | 50 | M | Non-specific moderate learning difficulties | Home: elderly parents | Voluntary organization providing supported employment | P/T work via supported employment through specialist training provider | Work, pub, café, voluntary organization disco | Manger voluntary organization supported employment provider, employer | Social life restrictions, benefits issues preventing increased hours of work |
| Bryce | 55 | M | Non-specific mild learning difficulties | Bed & breakfast: social work registered | Social work | Adult resource centre | Adult resource centre, swimming, voluntary organization recreational activities | Keyworker, landlady | Loneliness, difficulties of living arrangements, cycles of training |

*Abbreviations:* ES = Employment Service; F = female; FE = further education, F/T = full time; IT = information technology; LEC = local enterprise company; M = male; P/T = part time.

sheltered workshop spending goes on learning disabilities (Scottish Executive 2000b). An alternative route, followed by a few more able individuals, is into a special 'Skillseekers' programme followed by periods of unemployment. Such individuals tend to become increasingly invisible to the system as they move further away from transitional support. The lack of access to coherent post-school education, training and employment, all traditional sites for the formation of bridging social capital, has negative consequences for the social capital of people with learning difficulties. In terms of family relationships, it is evident that people with learning difficulties tend to move from strong bonding relationships, where they are often kept in a suspended state of childhood for far longer than their siblings, to a state of orphanhood following their parents' death or infirmity. Siblings are generally unwilling or unable to fulfil the role of the parent, and as a result the person with learning difficulties is forced abruptly into a potentially hostile environment without the gradual loosening of family ties which normally accompanies a shift into adulthood (see Figure 7.1).

Having described the commonalities in the lives of people with learning difficulties, it is essential to note the way in which the broad patterns, including the relationship to social capital, are infused by gendered social structures and relationships. First, it is important to note that men are much more likely to be identified as having learning difficulties than women. Scottish Executive statistics based on the schools census (Scottish Executive 2000b) show that

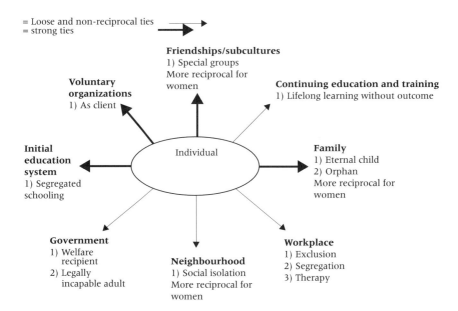

**Figure 7.1**  Principal relationship of individuals with learning difficulties to sources of social capital

**Table 7.2** Case studies from rural area

| Pseudo-nym | Age | Gender | Nature of impairment | Domestic circumstances | Primary responsible organization | Main daytime placement | Primary context studied | Interviews conducted with significant others | Major issues |
|---|---|---|---|---|---|---|---|---|---|
| Chris | 18 | M | Down's syndrome, non-specific moderate learning difficulties | Home: parents | FE classes | FE | Home, FE classes, work placement | Mother, father, FE course tutor, placement employer | Benefits of FE, limited options post-FE, subsequent return to day services |
| Maureen | 20 | F | Non-specific severe learning difficulties, severe mobility problems | Home: parents | Social work | Adult resource centre | Adult resource centre | Parents, manager at adult resource centre | Ongoing serious health difficulties, problems of diagnosis, day services provision |
| Jack | 21 | M | Non-specific moderate learning difficulties | Home then supported accommodation | Social work | Adult resource centre | Adult resource centre | Key worker at adult resource centre | Allegations of abuse within family resulting in move to supported accommodation, death of parent ended case study prematurely |

| Name | Age | Sex | Disability | Home situation | Provider | Employment | Setting | Key people | Outcomes |
|---|---|---|---|---|---|---|---|---|---|
| Lois | 21 | F | Non-specific mild learning difficulties | Home: with mother | LEC specialist training provider | Training for Work programme placement, then unemployed | Home, work, voluntary organization specialist training provider | Mother, employer, manager voluntary organization specialist training provider | Cycles of training, failure to gain employment, abusive relationships |
| Sally | 21 | F | Non-specific mild learning difficulties | Home: mother, father, brother | LEC specialist training provider | Skillseeker, Training for Work, ES supported employment, then unemployed | Work, home, job centre | Father, employer, manager voluntary organization specialist training provider | Cycles of training, sporadic training and support, abusive relationships |
| Greg | 26 | M | Serious eczema, non-specific mild learning difficulties | Home: mother, sister | LEC specialist training provider | Full-time work, ES supported employment | Work | Father, supervisor at work, manager of voluntary organization specialist training provider | Successful F/T employment, adaptive employer, benefits of ES supported employment |
| Imran | 27 | M | Down's syndrome, non-specific moderate learning difficulties | Residential group home | Social work & voluntary organization providing residential and day care | Adult resource centre/ voluntary work, 1 morning per week | Adult resource centre, home, voluntary organization recreational activities | Best friend, key worker, mother | Dissatisfaction with day services/ difficulties in finding alternatives, depression |

**Table 7.2** continued

| Pseudo-nym | Age | Gender | Nature of impairment | Domestic circumstances | Primary responsible organization | Main daytime placement | Primary context studied | Interviews conducted with significant others | Major issues |
|---|---|---|---|---|---|---|---|---|---|
| Mavis | 27 | F | Cerebral palsy, non-specific severe learning difficulties | Home: parents, siblings | Social work | Adult resource centre | Home, adult resource centre | Mother, key worker at adult resource centre, social worker | Allegations of abuse by family, inadequacy of day services provision |
| Lisa | 27 | F | Non-specific mild learning difficulties | Home: mother and father | Social work then voluntary organization specialist training provider | Day services, ES work placement, P/T voluntary work | Home, work placement, voluntary work placement | Parents, key worker, 2 employers, voluntary organization (employment support) manager | Withdrawal from inadequate day services, difficulties encountered in accessing ES/ voluntary organization work programmes |
| Kirsty | 28 | F | Non-specific moderate learning difficulties | Home: parents and sister | Social work | Adult resource centre | Adult resource centre, home, FE class | Parents, adult resource centre key worker, course tutor | Increasing independence, lack of differentiated services preventing progression |

| Name | Age | Gender | Learning difficulty | Living situation | Provider | Activities | Locations | Key people | Issues |
|---|---|---|---|---|---|---|---|---|---|
| Doris | 33 | F | Non-specific mild learning difficulties | Supported in own home by housing association | Social work | Adult resource centre, community education class, voluntary work | Home, adult resource centre, community education class | Boyfriend, community education worker, key worker, home support worker | Lack of differentiated provision beyond day services to enable increased independence |
| Iona | 41 | F | Non-specific mild learning difficulties | Home: parents, brother | Community education | P/T work | Work, community education class | Community education class coordinator and course tutor, employer | Increasing independence |
| Ewan | 46 | M | Non-specific mild learning difficulties | Residential group home | Social work & voluntary organization providing residential and day care | Day services, P/T work | Home, adult resource centre | Key worker, employer, adult resource centre staff | Restrictions on independence/ employment opportunities imposed by DSS/ social work/ voluntary organization funding |
| Kate | 47 | F | Non-specific moderate learning difficulties | Home: shares with husband | Social work & specialist housing association | Adult resource centre, looking for part time employment | Adult resource centre, home | Husband, key worker | Supported in long-standing marriage and own home |

**Table 7.2** continued

| Pseudo-nym | Age | Gender | Nature of impairment | Domestic circumstances | Primary responsible organization | Main daytime placement | Primary context studied | Interviews conducted with significant others | Major issues |
|---|---|---|---|---|---|---|---|---|---|
| Maud | 56 | F | Non-specific moderate learning difficulties | Group home: shares with three others | Social work | Adult resource centre | Adult resource centre | Key worker at adult resource centre, home support key worker | Lifetime in training |
| Ruth | 67 | F | Mild depression, non-specific moderate learning difficulties | Residential group home | Social work & voluntary organization providing residential and day care | Day services/ FE | Home, further education college, adult resource centre | Key worker, further education college tutor | Difficulties adjusting to group home following 20 years in institutional setting, long-term treatment for depression, restrictive nature of residential care preventing increase in social networks formed at FE |

*Abbreviations:* ES = Employment Service; F = female; FE = further education, F/T = full time; IT = information technology; LEC = local enterprise company; M = male; P/T = part time.

of the 9360 pupils in special schools in Scotland in September 1999, two thirds were male. Females accounted for 21 per cent of those with language and communication disorders, 16 per cent of those with social and emotional difficulties, 36 per cent of those with moderate learning difficulties and 40 per cent of those with severe learning difficulties. Moderate learning difficulties is by far the largest category, accounting for 28 per cent of all pupils in special schools. Reasons for this disparity, which rest on a complex mixture of men's heightened susceptibility to impairments associated with germs, genes and trauma, as well as complex cultural factors, have been discussed in the education literature (for example, Riddell 1996). However, there is a silence with regard to the gender disparity among adults with learning difficulties. To inform the work of the Learning Disabilities Review Group, the Scottish Executive commissioned an overview of epidemiological evidence (Espie *et al.* 1999), but this report made no mention at all of gender differences. Our research suggested that there is a lack of awareness and problematizing of the predominance of men in the population of people with learning difficulties. This does not imply that gender is irrelevant, but rather that it is ignored. A clear instance of this is the disparity in access to government training programmes by women and men with learning difficulties. Analysis of access to the Employment Service's Work Preparation programme, for example, conducted as part of a Department for Education and Employment funded project (Wilson *et al.* 2000), indicated that women made up only a quarter of people participating in Work Preparation in Scotland in 1999.

As noted earlier, the research project from which data are drawn in this chapter focused on the significance of the learning society for people with learning difficulties. There was much evidence that training and supported employment were structured by gender. For example, one of our case study individuals participated in a horticultural squad run by a voluntary organization which was made up exclusively of men. Men were also more likely to undertake heavy kitchen work and cleaning, whereas women participated in cooking, waitressing and clerical work. Particular issues which arose for the women in our case studies, such as sexuality and reproductive health, tended to be ignored or dealt with in a somewhat peremptory manner by social workers and carers. In the case of another of our research participants, who experienced a form of muscular dystrophy, there was no attempt to discuss with her the significance of her genetic condition, which was heritable and progressive, clearly having major implications for her reproductive decisions. At least two of the women in our case studies had been sterilized, and tentative discussions with them suggested that their understanding of the medical intervention was at best only partial.

In terms of relationships to social capital, particularly in the domains of family, friendships and neighbourhood connections, it was evident that women were much more likely than men to be engaged in reciprocal activities, such as babysitting and undertaking caring tasks for other family members (Riddell *et al.* 2001b). The only person in our case studies who was married was a woman, and several other women had boyfriends.

While these relationships were not unproblematic, they contrasted with the general male experience where relationships existed only at the level of fantasy. This of course may have been to do with the attitudes of carers and key workers, who tended to see women with learning difficulties as in need of sexual protection, while men were seen as a sexual threat.

To summarize, many aspects of the lives of men and women with learning difficulties are structured in such a way as to preclude or restrict opportunities for education and training, thus limiting the formation of bridging forms of social capital. Women, however, are more likely to be engaged in the type of reciprocal social relationships which contribute to the wider regeneration of social capital. This is likely to bring benefits to them in terms of a more meaningful and fulfilling social life, but is unlikely to have a major impact on their economic position. The following case studies illustrate how gender is experienced in the post-16 lives of a man and a woman with learning difficulties.

## Case studies of post-school experiences of women and men with learning difficulties

*Clare*

Clare was a woman of 43 who lived alone in an elegant city apartment inherited, along with a private income, when her mother died. She had Down's syndrome and spent her weekdays at a resource centre. Clare was an only child and both parents had been well paid professionals, with Clare's father dying some 25 years earlier. After special school, Clare attended a sheltered workshop doing domestic tasks before moving to the resource centre. The attempts by the resource centre to move Clare into more integrated settings were resisted by her mother; a paid job which Clare secured was stopped by her mother on the grounds of exploitation, while a similar, unpaid, job for a charity was allowed.

Clare's life situation changed dramatically after her mother's death. She was the sole beneficiary of a trust set up under the will, administered quarterly by distant family members and, on a day-to-day basis by a local lawyer. This trust not only gave Clare the right to live in the flat but was also capable of generating an annual income some one and half times average British earnings: Clare was a wealthy woman. However, as a result of Clare's categorization as an incapable adult (*incapax*) the trust was administered by the lawyer. Daily expenditure, including purchase of items such as birthday presents, had to be given prior approval, effectively denying Clare any degree of control over her finances.

Clare's timetable from the resource centre (see Table 7.3) was full, with commitments to special clubs every weekday night. She had a job on Sundays as a waitress and was in the process of getting another waitressing job on a Saturday. She banked her earnings and used this money, outside the trust, to buy items which she decided she would like. Clare very much wanted to

**Table 7.3**   Clare's timetable from the resource centre

|           | *Morning*                        | *Afternoon*                        | *Evening*                          |
|-----------|----------------------------------|------------------------------------|------------------------------------|
| Monday    | Drama:<br>FE college A           | Art Class: resource<br>centre A    | Games club                         |
| Tuesday   | Woodwork:<br>FE college B        | Swimming                           | Drama class: resource<br>centre B  |
| Wednesday | Free all day:<br>at home         | At home                            | At home                            |
| Thursday  | Yoga: youth centre               | Dance performance:<br>dance studio | Action group<br>(advocacy group)   |
| Friday    | Life skills course:<br>FE college C | At home                         | Resource centre C                  |
| Saturday  | Free all day:<br>at home         | At home                            | At home                            |
| Sunday    | Work as waitress in<br>fish restaurant | At home                      | At home                            |

*Abbreviations:* FE = further education.

marry a particular man, and confided in the researcher that 'one day he will buy me a ring'. However, this was hindered by a certain lack of reciprocity and the status of *incapax*. Clare also spoke about children, but said 'I can't have one at the minute'. Another plan was to have a flatmate to live with but the trust would not agree. The social work staff involved with Clare reported that every move which they and Clare made towards her being more independent was challenged by the lawyer on the grounds of *incapax*. Nevertheless, her private income meant that Clare could pay a daily home help, a key person in enabling her to live independently. Clare was expected, as a matter of course, to undertake housework and look after her personal possessions, in contrast to Bryce (see below).

It was evident from Clare's flat that her life was governed by a number of rules which she had written out in large coloured letters and pinned up as notices around the flat. Some of the notices were reminders to do certain things around the flat, such as 'Turn off the water heater' and 'Do not put metal in the microwave'. Another message on her bedroom door said 'No more sex'. She explained that this was a notice directed at a man who came to the flat who, according to the key worker, was exploiting her. The key worker's anxiety was driven by the fact that local authorities have a duty of care towards people receiving community care services. However, the effect of this duty was to construe all women with learning difficulties as potentially vulnerable to abuse and all men as potential abusers.

*Bryce*

Bryce lived in a large Scottish city. He was a slight man in his mid-fifties, who looked older than his years. He attended a special school where, during his later years, he learned to mend shoes, a trade which he was never able to put into practice. He had never worked or had a long-term girlfriend, sources of great sadness to him. The reason he was unable to work, he said, was 'I'm not very clever. I couldn't get a job no matter how I tried'. A former girlfriend had 'gone off with another man'. Bryce explained 'Now I'm going to be a bachelor because I haven't got a job'. His retirement ambition was to get a job. Bryce lived with his mother until she died, and then moved into accommodation under the community landlady scheme. His community landlady felt that his mother's death had been particularly hard for him to come to terms with because, until her death, he had lived in a very sheltered environment. She described the way in which Bryce's sister looked after him:

> Bryce's sister was in America but she was home when her mum was dying and we were on an outing . . . I was just getting to know Bryce at this stage and we were in one of the big restaurants and she sat and she actually took Bryce's coat off him, she drew back the chair, she sat him down, pushed his chair in, put the napkin, tucked it round his neck for him and then proceeded to cut up his sausages.

When his mother died, Bryce was forced to make a sudden move out of the family home into a hostel for people with learning difficulties, where he had problems fending for himself in an impersonal environment. At the time of the research, Bryce had no contact with any family members. He appeared reasonably contented at the community landlady's house, although staff at the day centre thought he might be frightened by the man with whom he shared a room. The authoritarian nature of the relationship between the landlady and the tenants was also evident, as shown by this comment from the landlady:

> If I go to give Bryce a row, I feel very guilty because he ends up standing there like a wee 10-year-old who feels as if he is waiting to be pounced on and you can see him – his eyes and he starts to get that stern look and his wee bottom lip starts to go and I say, 'Bryce, I am not going to pounce on you but you are wrong so you are getting a row'. Basically the things Bryce gets a row for is being unshevelled, unshaven and not keeping himself clean and tidy and it is an ongoing battle with him.

Part of the community landlady's job was to encourage the residents to become more independent by helping with household tasks. However, it was clear that the landlady subscribed to the view that it was inappropriate for middle-aged men to be involved in housework:

> At 55 – I mean I am told that I should be involving him more in doing cooking and doing their laundry, doing their ironing – at one point I had Bryce doing his ironing and he was just a nervous wreck and

**Table 7.4**   Bryce's timetable from the resource centre

|  | *Morning* | *Afternoon/evening* |
|---|---|---|
| Monday | Craft activity in centre | Quiz in centre |
| Tuesday | Going for a walk: FE college | Going for a walk: FE college |
| Wednesday | Adult basic education class | Centre: relaxation class |
| Thursday | ARC: art class | Placement in horticultural project |
| Friday | ARC: watch videos | Group meeting with key worker |
| Saturday | At home | At home |
| Sunday | At home | At home |

*Abbreviations:* ARC = adult resource centre; FE = further education.

> I thought – I am giving this man more grief because I am told I am try-
> ing to make him better – I am actually making him worse, so I am not
> doing it.

Bryce attended many centres and courses for people with learning difficulties around the city, and his resource centre key worker felt the long journeys
by bus and on foot were in danger of exhausting him. There was also concern
that he was repeating courses rather than finding new ones which would
extend him. Table 7.4 illustrates the range of activities in which he was
involved.

Most of Bryce's social life took place in special settings. On a number of
evenings each week he was taken to and from a club in a social work minibus.
His key worker at the day centre said that although the idea of segregated
social arrangements made her cringe, many people with learning difficulties
enjoyed these events because of the opportunity it gave then to network. In
addition to the social clubs, Bryce was taken for an outing once a week by a
befriender. The centre key worker described the purpose of the relationship
in the following way:

> They go out every Saturday together – Littlewoods for a cup of tea.
> In some ways having a befriender, for Bryce, is about meeting other
> people and doing other things. More of an equal relationship than
> controlling you and telling you where to go and what to do.

At other times, as this resource centre worker commented, Bryce, like other
people with learning difficulties, encountered hostility in his daily routines:

I know from people's experiences they are not treated as adults – they get abuse every day from kids on the bus and there is stuff that goes on which is horrendous. I think we are living in a society that fears people with learning difficulties. We never see anyone with learning difficulties as sexual so there is a huge battle there.

Bryce experienced periods of anxiety and depression, triggered by traumatic life events but also due in part to the monotony of his weekly resource centre timetable. He had become very depressed after the death of his mother, and a recent road accident (when he had been knocked down and had broken his leg) had again led to a sudden loss of confidence. At the time of the research, he was taking antidepressants and was also being taught relaxation techniques at the centre.

## Discussion and conclusion

In this final section, we first draw together some of the messages from the case studies presented here before considering the implications of this work for future research in the field of gender and education.

In the case studies of Clare and Bryce, there are clear commonalities in their relationship to social capital, and in their opportunities for further education and training, which were largely governed by the attributed category of 'person with learning difficulties'. Bonding forms of social capital, particularly in their families, restricted rather than promoted their personal growth and development. While these strong family bonds were a major formative influence in early life, in later life they prevented Bryce and Clare from forming their own families. According to Bryce, his lack of work made it impossible for him to fulfil the traditional male role of breadwinner: he interpreted this as the main reason why he had been unable to have a girlfriend. Factors arresting Clare's social development were rather different. Despite her inherited wealth, the legal status of incapable adult prevented her from using financial resources to support an independent life and friendship/family networks. Many aspects of her life, including the expression of her sexuality, were closely overseen by the trust. It appeared that the financial interests of the distant relatives who were the eventual beneficiaries of the trust came before Clare's right to self-expression and independence.

Despite these similarities, relationships to social capital for Clare and Bryce, as well as for other people with learning difficulties in our study, were overlain by gendered relationships and structures. Bryce's dependence, for instance, was exacerbated by the fact that he was not permitted to undertake domestic work for himself. Even though she was provided with a home help from trust funds, Clare was expected to participate in this aspect of her life and this contributed to her greater degree of independence. In addition, Clare was working as a waitress in a supported employment scheme and, although this made little difference to her financial situation, it was widening her social contacts.

We have argued throughout this chapter that, since social capital is germane to much government policy, it is important to engage in a critical assessment of its utility. It is characterized as an inevitably benign influence within official policy and by academics such as Putnam (2000) and Wilkinson (1999), who see the existence of egalitarian societies as a necessary condition for the formation and maintenance of social capital. However, it is very clear that social capital has a dark side, and that social cohesion may be based on the exclusion of particular groups on the grounds of gender, 'race' and dis/ability. Our analysis of the post-16 experiences of people with learning difficulties suggests that both women and men were excluded. However, women's social networks tended to be stronger than those of men. While not providing them with access to economic power, nevertheless women experienced greater social connection as a result of the expectation that they would act independently, at least in the social sphere. So, ironically, the expectation that domestic work is primarily women's responsibility, which acts as an oppressive assumption for many women, inadvertently provided a greater range of opportunities for women with learning difficulties than their male counterparts.

The work presented above provides an example of how key elements in the sociology of education, the sociology of disability and feminist social science may be drawn together to understand better the educational experiences of people with learning difficulties and disabled people more generally, whether located in school or postschool settings. These case studies have employed ethnographic methods to explore culture and identity, and there is a clear need for in-depth ethnographic accounts of the experiences of disabled children in school. At the same time, we believe there is a need for quantitative studies of, for example, patterns of achievement by disabled people in different settings, looking at the interaction of a range of variables including gender, 'race' and social class. The insulation of different fields of study has, in the past, limited our understanding. Drawing on the insights and methods of different theoretical approaches will challenge preconceived expectations and open up new possibilities for further study.

# Issues of gender and sexuality in schools

*Mary Jane Kehily*

## Introduction

This chapter will explore issues of gender and sexuality in school and will consider some of the practical ways in which the categories of 'gender' and 'sexuality' work together to structure the experience of schooling. The chapter is intended to address issues of practice and the concerns of practitioners in educational settings. Specifically the chapter aims to explore two key questions:

- How do issues of gender and sexuality manifest themselves in school?
- What are the implications for educational practice?

The chapter is based upon data drawn from school-based research in four secondary schools in the UK where fieldwork took place over a four-year period.[1] In all schools a range of qualitative research methods were used which included group discussions, participant observation and semi-structured interviews with groups and individuals. Some parts of the chapter are based upon my doctoral research (Kehily 1999a), an ethnographic study which explored the ways in which school students negotiate issues of sexuality within the context of the secondary school. Throughout the study I suggest that school students maintain a strong sense of agency and often organize their own cultural groups within the school in ways that give shape to pupil sexual cultures. In using the term 'pupil cultures' I am referring to informal groups of school students who actively ascribe meanings to events within specific social contexts. My approach suggests that the processes of meaning-making which students engage in produces individual and collective identities which carry social and psychic investments. The doctoral study documents the ways in which issues of gender and sexuality feature in the context of pupil peer groups and the implications of this for sexual learning and the construction of sexual identities. I pay particular attention to the interrelationship between gender and sexuality and the ways in which school students negotiate complex social relations that can be both creative and constraining.

To address the two questions posed above, the chapter is divided into three main sections. The first section looks at contemporary perspectives on gender and sexuality and suggests that these ways of looking provide a backdrop to issues of gender and sexuality in school. The second section focuses more specifically on issues of gender, sexuality and pupil experience. It draws upon ethnographic data and looks in detail at masculinities, femininities and the implications for sex-gender identities in school, the form they take and the ways they can be interpreted. The final section discusses gender and sexuality in relation to educational practice and considers the implications for teachers and teaching.

## Perspectives on gender and sexuality

Contemporary perspectives on gender and sexuality often point to a dichotomy between essentialist and social constructionist ways of looking. Essentialism is commonly understood to rest upon biological arguments to posit that gender difference is genetically determined and that each gender carries with it a set of physical, emotional and psychological characteristics. Social constructionist perspectives on the other hand suggest that gender is shaped by and through the society in which we live. There are many different social constructionist perspectives on gender, however they all share the idea that becoming male or female is a social process that is learned through culture: in the family, in school and in social interactions more generally. Viewing gender as culturally specific also suggests that notions of gender are not fixed but may in fact change over time and place. Social constructionist perspectives frequently point to the ways in which gender can be understood as relational. In other words, what it is to be male is often defined in relation to what it is to be female and vice versa.

Correspondingly, the gendered identities of masculinity and femininity can be seen in terms of a mutually defining and mutually exclusive relationship. In this respect the relational aspect of gender categories produces and sustains binary opposites which may be invoked in stereotypical ways:

| masculinity | femininity |
|---|---|
| strong | weak |
| active | passive |
| hard | soft |
| rational | emotional |

Dualisms such as those above may be seen as part of a tradition of western thought which has many consequences for us as gendered human beings. One often unacknowledged consequence has a direct bearing on sexuality and sexual identity. Sexual desire invoked through gender arrangements is premised upon the widely held assumption that if you are a man you will inevitably be attracted to a woman, and if you are a woman you will inevitably be attracted to a man. Adrienne Rich (1980) refers to this as 'compulsory heterosexuality': the largely unspoken policing of sexual desire in culture which makes same-sex relationships marginal and even taboo. The assumed dominance of a heterosexual order in societies places heterosexual relationships at the centre – as 'normal' and normalizing – and thereby indicates that all other forms of sexual relationship remain 'deviant' and 'abnormal'.

How do the ideas about gender and sexuality outlined above relate to schools? The concept of the 'hidden curriculum' has been used by educationalists to acknowledge that learning extends the boundaries of the official curriculum and may have inadvertent effects. What is learned by pupils may not fit with the intended aims of teachers and educational policy makers (see Hammersley and Woods 1976; Whitty 1985 for a discussion of these themes). Research from this period suggests that through participation in school routines, pupils learn to conform or resist the official culture of the school (see, for example, Rosser and Harre 1976; Willis 1977). I would like to suggest that the 'hidden curriculum' can also be seen in terms of the regulation of sex-gender categories. Within the context of the school much informal learning takes place concerning issues of gender and sexuality; the homophobia of young men, the sexual reputations of young women, and the pervasive presence of heterosexuality as an 'ideal' and a practice mark out the terrain for the production of gendered and sexualized identities. Furthermore, such social learning is overt and explicit rather than hidden.

A rich vein of research on gender and schooling has exposed the gender inequalities that exist between young men and women and the implications for school-based policy and practice (see, for example, Griffin 1985; Lees 1986, 1993; Connell 1987; Weiner and Arnot 1987; Arnot and Weiler 1993; Kenway and Willis 1998; Gordon *et al.* 2000). This body of work has the effect of 'making visible' the experience of girls within the schooling process and points to the need to account for gender inequalities in school. Gordon *et al.* (2000) explore issues of inequality as a spatial dynamic as well as an effect of power relations. Their innovative approach to themes of marginalization and participation demonstrates the complexity of gender arrangements and the need for a reformulated notion of 'citizenship' to be taken up in schools.

Further research has drawn attention to sexuality and particularly the heterosexist structure of school relations by acknowledging gay and lesbian identities in school (Trenchard and Warren 1984; Sears 1992; Mac an Ghaill 1994; Britzman 1995; Epstein and Johnson 1998). This literature provides us with valuable insights and ways of understanding gendered and sexual hierarchies in schools. Within sex-gender structures in schools, homosexuality may be marginalized and stigmatized through the curriculum, pedagogic practices and pupil cultures. This literature indicates that sexual identities are not biologically given but are created through institutional and lived practices. Moreover, schools can be seen as sites for the *production* of gendered/sexualized identities rather than agencies that passively reflect dominant power relations. More recent work on masculinities has contributed to the literature on gender and sexuality by exploring the recognition that boys too are gendered subjects, engaged in the struggle for masculine identities within schools (Mac an Ghaill 1994; Epstein *et al.* 1998; Gilbert and Gilbert 1998; Pattman *et al.* 1998; Lingard and Douglas 1999). Mac an Ghaill's study in particular illustrates the ways in which diverse sexualities can be spoken through the various *masculinities* young men come to inhabit (see Chapter 12 for problematics of this term). Being a lad may involve the cultivation of a hyper-heterosexual identity, while being a 'wimp' implies occupying a feminized or asexual identity that may easily translate into being called 'gay'. In this sense sexuality underpins the location of young men's masculinities within the schooling system and can be seen to structure gender arrangements more generally.

## Gender, sexuality and pupil experience

In this section we will explore the ways in which gender/sexuality is lived out in school, particularly within pupil cultures. Ethnographic data will be drawn upon to illustrate the ways in which gender and sexuality are interconnected and spoken through each other in the context of the school. In an earlier study (Kehily and Nayak 1996) we suggest that sexuality can be seen metaphorically as a *playground* which provides the site for a multiplicity of games and social interactions. Our analysis points to the ways in which sexuality can be seen as a resource that is frequently used by teachers and pupils to create symbolic boundaries for speech and action. The creation of boundaries, however, also produces the opportunity for multiple transgressions. Sexualized exchanges in school remain an everyday occurrence and invariably involve issues of power which are struggled over in the daily routines and rituals of schooling. Within pupil cultures sexuality takes on particular significance and is frequently linked to gender identity and issues of gender appropriate behaviour. Through the utilization of sexuality, school students may negotiate hierarchies among themselves and challenge the authority of teachers. In the following example two sixth-form students (age 16–17) reflect on the gendered and sexualized name-calling that they routinely encountered in school:

> *Miles*: Girls get called 'slag', it's just something to pass the time, they think. 'Oh look at him, he's quiet, not like everyone else and you get a laugh if you call him gay.'
> *Melissa*: It's for attention I suppose.
> *Miles*: And it makes them look big.
> *Interviewer*: And what do you have to do to be popular?
> *Miles*: Well you got to be disrupting lessons, be cheeky to teachers, otherwise you're looked upon as a wimp or something.

*Melissa*: 'Cos I worked hard people called me a snob, 'cos I got good grades but I didn't want to work on a checkout for the rest of my life.

The experiences of Miles and Melissa suggest that different social codes operate for young men and women in relation to the learning process. Their experiences of name-calling are gendered and sexualized; Miles is seen as 'gay' while Melissa is seen as a 'snob' for working hard and displaying an interest in academic achievement.

## Masculinities

In *Learning to Labour* Willis (1977) illustrates the ways in which conventional masculinity is gendered through class whereby 'manual labour is associated with the social superiority of masculinity and mental labour is associated with the social inferiority of femininity' (p. 148). Willis' study of male working-class pupils in the UK demonstrates that these associations were integral to preparing 'lads' for the culture of work they will participate in when they have completed compulsory schooling. Melissa and Miles suggest that young men engage in various forms of verbal abuse as an activity in itself, 'for attention' and to 'look big'. The concept of 'looking big' has a physical quality to it, acting as a symbolic form of body-building for 'pumping up' male reputations. In such exchanges students draw upon sexualized name-calling to distinguish between the 'lads' and boys who display a more positive attitude to the learning process.

During the research period I became aware of the pervasive presence of homophobia in interactions between young men and, to a lesser extent, young women. Homophobic jokes, banter and abuse featured regularly in male peer groups and have been the subject of earlier studies (Nayak and Kehily 1996; Kehily and Nayak 1997). We found that the potentially emasculating experience of being called 'gay' haunted young men in school and identified certain boys as 'different'. We noted the ways in which homophobic abuse could be carefully codified and ritualized within male peer groups and could incorporate a seemingly endless range of features such as clothes, posture, mannerisms, hobbies, tone of voice, patterns of friendship and attitude to schoolwork. Our analysis of homophobia in school draws upon Butler (1990) to illustrate the ways in which such recurrent rituals can be seen as *performance* – an attempt to convey a coherent heterosexual masculinity (see also Chapter 14).

We suggest that heterosexual masculine identities are sustained through fraught exhibition, where the highly dramatized performance is itself evidence of the insecurities and splittings within the male psyche. In his interview, Miles elaborated upon the social cost of 'getting on' at school in the following way:

*Miles:* It's a sort of stigma ain't it? A quiet person in a class would be called 'gay' or summat. I was for a time 'cos I was fairly quiet in the classroom and for a while everyone was calling me gay . . . To be honest it didn't really bother me. I've never been bothered by insults or that. I just thought they were stupid. I had my own group of friends so it didn't really bother me; it wasn't my close friends who were calling me gay . . . They [the name callers] should be allowed to leave and get a job, it would make life for everyone else a lot easier. I think my grades have suffered 'cos of the disruptive members of the class. They're not really interested in getting a qualification, so it's, 'Well, what can we do for a laugh today? Disrupt the history lesson or something like that'. It just makes it impossible for anyone who wants to get on with their work, 'cos of the things going on in the class, know what I mean?

Miles indicates that non-conformity is in fact a powerful mode of conformity for a certain group of young men in school. Being loud, disruptive and abusive becomes the norm for this group and can be seen as a style for the enactment of a particular heterosexual masculinity. Being quiet and hard working, by contrast, marks boys out as targets for homophobic abuse. Miles claims that the name-calling has had little effect upon him, however he also feels aggrieved that the sexual taunts have disrupted his education and that his grades have suffered as a result of the abuse. Miles' response suggests that he may be cultivating an academic identity as an alternative form of masculinity and could be drawing upon and investing in bourgeois ideological concepts of the work ethic, freedom of choice, individualism and self-sufficiency. Through mental labour Miles can be seen to embrace a version of heterosexual masculinity premised upon intellectual ability, achievement and rational argument. Redman and Mac an Ghaill (1997) refer to this class-cultural style of masculinity as 'muscular intellectual'.

So far we have discussed the links between gender and sexuality in relation to young men in school. I have suggested that homophobia and the threat of homophobic abuse regulates interactions among boys and produces a social hierarchy for the public appraisal of masculinities. In such a structure certain forms of masculinity achieve social status within male peer group cultures and provide a sphere for the enactment of dominant versions of heterosexuality. Other researchers (Mac an Ghaill 1994; Nayak 1997; Sewell 1997) point to the links between masculinities, sexuality and ethnicity. This literature documents the ways in which South Asian males may be 'feminized', seen as weak and placed in a subordinate relation to the perceived strength, dynamism and hyper-heterosexuality of African-Caribbean males. Miles reminds us of the social and psychic costs involved in the negotiation of sex-gender hierarchies and also suggests that other versions of masculinity are possible in school, if not entirely comfortable or high status.

*Femininities*

Studies exploring the social experiences of young women have documented the many ways in which young women's lives are shaped and lived through the notion of sexual reputation (see, for example, McRobbie and Garber 1982; Griffin 1985; Canaan 1986; Cowie and Lees 1987). Many of these studies stress the dominant regulatory power of young men to categorize young women in terms of sexual availability as 'slags' or 'drags'. Canaan's (1986) study of US middle-class girls in school points to the ways in which female friendship groups are also concerned with issues of sexual reputation. Canaan cites the example of a young woman in her study who was rumoured to have kinky sex with her boyfriend involving, among other things, the novel use of McDonald's french fries. Canaan documents the responses of other young women and suggests that they collectively 'draw the line' (p. 193) between acceptable and unacceptable sexual activity. In these moments female friendship groups incorporate spheres or practices they feel comfortable with and displace practices that do not concur with their collectively defined femininity. Young women who do not draw the line incur a reputation as 'the other kinda girl' (Canaan 1986: 190), the sexually promiscuous and much denigrated female figure whose lack of adherence to conventional morality serves as a 'cautionary tale' for young women to be ever vigilant in the maintenance of their reputation.

I have drawn upon the insights of feminist studies to further explore the ways in which young women define and establish a culture of femininity through engagements with popular culture, and particularly teen magazines. During the research period I found that young people frequently used popular cultural forms as a resource and a framework for discussing issues of sexuality. Plots from soap operas, advertisements, celebrities and magazines were cited and used as reference points in discussions of physical attraction, sexual relationships, parental constraints and sexual orientation. In such discussions cultural references acted like road maps, charting the hazardous terrain of sexual taboo and prohibition. The discussions also provided a frame or a way of looking at sexuality whereby students could juxtapose their personal experiences to media constructions. Magazines aimed at a teenage, predominantly female market can be seen as part of this broader social context of popular, mass produced and publicly shared media products which speak to young people in particular ways and enable them to talk back. In this sense teen magazines form a cultural resource for young women which they can, at different moments, 'talk with' and 'think with'.

The explicit treatment of sexual issues in contemporary girls' teen magazines has been a source of controversy and comment (see Kehily 1999b for a further discussion of these themes). Teen magazines containing features on sex and readers expecting to be informed and entertained by the sexual content of the magazine can be seen as a form of partnership, or 'contractual understanding' as Barker (1989) refers to it. The young women I spoke with suggested that this source of sexual knowledge is viewed critically by individuals and mediated by friendship groups. *More!* magazine in particular aroused controversy among the young women. In the following example a group of friends (age 14–15) discuss the differences between two magazines and the ensuing effects on their behaviour as readers and friends:

*Clare:* But that *More!* really goes into it. I mean some of the stories are, you know, you wouldn't want to tell anybody about 'em. Like, if you look in those other magazines they say, 'My boyfriend did this and what can I do?' and a story and there's other stories you would want to tell your friends at your age. But that *More!* magazine, it's more, you know, for 17-year-olds to read 'cos it goes too into depth with them.

*Amy:* In fairness to *More!* though, it aims at a higher age group, so, like, it's younger people's fault if they read it, or their mom and dads' fault.

*Interviewer:* But you'd find, like, things in, say, *Sugar,* you'd all talk about among yourselves?

*Clare:* Yeah.

*Amy:* Yeah we would.

*Ruth:* Yeah.

*Amy:* But you couldn't do the same with *More!* magazine.

*Interviewer:* Because of embarrassment?

*Amy*: It is yeah. You say, 'Oh I saw this in this magazine' and then everybody starts laughing at you.

*Clare:* Yeah, it just goes over the top really.

In this discussion Clare, Amy and Ruth suggest that *More!* breaks the contract between magazine and readers by being too sexually explicit. By printing stories 'you wouldn't want to tell anybody about' *More!* is placed beyond the collective reading practices of these young women. Their embarrassment suggests that their reputations may be tainted by reading and embracing *More!* magazine. Amy's comments, particularly, indicate that to repeat features to friends may result in embarrassment and humiliation: 'everybody starts laughing at you'. This collective action which relies on humour to deride and 'other' a member of the group is illustrative of the ways in which these young women negotiate some subjects deemed appropriate for discussion and successfully marginalize others (see also Chapter 14). This active engagement with issues arising from the reading of magazines suggests that female friendship groups provide a site for the enactment of particular cultures of femininity (Hey 1997; Skeggs 1997). This culture of femininity may, at times, work to expel other cultures of femininity such as those contained in the pages of *More!* magazine and external to the friendship group. In this context the 'too in depth' and 'over the top' features of *More!* transgress the boundaries of legitimacy defined by these young women as suitable for their age group and feminine identities. Cindy Patton (1993: 147) has commented on the ways in which identities carry with them a 'requirement to act which is felt as "what a person like me does"'. Clare, Amy and Ruth indicate that female friendship groups adopt a collective 'requirement to act' in relation to issues of sexuality which appears to be anchored in an agreed notion of 'what girls like us do'. This action can be seen to be concerned with the establishment and maintenance of a particular moral agenda which marks out the terrain for discussion and/or action.

The collective activity of female friendship groups in relation to the reading of teen magazines can be seen as part of a constant and sustained engagement in the production of school-based femininities. These processes involve the continual negotiation and delineation of acceptable and unacceptable forms of behaviour/action which bespeak and thereby bring into being feminine identities. The collective investment in particular feminine identities as expressed by the young women I spoke with reveals the associative link between magazine reading and identity work as mutually constitutive acts in their everyday social interactions in school. The creative energy involved in the constitutive enactment of a particular femininity is suggestive of the labour involved in the production of sex-gender identities and can be seen as an attempt to fix and consolidate continually shifting social and psychic locations. The next section looks at gender and sexuality in relation to educational practice and discusses some of the implications for teachers and teaching.

## Some thoughts on pedagogy

Research in the field of gender and education has been instrumental in pro-posing strategies for gender reform and intervention in schools. Kenway and Willis' (1998) Australian study on the effects of gender reform in schools indicates that the remaking of gender can have positive outcomes for the school as a whole. Their study concludes that schools where gender reform was successful were open and refreshed by new ideas; encouraged and cele-brated difference; and recognized the importance of changing their practices and themselves. Applying the success of gender reform initiatives to the area of sexuality has not been easy, though the concept of cultural and sexual citizenship proposed by Gordon *et al.* (2000) remains an interesting and worthwhile project. In terms of present practice, the work of the Sex Education Forum (1995, 1997) in the UK points to many examples of good practice and highlights the importance of sexuality/relationship education to the lives of young people.

In the context of a discussion about changing masculinities Lynn Segal (1990) suggests intensive, anti-sexist consciousness raising for young people in schools and youth organizations as a way of developing awareness of sexual power, especially in relation to date rape. The ethnographic study I conducted suggests that such an approach could be usefully extended to include a critical take on gender and gender appropriate behaviour where some of the insecurities and contradictions of gender identity could be broached. The following points for consideration in the development of sexuality education arise from discussions I have had in in-service work with teachers:

- A recognition of pupil sexual cultures offers a starting point for teachers. It may not be helpful to presume that pupils are 'innocent' in the domain of the sexual – some are sexually active and *all* pupils will be aware of the significance of sexual cultures to their lives and identities.

- Student-centred approaches may be helpful for teachers and pupils to develop their own moral/political positions.
- Popular culture can be seen as a resource for sexual learning and can be utilized by teachers for discussion. Young people do not absorb ideas passively but are active in constructing beliefs from a range of sources.
- It is important to recognize schools as sites for the production of sexual identities.
- Ground rules need to be established with students for discussion and behaviour. Teachers need to respect differences and be aware of power relations.
- Teachers should work with colleagues, governors and parents to create a progressive policy supportive to practitioners.

## Concluding comments

This chapter has discussed the links between gender and sexuality and the ways in which these categories work together to structure the experience of schooling. The introduction posed two key questions:

- How do issues of gender and sexuality manifest themselves in school?
- what are the implications for educational practice?

Based on ethnographic data drawn from interactions with young people in schools the chapter suggests that issues of gender and sexuality affect the everyday routines of schooling and as such become a significant site of social learning. Much of this social learning can be seen in terms of the regulation of sex-gender categories. Students develop an understanding of the meanings and implications of sex-gender categories and also create their own meanings in a range of informal encounters. The chapter suggests that gender differentiated social codes operate in schools and serve to regulate the experiences of pupils. Whereas homophobia acts as a structuring presence in the lives of young men, notions of sexual reputation shape young women's experiences. Finally the chapter addresses issues of pedagogy and suggests some points for consideration in the development of sexuality/relationship education.

## Note

1 Earlier parts of this research and analysis were carried out jointly with Anoop Nayak. I would like to acknowledge his creative contribution to this work.

# Racialization and gendering in the (re)production of educational inequalities

*Ann Phoenix*

## Introduction

'Race' and education are long-standing subjects of debate in Britain. For example, in the 1960s black and South Asian parents campaigned against policies of bussing their children in order to disperse them among different schools. This practice started in Southall, London, and was then supported more widely by the Department of Education and Science (DES). The publication of *How the Black Child is Made Educationally Subnormal in the British School System* (Coard 1971) drew attention to the concerns that black parents and teachers had long been expressing. This disquiet eventually led to the publication of the Rampton (DES 1981) and Swann (DES 1985) reports into the educational underachievement of black children.

In the years since then, debates on 'race' and education have shifted as theoretical understandings and accepted practices have changed. It is, for example, no longer possible to speak generally of 'race' as undifferentiated in relation to education. Racialized and ethnicized differences have to be considered, and gender is now widely recognized to intersect with 'race' and ethnicity in differentiating educational experiences and attainment. However, many of the issues that concerned black and South Asian parents in the 1960s remain features of the British education system. In particular, educational attainment continues to be racialized and ethnicized.

This chapter discusses 'race' and gender in education. It first considers why an understanding of both 'race' and gender is helpful in taking forward educational debates. It then looks at current theorizations of 'race' and the terminology associated with it. The third section examines what we know about 'race', ethnicity and educational attainment. The final section uses the example of masculinity and schooling to examine a possible contributory factor in the persistence of racialized, gendered educational inequalities: teachers' racism – whether intentional or not.

## Theorizing 'race' and gender

It is now commonly recognized that both 'race' and gender differentiate people's experiences and life chances. A major impetus for the linkage of 'race' and gender was the dissatisfaction expressed by black feminists with the constructions of 'women' made by white feminists and of 'black people' made by black men. These often took white women's experience as paradigmatic of gender and black men's experience as paradigmatic of 'race' so that, for example, black women's experiences were rendered invisible while white men's were taken for granted as the 'norm' (Hull *et al.* 1982). The US Combahee River Collective statement ([1977] 1997) put racialized and gendered difference and the politics of alliance on the feminist and black political agenda when it argued for recognition of differences, as well as of commonalities between black women and black men and black women and white women. It raised the simultaneity of racialized and gendered power relations and gave a powerful challenge to essentialist thinking about women (hooks 1981).

More recent theorizing has attempted to treat both 'race' and gender as dynamic, relational processes (for example, Rattansi 1994; Brah 1996). Ethnicity has also been recognized as a central feature of differentiation (Anthias and Yuval-Davis 1992). A focus on the complexities of difference has allowed better analytical understandings than were enabled by a dualist focus on difference as bipolar (for example, black/white or men/women). One of the most important insights from this has been that gender categories are differentiated by 'race', culture, social class and sexuality as well as by personal experiences and desires. Masculinities and femininities are, thus, now viewed as plural – racialized, ethnicized and always expressed through a social class position (Westwood 1990; Palmgren *et al.* 1992; Edley and Wetherell 1995). A full understanding of gender and education is, therefore, only possible if gender is treated as plural processes that find expression in relation to the other ways in which children and young people are positioned.

Yet, recognizing the simultaneity of 'race' and gender is the beginning, rather than the end of a process: 'There is still a paucity of research data on the interrelationship between "race" and gender' (Afshar and Maynard 1994: 1). Indeed, difference has often been treated in tokenistic or marginalizing ways in research (Anthias 1996).

## Current ways of understanding racialization and ethnicization

The terminology of 'race' and ethnicity is in continual flux, largely because no terms are entirely satisfactory. 'Race' and ethnicity are both about processes of boundary maintenance (Anthias and Yuval-Davis 1992). Ethnicity refers to a collectivity or community that makes assumptions about shared common attributes to do with cultural practices and shared history. Thus religion, language and territory are all included in the term 'ethnicity'. It is, to a large extent, insider defined. While ethnic group is sometimes used as if it refers to people who are in less powerful positions within society and who are often subjected to racism, it actually refers to everybody. Thus the term 'majority ethnic group' is sometimes used to refer to ethnic groups which have relatively more power because their cultural practices and presence is taken for granted as natural in a society. In Europe and the USA majority ethnic groups are white, but there are also white (as well as black) 'minority ethnic groups' such as Irish and Jewish people. However, the term 'minority group' has been much criticized for its pejorative overtones and the ways in which many people confuse the majority/minority distinction with numerical proportions, rather than power relations. Brah (1996) uses the term 'minoritized' to indicate that people are constructed as 'minorities' and hence to encompass the pejorative overtones this entails – a usage that is followed in this chapter.

People designated as belonging to the same 'race' are constructed as belonging to the same human stock. 'Race' is seen as inherited and often is considered to be manifested in biological or physical difference or culture. Skin colour, physiognomy, culture or territory have all been used as markers of the boundaries between 'races' (Anthias 1996). Hence, 'race' overlaps with ethnicity. Many people put the term 'race' into quotation marks to signify its social constructedness and to reject notions that it signifies 'natural' biological or cultural difference. The ways in which 'race' and ethnicity are designated shift over time. However, 'race' is often used to mean no more than 'black' and 'white'. The currently widespread use of the terms 'racialization' and 'ethnicization' signify the recognition of these as socially constructed socioeconomic processes. 'Race' and ethnicity can become particularly confusing since ethnic groups also have racialized positions and racialized identities and since they are sometimes used interchangeably.

Avtar Brah's (1996, 1999) notion of 'diaspora space' provides another way of thinking through ethnicized and gendered identities and theoretically foregrounding each. It constitutes the space in which all our genealogies are entangled – those with known histories of migration and those without. It therefore provides what Brah calls a 'creolized theory' which allows a 'figuration of power in its multiple modalities' (of class, gender, 'race', sexuality etc.) – what Brah calls 're-figuring the multi'. As Brah points out, this notion requires attention to 'how differences, multiplicities and commonalities are played out; how these are constituted, contested, reproduced or re-signified in many and varied discourses, institutions and practices' (1996: 246). It also requires the reconceptualization of 'cultural difference' in non-essentialist and non-reductive ways which undermine 'minoritizing impulses'.

The rest of this chapter aims to contribute to 're-figuring the multi' by examining the multiplicities associated with racialized, gendered educational practices.

## 'Race', ethnicity and educational attainment

When the Rampton and Swann reports were published in the 1980s they focused on the 'underachievement' and high rates of exclusion of black children (then called 'West Indian') in British schools. By way of contrast they emphasised the satisfactory achievement of Asian children. Yet, even at the time this was too simplistic a division, for it was already known that Bangladeshi and Mirpuri Pakistani children did not do well at school, although East African Asians did very well and Indian children were also doing well (Rattansi 1993). Furthermore, work had already been published indicating that for 'West Indians' girls did better than boys and were less frequently excluded (Driver 1980a, 1980b; Fuller 1980, 1982, 1983). More recent work on 'race', ethnicity and attainment indicates that, as theories of 'race' and ethnicity also indicate, we need more nuanced and less essentialist understandings.

While national school educational statistics are collected on gender differences, 'race' and ethnicity are not recorded. This may be because white people constitute 94 per cent of the British population (Schuman 1999 – although not all white people are from the ethnic majority) and some local education authorities have almost exclusively white pupils within them. The result, however, is that we have to depend on surveys done at different times and using different samples in order to assess the evidence available.

The Office for Standards in Education (Ofsted) conducted a survey of 25 local education authorities in Britain (Ofsted 1999). They found that the performance of all minoritized groups is improving, but that Bangladeshi, Pakistani, black Caribbean and gypsy traveller children attain poorly at GCSE. Gypsy traveller children's performance was the worst and the performance of black Caribbean pupils started well in primary schools, but showed a marked decline in secondary schools. In general, Ofsted found that girls from minoritized groups attain more highly than boys.

Gillborn and Mirza (2000) drew on a range of different sources in their analyses of 'race', class and gender in educational inequality. They used data supplied by the Department for Education and Employment (DfEE); local education authority applications to the Ethnic Minority Grant (EMAG) and the Youth Cohort Study of England and Wales (YCS). They concentrated on six minoritized groups (black Caribbean, black African, black Other, Indian, Pakistani and Bangladeshi) and compared them to the white students.

Gillborn and Mirza found enormous local variation in attainment levels by ethnicity. For the 118 local education authority submissions to EMAG analysed, each of the minoritized groups they studied was the highest attaining in at least one local education authority. Thus, black students were more likely to attain five GCSEs than white students in 11 per cent of authorities;

Indian students were more likely to do this in 83 per cent of the authorities as were 43 per cent of Pakistani students and 26 per cent of Bangladeshi students. Using the YCS to look at trends in attainment levels over a ten-year period (1988–97), Gillborn and Mirza found that all ethnic groups have improved their performance at GCSE. However, African-Caribbean, Bangladeshi and Pakistani students had periods where their attainment levels worsened as well as periods where they improved. Students of Indian origin have made the biggest improvements and now tend to do better than their white peers. Bangladeshi students have improved their attainment, but the gap between Bangladeshi and white pupils has not really changed. By way of contrast, the improvement of African-Caribbean and Pakistani students did not allow them to keep pace with their white peers and the gap between them and white students has increased. As in the Ofsted report, Gillborn and Mirza found that the inequalities in attainment worsen for African-Caribbean students as they go through secondary school.

Although gender and education has recently become an issue of enormous popular concern to some journalists and commentators as boys have been shown to gain slightly fewer GCSEs overall than girls, Gillborn and Mirza (2000: 21, 23, 24) argue that:

> The analysis reveals new inequalities: showing that Black pupils from relatively advantaged backgrounds are little better placed, as a group, than white peers from manual backgrounds . . . In contrast to the disproportionate media attention, our data shows gender to be a less problematic issue than the significant disadvantage of 'race', and the even greater inequality of class . . . it is important not to fall into the trap of simply arguing *between* various inequalities. *All* pupils have a gender, class and ethnic identity – the factors do not operate in isolation . . . In 1997 the gap between boys and girls attaining five or more higher grade passes was nine percentage points. The difference between managerial/professional and unskilled manual was 49 percentage points . . . the data highlight a particular disadvantage experienced by Pakistani/Bangladeshi and African-Caribbean pupils. Here the girls attain rather higher than their male peers but the gender gap within their groups is insufficient to close the pronounced inequality of attainment associated with their ethnic group as a whole.

The census of the UK population, which is conducted every ten years, records highest educational qualifications and the 1991 census was the first to record ethnicity in Britain. In their analysis of the 1991 census, Mortimore *et al.* (1997) found that Black-African and Chinese people were consistently among the best qualified and that Black-Caribbean, Pakistani and Bangladeshi groups were consistently among the worst qualified. People born in Britain were as a rule less well qualified than those born outside Britain. In general, men were better qualified than women, with the exception of Black-Caribbean women who were better qualified than were their male counterparts.

Gillborn and Mirza (2000) caution that the data available for their analyses are flawed in various ways. It is also the case that different analyses focus on slightly different ethnic groups. None the less, taken together, the findings from the three publications discussed in this section (Mortimore *et al.* 1997; Ofsted 1999; Gillborn and Mirza 2000) demonstrate that of those groups studied, black students fare the worst and Indian students the best in the British education system with regard to educational qualifications. They indicate that 'race', gender, social class and attainment are more complicated, dynamic processes than suggested in the Rampton and Swann reports. Furthermore, they show that both ethnicity and 'race' are simultaneously important since different ethnic groups from within the same racialized group fare differently (for example African cf. Caribbean people in higher education and Pakistani and Bangladeshi cf. Indian students). It follows that explanations for these results also have to be multi-faceted and nuanced. Explanations put forward frequently look for reasons in the supposed inadequacies of black students and their families compared with the assets of Indian families (sometimes undifferentiated in the term 'Asian'). This implicit praising of Asian families is contradictory in that Asian school children are also often problematized as too quiet and passive (Brah 1996). Yet, as Gillborn and Gipps (1996) point out in a review, black students have generally been found to be more motivated and less alienated from school than their white peers of the same gender and social class background, and their parents have been found to be supportive of education for their children.

The next section explores another possible reason for these 'race' and gender intersections: that racism is an important contributory issue.

## The place of racism and gender inequality in education

In 1999, the publication of the Macpherson report into the flawed investigation of the racist murder in Britain of a black 18–year-old, Stephen Lawrence, brought the issue of institutional racism to public attention. Although, as the report makes clear, institutional racism was not a new term (having been coined by Carmichael and Hamilton in 1967), it reopened the issue of how institutions may contribute to the reproduction of racialized inequalities. MacPherson argued that urgent action needs to be taken if racial disadvantage and racism (overt and covert) are not to threaten the survival of society. While it was dealing with the investigation of a murder, the Macpherson report drew attention to the prevalence of racism in schools and highlighted the well documented finding that members of particular ethnic groups are disproportionately excluded from schools. It also recommended that the National Curriculum should aim to value cultural diversity and prevent racism, in order better to reflect the needs of a diverse society. The Race Relations Amendment Act 2001 puts on schools (as on all public institutions) the new duty (enforceable by the Commission for Racial Equality) to avoid indirect discrimination and to promote equality. The issue of racism in schools is, therefore, likely to become increasingly important.

*Indirect racism?*

There are numerous studies that identify racism in schools (see the review by Gillborn and Gipps 1996). Some of these studies demonstrate that some teachers do discriminate against black and South Asian students – either treating them in stereotypic ways or being hostile towards them (Griffin 1985; Lees 1986; Mac an Ghaill 1988; Wright 1992; Connolly 1995a, 1998; Sewell 1997).[1] It is difficult to establish a cause and effect relationship between teacher racism and poor educational attainment. None the less, differential treatment, whether intended or not, is part of the context within which learning occurs. This section looks at three rare research examples (Ogilvy 1990, 1992; Wright 1992; Sonuga-Barke *et al.* 1993) where racism may not be intended by teachers, but appears to have an impact on the opportunities for very young children to learn. In each example, gender intersected with racialization. These are the sorts of instance that will have to be dealt with by the new Race Relations Amendment Act.

Most of the research on racism in schools has been done in secondary schools. However, Carol Ogilvy and her colleagues (1990; 1992) at Strathclyde University studied nursery staff and children from eight Scottish nursery schools. In half of these schools over a third of the children were from minoritized ethnic groups, while the other half had less than one sixth of children from such groups. Ogilvy *et al.* (1990) reported differences in the way that staff members talked about and treated South Asian and white children, which could have an impact on the children's experiences and educational progress, even though some of these differences were subtle. They found a consistent tendency for staff to report that the South Asian children had more difficulties than the white Scottish children did. These difficulties were more likely to be reported to be emotional/behavioural rather than cognitive. This interview finding was confirmed by the findings on the behavioural checklist (filled in by headteachers and nursery staff). Yet, the language problems identified by the researchers that the Asian children had were not recognized by the staff.

In the staff members' interactions with the children, Ogilvy *et al.* (1992) found that in one-to-one conversation staff gave more directives to South Asian than to white children and asked Asian children more questions overall, sometimes bombarding them with so many questions they could not answer that children became upset. In joint book reading sessions, they spent more time talking about the book with Asian children and less time talking about the children's experiences or other things than they did with white children. By way of contrast, on a teaching task, the staff gave more questions to white children while they used more directives, negative feedback, demonstration, physical control and visual cues with the Asian children. When the observed staff member had to help a group of three children (two white and one Asian) they responded more to Scottish children's bids for attention. As a result, white Scottish children experienced more interactions with nursery school teachers.

Gender interacted with the ethnic mix of the school in that Asian girls were more likely to make bids for attention in schools with one sixth rather than one third of minoritized children. Over half the Asian girls' bids in 'low mix' schools and over half of the Asian boys' bids in 'high mix' schools met no response from staff members. Staff were more controlling of the Asian children in all situations.

A study by Sonuga-Barke *et al.* (1993) with slightly older children throws some light on how teachers may view Asian and white boys differently. They compared teachers' ratings with 'objective' measures of hyperactivity in Asian and white British boys aged 6 and 7 years, who attended schools in London. Boys are more likely than girls to be considered hyperactive by teachers and parents. The objective tests in the study included actometers strapped to the boys' non-dominant wrist and ankle; observations of activity and inattentiveness during a task; and a neurological test of clumsiness. Sonuga-Barke *et al.* found that teachers were equally likely to rate white and Asian children as hyperactive, but that the Asian children rated as hyperactive actually had levels of activity and inattention which were no different from the English controls.

Older children's experiences of racism from their teachers have received more attention than have those of very young children. Cecile Wright (1992) studied four schools (nursery, first and middle) in one British local education authority. She found that 'both Afro-Caribbean and Asian children faced negative teacher interaction in the classroom' (p.100). However, they were subject to different assumptions and hence different treatment. Asian children were expected to have language problems, poor social skills and difficulty interacting with other groups of children in the classroom but they were also expected to be industrious, keen to learn and courteous. African-Caribbean children (particularly boys) were expected to be disruptive in class and were more likely to be the ones singled out for reprimand, even if they were among a group of children behaving in the same way.

Given this evidence – that very young South Asian, black and white children are treated differently by their teachers – it would be extremely surprising if, for at least some children, racism did not have an impact on educational attainment. Its effects are, however, not straightforward and are difficult to quantify, particularly since gender intersects with racialization and ethnicization.

### Students' perceptions of teachers as racist and sexist

This section focuses on data from a study of 78 11–14-year-old boys from a range of ethnicized and racialized groups who attended 12 London schools. It explores the ways in which masculine identities are constituted within everyday school cultures. For more details of the study see Frosh *et al.* (2001). To some extent, each school in the study produced its own local, situated culture. Yet, it was striking that boys in many schools expressed resentment against teachers for their perceived discrimination against boys in general, and in ethnically mixed schools, particularly against black boys.

For some boys, this perception of unfairness bolstered their opposition to teachers and to getting on with their work. It is, of course, difficult to untangle narratives of unfairness. It has, for example, repeatedly been found that white people who produce racist discourses often justify them on the grounds that they have been treated unfairly by black people who they argue are really the ones who are prejudiced (for example van Dijk 1993; Hewitt 1996; Cohen 1997). There has also long been research which demonstrates how easy it is for teachers and boys to be convinced that girls are getting a disproportionate amount of attention when teachers are giving equal attention to girls and boys (for example, Stanworth 1981; Spender 1983). It may also be the case that current talk of a 'crisis' in boys' attainment has led some well motivated teachers to deal more firmly with boys than they otherwise would. Yet, as indicated by the studies discussed in the previous section, some black children are subjected to racism from their teachers. Such issues are integral to considerations of gender and education.

It was not only black boys who produced discourses of unfair treatment against black boys. The following example is particularly interesting because girls (white and black) and white boys also produced discourses of teacher racism and sexism. The children argue that boys are treated unfairly in comparison with girls and that this is particularly the case for black boys. The segment of group interview from which we quote below is from 13-year-olds attending a mixed private school. The group consisted of two white girls, one black girl, one Asian boy, one black boy and two white boys:[2]

*Black girl:* A lot of them tend to be sexist as well.
*Interviewer:* Sexist are they?
*Black girl:* They give the boys harder punishments. Like they book them in Saturday. The girls they would just be 'Don't do it again'.
*Interviewer:* Oh really? Does that happen yeah?
*White boy:* Yeah. It's like in my maths. Suppose like one boy comes late, for registration and, um, the teacher goes like, 'Come and see me after school' and like five minutes later the girl could come even later and like she doesn't even notice her.
*White girl:* No, but like the girls like usually apologize and I think the girls are usually more polite to the teachers.
*White girl 2:* The girls are usually politer. I find in this school that –
*Black girl:* And then one teacher, I'm not going to say which one, they call all the boys by their second names and all the girls by their first names.
*Interviewer:* What do you think of that?
*Two girls:* It's annoying and also [*inaudible*] it's stupid. I think it's a way of disciplining them though.
*Black boy:* My teacher calls everybody else by their first name and he keeps calling me by my second.

*Interviewer:* Right. Does he call all the boys by their second name?

*Black boy:* Some boys whom he doesn't like. He calls them by their second, but all the others, he calls by their first.

*Interviewer:* Right.

*Black boy:* It's so annoying. Once I got into trouble for talking in class and then the teacher give – gave me a detention and then the girl owned up and said it was her talking, but he never gave her a detention.

*Black girl:* No, but another thing is that does come back into race though, because like you're the only black boy in your class.

*Black boy:* I know yeah!

[*A lot of joint giggling continues at the start of the next turn.*]

*Black girl:* No, no seriously, like, no seriously, like certain things like, there's this black boy in my class and there's this other white boy, they're always, like, like they're always in trouble together. The both of them and one of them was allowed to go on a trip, the other wasn't and this one who wasn't was actually black, you know. I don't know why that is 'cos that's sexism and racism put together.

*White girl:* There's a group, yeah in our class and, um they don't do any-thing and it's like black boys and white boys and some half-castes and there's, um one black boy in it and, um like they all do the same things, but he's the one who's been threatened to be expelled and stuff, but no one else has. He's the one who has been threatened and all the others haven't and um . . .

*Black girl:* The mixed race one has though.

*Black boy:* Oh yeah, it's like the other boy in my class.

[*All talk together, inaudible*]

*White boy:* If a boy does something wrong like once, the teachers hold the reputation and they get, they're like they're the ones that get in trouble all the time, even if it's not them.

*Interviewer:* Oh do they! Have you got a reputation?

*White boy:* No.

*Interviewer:* Have *you* got a reputation from any teachers? Have you got – sounds as if you've got a reputation with some teachers?

*Black boy:* What to get in trouble? Yeah, some teachers just keep blaming it on you. Like there's a new teacher who's just come in, Miss ——, my form tutor and I *always* get in trouble even though I don't do nothing. It's like I go to pick up my bag and she says 'Sit back in your seat', and when somebody else is talking, I get in trouble for it, 'cos I know she doesn't like me, 'cos once, there was me and there was another boy and we both didn't hand in our homework and she gave me a detention and the boy said he lost it and she believed him, so he was allowed to hand his homework in tomorrow, but I got a detention and I handed mine in tomorrow as well.

This example highlights the simultaneous operation of racialization and gender. It also demonstrates the importance of theorizing and treating racialization as differentiated by gender. Black girls and black boys are constructed differently by teachers and, hence, treated differently, even though both groups are sometimes subjected to racism.

Our study is not the only one to have found that black boys consider that teachers are racist to them (for example, Mac an Ghaill 1988). In his study, Sewell (1997) viewed black masculinities as collective responses in a racist culture. He found that many of the 15-year-old black boys he studied resented being 'othered' by teachers, being perceived as threatening and being picked upon for no other reason they could see other than the fact they were black. However, for some, the knowledge that teachers were afraid of them was a source of power and an incentive to perform in ways that signified threat.

It is difficult to disentangle the factors that start the process of what comes to be reported as unequal treatment. None the less, it is clearly unsatisfactory that boys (and black boys in particular) should feel that they are subjected to discriminatory treatment which, in mixed schools, is also sometimes noted by girls. Teachers to a large extent play important parts in what Connell (1996: 213) calls 'schools as agents in the making of masculinities'. They are also agents in the making of racialization. The masculinities they make are racialized and the racialization produced is gendered.

*Teachers positioning students: racialization, gender and opportunities to learn*

Other racialized gender differences in education were identified in the 1980s. A longitudinal study of black (African-Caribbean origin) and white London children from infant schools (Tizard *et al.* 1988) found that while all the children started out pretty much the same with regard to reading and maths, differences opened up between them by the end of infant school. These differences were 'race'/gender specific so that black girls were best at reading, white boys were best at maths, black boys were worst at both and white girls seemed to be the most anxious. In order to follow up some of the issues raised in the infant school study, Plewis (1996) conducted a larger study of 500 Year 1 pupils (aged 6 years) and 173 Year 2 pupils. He found that the gap between African-Caribbean girls and boys had increased since the time of the Tizard *et al.* (1988) study, with boys doing worse than girls. As a group, African-Caribbean pupils were spending less time than white pupils doing maths, but African-Caribbean boys were covering less of the maths curriculum than African-Caribbean girls or any of the white children.

The interpretation of these findings is not straightforward. Plewis suggests that it appears to be related to the fact that black boys start Year 2 behind the other three groups in maths. At the beginning of the year, teachers decide how much of the curriculum they will cover with each pupil on the basis of what they have already done, so if black boys are already behind, teachers are likely to decide to give them less maths to do. Possibly because of this, the more African-Caribbean pupils there were in the classroom, the less likely it was that much of the maths curriculum would be covered in that classroom, or by that teacher. More African-Caribbean boys were, there-fore, in classrooms where teachers covered less of the maths curriculum. However, Plewis suggests that teachers did not discriminate between pupils in the same classroom. There was no systematic difference in the amount of the curriculum covered in any classroom containing both African-Caribbean and white pupils. Plewis (1996: 144) suggests that what seems to be happen-ing to African-Caribbean boys can be termed a 'Matthew' effect or a 'rich get richer' (and poor get poorer) effect, where they are likely to be cumulatively disadvantaged over the course of their school career. He found that African-Caribbean girls were also doing worse at maths than were white girls, but the gender/ethnicity gap between girls was less than that between boys. Plewis concludes that socioeconomic variables are likely to have some impact on findings such as these, but says:

> It is unlikely that this situation can be explained by just one factor and I do not purport to give a complete account of all the reasons. However, I do give some evidence which indicates that it is differences in the way in which teachers are now covering the curriculum which could, quite unwittingly, be leading to increasing inequality.
>
> (Plewis 1996: 147)

The findings of Plewis' study illustrate well the complexity of trying to promote equality of outcome for black and white children, girls and boys, regardless of social class. For doing so is not a matter of 'changing attitudes' but of understanding how, so early, children come to be positioned in ways which can cumulatively disadvantage them through intersections of 'race', gender and social class. The factors that produce such cumulative disadvan-tage can surely be thought of as institutional racism, however unwitting and unintended.

## Concluding thoughts

This chapter has argued that 'race' and gender intersect in education to pro-duce differential racialization and differential gendering. This is evident in analyses of edcational performance by ethnicity and in how children are treated in schools. Whether wittingly or unwittingly, some teachers discrimi-nate against black and Asian children by treating them in ways that disadvan-tage them while privileging their white peers. Since there are examples of this happening at the start of their school careers, it is not surprising that analyses of school attainment by ethnicity find that black children and Pakistani and Bangladeshi children fare badly. The examples presented give some insight into possible reasons for research findings in the 1980s that black girls were attaining better than black boys (Driver 1980a).

Of course, while it is of central importance, how teachers treat children is not the full story of how 'race'/ethnic/gender inequalities are produced. Children and young people are, to some extent, active agents in the school context. For example, Fuller (1983) argued that some black girls were pre-pared to 'qualify' their criticisms of racism and the inappropriateness of schools because they considered the attainment of qualifications to be critical to their future chances. Mac an Ghaill (1988) also found that some young black women used this strategy of 'resistance within accommodation' in order to deal with racism while still passing examinations. Young black men, however, were not prepared to 'accommodate' or to 'qualify criticisms'. Another layer of complexity is added to this picture by current school cultures, in which the performance of masculinity (for all boys) frequently entails behaviour that makes it difficult for boys to be seen to be working at school (Frosh *et al.* 2001). We also know that social class continues to be important to educational outcomes (Gillborn and Mirza 2000) and may at least partly explain differ-ences in educational outcomes between children of Indian and Pakistani origin.

However, despite these complexities, it remains vital that educators con-sider issues concerning 'race' and gender such as those raised by the examples discussed above. Increasingly they will be expected to demonstrate that they are not being indirectly discriminatory and are promoting equality, as required by the Race Relations Amendment Act. The research considered in this chapter demonstrates that it continues to be necessary to try and find ways of addressing 'race' and gender in schools that promote equality of outcome.

## Notes

1 Note however that Tizard *et al.* (1988) found no differences in the treatment of black and white children by teachers in their study of infant schools, even though they looked for it.
2 Thanks to Aisha Phoenix for this interview transcription.

# 10 | 'Ice white and ordinary': new perspectives on ethnicity, gender and youth cultural identities

*Anoop Nayak*

## Introduction

The bulk of educational research on race and ethnicity conducted during the 1980s and 90s has centred firmly – one may say exclusively – upon visible minority groups. This approach has enabled valuable studies to be completed on those generations heralding from Africa and the Caribbean in particular, as well as former migrants from the Indian subcontinent (Fuller 1980; Mac an Ghaill 1988; Gillborn 1990; Sewell 1997; Connolly 1998). At the same time, the established literature on race and education remains curiously silent on the issue of whiteness. More recently, the political antiracist certainties established in these early accounts have been called into question. In the light of recent postmodernist and postcolonial debates on cultural identity – and the paradigmatic concern with contingency, fluidity, fragmentation and multiplicity – the emergent research on race has begun to grapple with an agenda that challenges the acceptance of a black/white racial dualism. In these new global times of hybrid cultural exchange it is no longer sufficient to abstract our understandings of race, class and gender from a complex, transnational understanding of diasporic movement and settlement.

While work on minority groups has continued apace in a number of disciplines, the striking contradiction is that we now seem to know far less about the racialized identities of the ethnic majority (notably English whites) and who they are in the present postimperial era. This chapter seeks to address this oversight by drawing inspiration from recent poststructuralist and psychoanalytic perspectives in the area to encourage researchers on gender to become more reflexive about the construction of white identities in schools.

At the same time, the discussion is historically located in the local material cultures of young people and maintains a commitment to elaborating at least some of the strands excavated by the tracts of early multicultural and antiracist tendencies.

A recent watershed moment in British race relations has been the tragic murder of Stephen Lawrence at the hands of a gang of white youths in Eltham, London. This racist murder raised fundamental questions about the nature of Englishness, racial intolerance and the violence of masculine youth peer groups.[1] But this is not the first time that a racist murder of a young person in Britain has become the vehicle for social change and the site for a national inquiry. Many lessons can be learned from a previous, poignant study of Burnage High School in Manchester, which followed the fatal stabbing of an Asian youth, Ahmed Iqbal Ullah, by a white male, Darren Coulburn in 1986. The team-led inquiry into the reasons behind the *Murder in the Playground* (MacDonald *et al.* 1989) produced a comprehensive account of student race relations in what was to become known as the Burnage Report. The Report highlighted the lack of attention paid by anti-racist initiatives to the needs and perspectives of white (especially working-class) students who were treated as 'cultureless', wandering spirits.[2] The gravity of this omission meant that 'many of the students, especially those in the "English" category had little or no notion of their own ethnicity and were agitated and made insecure by their confusion or else showed anger and resentment' (McDonald *et al.* 1989: 392). In short, the school's attempt to disavow white, English ethnicity did not make it magically disappear altogether – instead, these emotional investments fatally returned in the guise of a racist murder. It was not the institution's antiracist policies that were to blame, but rather the limited extent to which these initiatives touched the everyday lives of all students.

For these reasons, this chapter seeks to demonstrate how a new critical understanding of whiteness can develop those aspects of feminist theory and pedagogy on violence that have at times struggled to ally anti-oppressive policies on gender with those of race, class and regional identity in particular. The aim is to understand the meaning of whiteness in young lives and demonstrate how white identity can be strategically reconfigured for a new and inclusive politic of antiracism befitting of these coming times. The research points to the need for the development of critical projects on whiteness which may take their lead from feminist and poststructuralist accounts, and so move beyond 'the jaundiced view of Whiteness as simply a trope of domination' (Giroux 1997a: 302). Instead, I want to suggest that we need to radically reconsider what it is to be white and English in the current post-colonial period, a project that requires us to rethink conventional binaries of race and gender. Such an approach may enable us to move beyond the traditional foci of social science research that construes the ethnic majority to be leading transparent 'ice-white' lives: coolly untouchable, neutral and plainly 'ordinary'.

## Rethinking the black/white binary: poststructuralist and psychoanalytical perspectives

Recently poststructuralist approaches in the area of ethnicity have begun to challenge the fixity of black/white models of race and racism. For example, contemporary cultural theorists have indicated that racism is not something that is inherent among white youth as a consequence of racial privilege, but, rather, that all ethnicities are 'suffused with elements of sexual and class difference and therefore fractured and criss-crossed around a number of axes and identities' (Rattansi 1993: 37). This approach has called for the need to further develop anti-oppressive models of identity politics that were formerly concerned with the social exclusion of minority groups and how relations of power constructed these subjectivities as subordinate. In this read-ing, whites and blacks, for instance, are inherently located in a respective power dynamic of dominance and subordinance. It is the social inequalities of racism that mark out the terrain upon which black and white actors are located. Here, power is a dangerous, determining force that benefits white citizens at the expense of oppressing their black counterparts.

Such a rationalist account of the effects of power, and how it is lived out, has been most thoroughly critiqued by the French analyst Michel Foucault (1980, 1988b). For Foucault, power is not uniformly experienced, nor is it a wholly negating activity. Instead, power is conceptualized as *productive* since it 'doesn't only weigh on us as a force that says no . . . it induces pleasure, forms of knowledge, produces discourses' (1980: 119).[3] Here, power relations are continually produced and reproduced in often unpredictable ways as the contours of oppression and resistance shift and intertwine. Rather than seeing power as a simple matter of closed binaries – white/black, men/women, straight/gay, bourgeoisie/proletariat – where the former categories come to dominate and subsume the latter elements of the dichotomous equation, post-structuralist analyses investigate the multiple interconnections between race, gender, sexuality and social class, to ask how these processes can be seen to interact, and so inflect one another.

More lately, some writers have used psychoanalytical approaches to avoid overly rational, simplistic conceptions of young people's social power relation-ships. In so doing they have pointed towards unconscious investments, unspeakable fears and desires and complex structures of feeling (Walkerdine 1990; Cohen 1993; Hall 1993). Psychoanalytical responses mark a crucial step forward in the movement from a fascination with black subjectivity towards a renewed interrogation of whiteness. As such, accepted discourses of racism are turned upside down, or, to be more accurate, 'inside out'. It is within the internal landscape of subjectivity then that racial identities come to be given deeper meaning and expression. As the writings of the French-Martinque psychiatrist Frantz Fanon ([1952] 1970) have shown, the construction of one particular racial or cultural identity (black, white, racist or antiracist) is relationally dependent on the displacement of another, unspoken, often less desirable identity. So this process of rejection is not a neat, clinical method of expulsion. Like a shadow cast by a moving figure, the sublimated identity is ever present in the act of subjectivity, operating in the dark margins of the unconscious. This inability to truly escape the shadow of whiteness means that the Negro that is the subject of Fanon's enquiry, 'is forever in combat with his own image' (p.136) as the split between Self/Other comes to rupture essentialist notions of black subjectivity.

Thus, in psychoanalytic understandings of subjecthood, identity must be understood as a perpetual process of symbolic interplay and recurring ambivalence. The established racial polarities that come to make up the black/white binary then dissolve in the knowledge that they are each partially constituted by – and come to embody – the inner configurations of the Other, albeit as image or imago. For, as Fanon so lucidly reveals, it is not just a question of external interactions (black skin/white skin), but rather a dynamic that now encompasses inner compulsions, better encapsulated as *black skin/white masks*. In this example, it is the suppressed emotional connections to whiteness that continue to cause anxiety to the Negro long after the process of decolonization has taken place. Small wonder that Fanon compares his own encounters with whites in terms of a fractured epidermal schema that evokes corporeal metaphors of psychic scarring, splitting and internal rupture. He recalls, 'What else could it be for me but an amputation, an excision, a haemorrhage, that spattered my whole body with black blood?' (1993: 222).[4]

As such, the poststructuralist and psychoanalytically informed arguments have produced refined understandings of young people's lives that may be of primary relevance to antiracist and feminist practitioners alike. Thus, in their landmark study of school antiracism, the authors of the Burnage Report found they could no longer view the death of Ahmed Iqbal Ullah as simply a matter of white power (although this dynamic informed the attack). Instead, they were led to consider, 'Did Ahmed Ullah die at the cross-roads where the power of masculinity, male dominance, violence and racism intersect?' (McDonald *et al.* 1989: 143). Here, issues of gender and power form part of the cultural nexus through which racist violence can be understood, where epithets such as 'Paki' may be shot through with 'feminine' or 'homosexual' connotations. On the other hand, teachers and pupils representing blackness as dangerous, physically aggressive and sexually alluring may encode certain black masculinities in a stridently 'phallic' manner (Mac an Ghaill 1994; Sewell 1997). However, this phallic assemblage occurs in the realm of the imaginary and is only articulated beyond the level of the symbolic order through tropes, motifs and the mythologies that come to surround black masculinity. The silent underside of this psychic manifestation is the construction of whiteness as simply absence or 'lack', an issue that will become apparent in the empirical sections of this chapter. Extrapolating from Fanon, then, it may not only be the Negro that is now in conflict with his or her own image, but the post-imperial generation of white English youth who are struggling to fashion a new sense of place and identity in these changing global times.

Significantly, such critical readings on gender and ethnicity can furnish feminist scholars and practitioners with new theoretical perspectives to interpret the cultural identities of young people. In particular the poststructuralist and psychoanalytical appreciation of ambivalence in the face of a deterministic rationalism can inform us of how young people may express a fetishistic fascination towards selective aspects of black popular culture while retaining an unbridled investment in white chauvinism (Hebdige [1979] 1995). Seeing whiteness as a discursive formation – and a most contradictory one at that – can widen the aperture of feminist analysis. In such readings, young people's racist expressions can be understood as 'situated responses', further articulated through the discursive matrices of gender and sexuality. Here, issues of context, power and subject positionality come to complicate any 'simple' understandings that invoke a racial binary.

Recently, a number of writers have expressed dissatisfaction with black/white models of racism. A key proponent in the UK remains Tariq Modood who offers a robust challenge of the common usage of the term 'black' (or more conventionally 'Black'), indicating that policy debates within this frame occlude the diverse experiences of South Asian peoples in particular (see, especially, Modood 1988). Thus, Connolly (1998: 10) has gone on to remark how:

> We cannot assume that racism will always be associated with beliefs about racial inferiority; that it will always be signified by skin colour; that it will be only White people who can be racist; or that racism will always be the most significant factor in the experience of minority ethnic groups.

Here, the multicultural and antiracist factions that conveniently came to congregate beneath the shared umbrella of a black/white dichotomy are now finding that such assumptions are increasingly strained at the level of theory, political practice and cultural identity formation.

In particular, recent work on 'new ethnicities' and global change has offered a not wholly unproblematic challenge to these earlier models of race and racism.[5] This research has been more attentive to emerging forms of cultural syncretism, hybridity and a new urban ecology (Hall 1993; Back 1996; Cohen 1997). Notably 'new ethnicities' studies have sparked a poststructuralist clamour to do away with 'the innocent notion of the essential black subject' (Hall 1993: 254). But if this line is to be pursued, by the same token is there not now a need to do away with essentialist notions of white youthful subjects as either 'antiracist angels' or 'racist demons'?[6] Such questions point to a move away from binary relations of racism (black/white) towards composite forms of discrimination and internal gradations within the categories 'white' and 'black'. By deconstructing whiteness in this way one may allude to inter-ethnic nuances such as the tainted status of the 'bogus' Eastern European asylum-seeker or those white minority groups whose cultural experiences do not chime easily with the ideological harmonies adhered to by the Anglo-ethnic majority. We may consider this shift as the emergence of a plural concept of racisms.[7] Here, established types of racism may continue but they have also fragmented and multiplied into new, sometimes contradictory, expressions of hostility as we shall go on to discover later in this chapter.


## The research

Having mapped the developing theoretical and conceptual field I will now utilize empirical evidence drawn from an extensive ethnography undertaken with young people in two schools in the North-East of England. The data will be used to illustrate the saliency of whiteness in what are ostensibly 'ordinary' young male and female lives. The approach departs from that paraded by certain researchers in the past, who may too easily have been seduced by the colourful, often 'spectacular' subcultures now vividly preserved in the purple prose of academic youth literature. By focusing on the supposedly mundane ethnicities of white male and female youth, the investigation aims to get beneath the glassy residue of ice-white ethnic invisibility.

Methodological aspects of the study have been discussed elsewhere to provide a detailed breakdown of the school sample, referring to the number of students in each school, their gender, class and ethnic background and the social historiography of the local community (Nayak 1999). For the purposes of this chapter it is worth noting that an approximately equal number of girls and boys were observed and directly interviewed from three classes comprising age batches 9–10 years, 11–12 years and 16–17 years. The older participants were self-selecting, while form teachers were instructed to provide a diverse and wide-ranging sample derived from the two cohorts of younger students. Interviews were conducted by way of focus group sessions with three to five students in each group. The method was an attempt to engender serious discussion on the sensitive question of white identity without recourse to making individuals feel overly uncomfortable.

The investigation was undertaken at a time when banal expressions of racism were no longer seen as socially acceptable in educational institutions. As such, schools can historically be seen as agencies for the *production* of racial (as well as gendered) identities via the curricula, beliefs, values and attitudes propagated. In this sense, they cannot be regarded as institutions that passively reflect or mechanically reproduce social relations of race.[8] School pedagogy and practice shapes and informs the 'acceptable' and 'non-acceptable' forms of racial/gendered identification and behaviour permitted within the institution. Moreover, racial identities are continually negotiated through student/teacher interactions, and the complex interplay that occurs within student cultures. While work upon the ethnicities of white youth remains frustratingly scarce, Henry Giroux has asked, 'What subjectivities or points of identification become available to white students who can imagine white experience only as monolithic, self-contained, and deeply racist?' (1997b: 310). This point was further brought home to me during the three-year ethnography when I provocatively asked young people what the stereotype of a white person was, to counteract the deluge of typologies surrounding blackness. It is worth noting that the stereotypes of whiteness were intersected by stereotypes of gender:

John [age 17]: You've got like the blonde bimbo; you've got like the skinhead. You think, 'Oh God'.
Chris [age 16]: You think like racist, Nazi kind of stuff, skinheads.

These responses reflect the perceived limitations of white cultural identity and reveal how whiteness can crystalize along the axis of highly emotive gender typologies. Here, the subjectivities of young people appear far from fluid but as ice-white – frozen within the polar extremities of racial intolerance. Furthermore, the comments indicate a need to splinter the nexus that seemingly binds racism, English nationalism and gendered whiteness together. We will now consider the first-hand perspectives of white youth before exploring new possibilities on or within the identity 'white'.

## Positioning whiteness: racism, power and subjectivity

The empirical research I undertook in English schools seemed to indicate that whiteness was frequently deemed ordinary and unremarkable to teachers and students. There was a sense from teachers that white youth lived racially unstructured lives, trapped behind a colourless glass that kept them from participation in meaningful cultural experiences. However, the rich working-class culture of the North-East region where the research was undertaken was all too rarely seen as a valid point of connection for young people. At its most extreme, some white youth expressed a belief that 'their' culture was under attack from the prevailing institutional policy. Indeed, a number of white working-class students I spoke to seemed to believe that the school's antiracist policy was in fact 'anti-white' – that is, it was designed to curb any positive expression of white ethnicity. Moreover, these students did not perceive whiteness to be a privilege but rather a cultural disadvantage in classroom contexts. Their responses also indicated that although their experience was informed by gender, it was rarely spoken of in gendered ways (see also Wright et al. 1998). The following discussion took place with 11–12-year-old students:

Interviewer: Are there any advantages to being white in this school?
Nicola: Well, no.
Michelle: 'Cos coloured people can call us [names].
James: It's not fair really, 'cos they can call us like 'milk bottles' and that, but us can't call them.

*Sam:* The thing is in this school, is like if you're racist you get expelled or something, but they [blacks] can call us names and the teachers don't take any notice of it.
*James:* They take no notice.

In this case the school's sensitivity to racist harassment appeared to bolster a feeling of injustice among white respondents, and create a feeling that such forms of 'moral' antiracism were 'not fair' (see also MacDonald *et al.* 1989; Hewitt 1996). That teachers were said to ignore name-calling by black students, yet expel white students for using racist taunts, affirmed a sense of white defensiveness (see Gillborn 1996). Moreover, white students could at times make charges of 'reverse racism' in name-calling disputes with black peers. In discussion with 11–12-year-old students:

*Interviewer:* So what do the name-callers say?
*Michelle:* Things like 'milk-bottle'.
*James:* And 'whitey'.
*Michelle:* And 'milky way' and things.

Such discussions reveal the unspoken grievances that white youth may harbour and their acute sensitivity to any forms of perceived unfairness. Alongside the opinion that antiracism was 'unfair' to the needs of white youth, ran an overwhelming feeling that black male students had an identifiable culture that they could draw on which was denied to English whites. A positive assertion of this culture by minority ethnic youth would tend to be sceptically interpreted by white students as a deliberate act of exclusion. At the same time, global images of masculine 'black cool' could be appropriated by white male youth subcultures via the consumption of hip-hop music, basketball and the sporting of particular hairstyles. These contradictions indicate how blackness, and more specifically male black culture, momentarily achieves peer group prestige in certain sites such as the street, playground or dance hall (see also Gilroy 1987; Sewell 1997 on black masculinities). In Foucauldian terms, established relations of power (here, black/white) can then have unpredictable consequences, generating a proliferation of new sites of resistance and desire.

Revealingly, both male and female white students were keen to make a careful distinction between racism as a discourse of power available to them through regimes of representation (in language, speech, metaphors and imagery); and racism as a 'chosen' subject position that was explicitly ideological and practised in daily, vehement exchanges. Whereas the former stance offered a latent potential for racist enactment, triggered only at certain moments, the latter position was more readily condemned as explicitly racist and wholly unegalitarian. It is this 'unevenness' of racism in young people's lives that became increasingly apparent. The grainy line separating what white students said to their black peers in certain situations, and how they felt towards them more generally, became a source of tension when episodes of racism surfaced in classroom contexts. Most specifically in fraught, personal exchanges between students, racist name-calling offered an inviting mode of redress for whites:

> *Sam:* We canna sey anythin' cos they [black students] can get us annoyed and it's hard not calling them a racist name or somethin'. I never bin racist 'cos I don't think it's right but some people jus' think it's hard to not call them a racist name if an argument starts.

The student responses shown here signal a confusion regarding the issue of why white racial epithets such as 'whitey', 'milk-bottle' or 'milky way' are not construed as forms of racist name-calling. As other researchers have implied, the meanings carried in white, derogatory terms rarely carry the same weight as anti-black racist terminology (Back 1990; Troyna and Hatcher 1992a). Troyna and Hatcher (1992a, 1992b) argue that *racial* insults such as 'white duck' or 'ice-cream' must be carefully distinguished from *racist* terms such as 'Paki', which are saturated with ideological power:

> Black children wanting to call racial names back faced several problems. First, the white racist vocabulary was much richer, as many children recognized . . . Second, white children knew that there was no social sanction against white skin . . . The third problem concerns the issue of 'nation'. There was no reverse equivalent to the racist name-calling of 'Paki'. . .
>
> (Troyna and Hatcher 1992a: 158)

In Troyna and Hatcher's (1992a, 1992b) structural definition, it is precisely because black and white/male and female students occupy different positions of dominance and subordinance in race relations that white epithets are considered 'racial' name-calling forms and black epithets are viewed as 'racist' name-calling terms. Here, there is no equivalence between black and white name-calling as ultimately, 'Racist attacks (by whites on blacks) are part of a coherent ideology of oppression which is not true when blacks attack whites, or indeed, when there is conflict between members of different ethnic minority groups' (Troyna and Hatcher 1992b: 495). However, this anti-oppressive model reifies race, and may have less import at a global level where it is subject to alternative forms of racism and differing relations of power. A further concern remains with how identity is deterministically conceptualized in this paradigm where 'an individual's subjectivity is conceptualised as coherent and rationally fixed' (Mac an Ghaill and Haywood 1997: 24).

While some students may have engaged in a 'white backlash' against moral forms of antiracism, others disclosed a more complex understanding of power. Ema, a 16-year-old female, white, working-class student explained how if someone used a term like 'black bastard' 'I'd say something and get 'em done'. However:

> *Ema:* If someone says, 'She's just called me "white trash"', I'd say, 'And
> what's wrong with that?' I'd probably think, 'Well maybe it would
> hurt them, but to me it wouldn't be anything to say "white"'. I'd be
> proud of it.

Ema made a qualitative distinction between the use of a black or white racial
epithet before an insult. She indicates that white has a neutral or even positive
signification that cannot be easily overturned ('I'd be proud of it'). As Troyna
and Hatcher (1992b) would have it, the prefix 'white' does not draw on a
historical, 'coherent ideology of racism' (slavery, imperialism, apartheid,
discrimination, xenophobia, nationalism) in the ways that the term 'black
bastard' might.

   While Troyna and Hatcher's definition foregrounds the 'asymmetrical
power relations' (1992b: 495) between blacks and whites and is a welcome
improvement on liberal, power-evasive models of racism, there remain potential shortcomings with the anti-oppressive framework. To begin with, there is
an immediate reification of race as an insurmountable point of embodied
difference that too readily equates whiteness with oppression and blackness
with victimhood. Moreover, whites are endowed with the privilege of being
the central architects of history and the key agents of social change. The
multiple positions that blacks and whites may come to occupy – and how
these subjective locations are nuanced by class, gender, sexuality and generation – are subsequently condensed into a racial dichotomy of powerful/
powerless. Furthermore, the tendency to construe racism across a black/
white binary may in turn occlude other examples of racist hostility such as
anti-Semitism, the 'ethnic cleansing' that has taken place in parts of Eastern
Europe, or the ritual persecution of the Irish. Indeed, an engagement with
whiteness beyond racial polarities may allude to a complex understanding
of racism that may invoke aspects of nationhood or religion as further
points of discrimination. Placing the issue of racism and ethnicity in a wider
context of global change, unequal development and the legacies of 'new'
and 'old' diasporic movements suggests that black/white binaries of race,
however convenient or strategically useful they may appear in the short-
term, are strictly limited.

## Pedagogic strategies for engaging white ethnicities

How can we delicately capture the varied experience of white male and
female ethnicity without alienating white youth? This question becomes all
the harder to address as whiteness and Englishness have come to represent
*the ethnicity that is not one*. In order to sensitively engage with white, English
ethnicities I will elaborate upon the local, historical and material cultures of
young people.

   Exposing the diverse histories of white students could be a productive
exchange where the immediate heritage of respondents was discussed. The

recognition that 'English' identities had changed over time allowed these students to feel less threatened by the prospect of black British settlement. Projects directed by young people which draw on familial life-history accounts may be of particular interest to feminist practitioners, whom may wish to share their own racially inscribed biographies in a mutual recognition that the personal is political. Encouraging students in mainly white preserves to sensitively trace their ethnic and social class lineage remains a fruitful way of deconstructing whiteness. However, as David Gillborn (1995: 89) has noted, first, 'no strategy is likely to be completely successful, and second . . . an effective strategy in one context, may fail in another context or at another time'. With these provisos in place, the approach deployed was sensitive to the local culture of the community and subject to my particular relationship with students. I found that imploding white ethnicities offered a way of contextualizing antiracism, and helped to develop an interest among students in race relations they felt they could have a personal stake in. Such a pedagogy is imperative, for as Stuart Hall has noted, 'We are all, in that sense, *ethnically* located and our ethnic identities are crucial to our subjective sense of who we are' (1993: 258).

The value of feminist auto/biography and life-history method were made known to me when new inflections upon an assumed, coherent English ethnicity began to unfold. It seemed that such counter-narratives could enable a critical appreciation of whiteness to emerge out of the fractured, cross-cutting pathways that come to intersect peoples daily lives (hooks 1993; Nayak 1997; Nebeker 1998). For example, the responses generated during the fieldwork period indicated that the implosion of white ethnicities could offer alternative historical trajectories that many students had a self-fascination with. Tracing their familial past was a means of personalizing history, making it relevant to their life experiences to date. In the course of this process it was not unusual for students to refer to generational elements of racism within their family lineage. Many students mentioned parents or grandparents with pronounced racist opinions and this allowed for further points of critique and discussion between young people.

Although the fragmented, 'hyphenated' identities of white male and female youth (Anglo-Irish, Scotch-Irish, Anglo-Italian) has particular resonance to the local culture in which the research was undertaken, this did not mean that Englishness itself was left untouched. Conversations concerning local identities ('Geordies', 'Makums', 'Charvers', 'Smoggies' etc.) and the labouring heritage of the area were particularly productive. Moreover, with older students it was possible to engage in a critical dialogue with whiteness. Ema and Jolene (both 16 years) each identified themselves as working-class young women. Both engaged in an appraisal of their own racial identities, which at times disrupted the association of Britishness/Englishness with whiteness:

> *Jolene:* There's different colours of white.
> *Interviewer:* What d'you mean?

*Jolene:* Like Chinese. Do you know what I mean, what colour are they? There isn't a colour – we're not proper white.

*Ema:* Different shades really.

*Jolene:* There's Chinese; there's other people; there's us; naturally dark skins who are white.

*Ema:* People say like, 'I'd hate to be black' and everything but when they go on the sunbed and get tanned, they love to be tanned.

*Jolene:* Yeah! People go on the sunbed just to get browned.

The critical deconstruction of whiteness undertaken by Ema and Jolene fractures the conception of white identity as icy-neutral by imparting the knowledge that so-called 'whites' are comprised of 'different shades really'. Instead of seeing white as colourless, as it is all too frequently regarded, the young women introduced a wide spectrum of colour symbols which at its most extreme included bronzed, sun-tanned figures who still manage to 'claim' the elusive emblem of whiteness. The question of what 'colour' are Chinese people further disrupts the fixed polarization of race as a discourse shared solely between black and white citizens. Moreover, whiteness is seen as a term socially ascribed to certain groups rather than an accurate mode of racial classification. The social construction of whiteness is also apparent here, where students recognize that strictly speaking they were not 'proper white' (whatever that might be). I would suggest that making slippery the frozen status of white, English ethnicity in the ways outlined could allow for new points of connection to emerge for white youth.

## Concluding remarks

Referring to Paul Gilroy's (1987) book *There Ain't No Black in the Union Jack* (a title derived from a National Front slogan), Stuart Hall (1993: 258) closes his essay 'New Ethnicities' with the claim that until relatively recently he 'didn't care, whether there was any black in the Union Jack. Now not only do we care, we must'. By the same token, if white students are to feel able to contribute to a policy of social justice whatever their nationality may be, they must have subjective investments in a politics that at times has passed them by. Deconstructing the identities of ethnic majorities with as much purpose and vigour as that of minority groups should be a vital component of feminist, antiracist practice. A failure to engender the perspectives of white students only serves to encourage confusion, and the claims of unfairness we have witnessed. A stumbling block that needs to be removed is the perception held by many white students (and parents) that antiracism is a bourgeois, *anti-white* practice. Here, suppressed white grievance could give way to an understanding that while racism 'works both ways', but antiracism does not. A more fruitful route to pursue may be to connect anti-oppressive policies with local histories and the 'lived' culture of the community. As Raphael Samuel has noted, 'Local history also has the strength of being popular . . . People are continually asking themselves questions about where they live, and how their elders fared' (1982: 136–137). Embracing the popular in this way may entail a clearer understanding of the cultural specificities of white, English ethnicities, and engender a perspective that is more sensitive to marginal working-class experiences. Moreover, the multiple styles of whiteness evoked by young people even in largely white enclaves implies that a more sophisticated treatment of racism and antiracism is required. Exposing the multiplicity and mutability of white experience remains imperative where the only recognizable forms of white, English identity appear to be the racially loaded and gender scripted 'Nazi skinhead' or 'blonde bombshell'. Contemporary research now requires a meaningful engagement with white ethnicities beyond the plain and ordinary in order to critique the glistening privilege of whiteness and do justice to the complex life experiences of young people.

## Notes

1 Some of these issues have been revisited in the UK national press in the aftermath of the murder of Daminola Taylor in South London.
2 The Report was later hijacked by sections of the press to make the spurious claim that the school's antiracist policy led to the murder of Ahmed. This of course had been a misreading of the findings proposed by the inquiry, which stated almost the reverse: anti-racims needed to be *extended* to incorporate white youth rather than retracted (see Rattansi 1993 for details). To avoid further confusion, any theoretical and pedagogical criticisms made of antiracism/multiculturalism here must be carefully placed within this caveat.
3 At the micro-political level of schooling cultures, some researchers have utilized these notions of power to provide evidence of how teacher/student relations may incite 'unexpected happenings' (Walkerdine 1990; Skeggs 1991; Kehily and Nayak 1996). In each of these studies power is not a given constant, but worked and reworked through its potential possibilities in what are often imaginative ways.
4 In the light of the racist violence meted upon Stephen Lawrence, Rohit Duggla and Ricky Reel in the UK, such bodily simile has come to take on a frightening corporeality.
5 Space does not allow for a critique of the research that has emerged from this paradigm.
6 As Alastair Bonnett asserts, 'To subvert "blackness" without subverting "whiteness" reproduces and reinforces the "racial" myths, and "racial" dominance, associated with the latter' (1996: 99).
7 For a thorough account of definitions of racism and how it is variously practised see Miles (1995).
8 There is now an extensive literature concerning how teachers use racist labels to interpret the behaviour of black youth and how these typologies influence black academic performance (Fuller 1980; Coard 1982; Driver 1982; Mac an Ghaill 1988; Mirza 1992; Sewell 1997).

# The paradox of contemporary femininities in education: combining fluidity with fixity

*Diane Reay*

## Introduction

The contemporary concern with 'a crisis of masculinity' has successfully eluded in-depth scrutiny of what is happening to girls and women. However, at a time when masculinities appears to be an ever growing preoccupation within education, it is important to refocus and ask how femininities are lived and regulated at the beginning of the twenty-first century. Recent research studies suggest that contemporary gendered power relations are more complicated and contradictory than the new orthodoxy that girls are doing better than boys suggests (Kenway and Willis 1998; Blackmore 1999; Francis 2000a; Walkerdine *et al.* 2001). There is much to celebrate in both the emergence of new, strong, assertive femininities and the continuing pleasure and reward that the performance of femininity brings many women and girls. At the same time, the contemporary orthodoxy that girls are doing better than boys masks the complex messiness of gender relations. Despite girls' better educational attainment, recent research studies point to a vast majority of boys, as well as a significant number of girls, still adhering to the view that it is preferable to be male than female (Reay 2001).

### A historical perspective on femininity

Historically it has always been the case that masculinity is the preferred 'superior' subject positioning. In fact there is a long mainstream tradition which views female identity as 'non-identity'. Tseelon (1995: 34) argues that this tradition, which pervades psychoanalytic, theological and social theory, defines femininity as an 'inessential social construction'. Thus in the theological discourse femininity is fake. It is duplicitious. In the psycho-analytic discourse femininity is masquerade. And, as Doane (1988) argues, implicit in understandings of femininity as masquerade is the notion of woman's status as spectacle rather than spectator. But many psychoanalytic understandings, premised on the Freudian notion that the libido is male (Freud 1905) move beyond conceptions of femininity as spectacle into theo-rizations of femininity as a dissimulation of the female unconscious masculi-nity. It is argued that women's anxiety about retribution for challenging male power leads them to disguise themselves as objects of desire (Heath 1989). Women can only equal men if they renounce all that is quintessentially female (Bloch 1992). Thus as Tsselon asserts, as the real 'woman' is a man, the feminine woman must be a masquerade. Or as Lacan (1977: 290) asserts: 'It is in order to be the phallus, that is to say, the signifier of the desire of the Other, that a woman will reject an essential part of femininity, namely, all her attributes in the masquerade. It is for that which she is not that she wishes to be desired as well as loved'.

Implicit in all these approaches is the issue of authenticity. Historically, and currently, femininity is a category full of masculine projections in which 'woman' has been simultaneously constructed and condemned as deceitful artifice.

## Femininity or femininities?

Femininity is the process through which girls and women are gendered and become specific sorts of female. But, 'being and becoming, practising and doing femininity are very different things for women of different classes, races, ages and nations' (Skeggs 1997: 98). Femininity is always overlayered with other categorizations, generating understandings in which minority ethnic women and working-class women of all ethnicities are often positioned against normative conceptions of femininity. Within an ideal of femininity as a bourgeois sign they are perceived to be what femininity is not (Walkerdine 1990). Following Connell (1995) and Kenway and Willis (1998) I would argue that there are different formations of femininity. As Pyke (1996: 531) argues, 'hierarchies of social class, race and sexuality provide additional layers of complication. They form the structural and cultural contexts in which gender is enacted in everyday life, thereby fragmenting gender into multiple masculinities and femininities'.

Femininity is not a unified discourse, although dominant forms of femin-inity will usually be configured as rational and coherent; often as so obvious as to be taken for granted. For instance, it is generally believed that all women are naturally nurturant and caring. In contrast to such dominant understand-ings, femininity is dynamic, various and changing and it is perhaps helpful to think in terms of multiple femininities rather than one femininity. As Laurie *et al.* (1999) argue, this recognition of a multiplicity of femininities suggests that while dominant forms of femininity often draw on 'natural' and 'essential' associations between the biological sexed body and gender identities, these associations are not straightforward. Rather, we might consider sex and gender as dialectically interrelated (Butler 1993). Thus, while recognizing various forms of femininity, it is important not to view them as fixed categories. Furthermore, the practices and emotional, psychic relations through which femininity is constituted are historically and contextually specific.

Context has always mattered in eliciting traits traditionally associated with being female (Epstein 1988; Rhodes 1992). It has been suggested that women are more often able to behave in supportive, caring ways at work because they are locked into low-paid, low-power jobs (Hansot and Tyack 1981). Such jobs, for example nursing and child care, rarely require competitive ways of operating. In contrast, studies of women in high-level management posts across the labour market report that they frequently adopted a career orientation more traditionally associated with men rather than women (Fogarty *et al.* 1972; Evetts 1990; Cox 1996; Schmuck 1996). The possibilities for the realization of particular femininities differ according to position, context and moral environment. Williams (1986) has written about the North American Berdache, men who assume the tasks and roles of a woman and thus come to be seen within their native American culture as a third gender categorization, stressing how the performance of gender influences the ways in which it is symbolically constructed. The point being that when girls and women take up specific roles and bring gender identity and behaviour to bear, there is no simple, essential playing out of fixed gender behaviour and relations but rather a process of accommodation and mutual acceptance. However, the conventional position is rooted in binaries which mitigate against seeing how both changes in roles and performativity result in new evolving gender identities which transgress normative gender divisions.

Femininities are best understood as being in process, constantly being made and remade in different times and places. They are always highly variable and changeable. Class, 'race', age and sexuality never mediate gender in formulaic or predictable ways. Girls and women are never simply positioned within one femininity while remaining untouched by others. Yet the acting out of particular sets of ideas about how girls and women should behave and be is not as voluntary as notions of variability and dynamism imply. The addenda in any account of femininity are 'the economic, political and social structures through which dominant femininities are determined' (Laurie *et al.* 1999: 4.)

These social structures implicate 'race' and racism in the construction of minority ethnic femininities. As Vron Ware (1991) demonstrates, constructions of femininity cannot be separated from the racialization of identity. Heidi Mirza (1992) argues that the cultural construction of femininity among black girls fundamentally differs from the forms of femininity found among their white peers. The young black women in her study made few distinctions between male and female abilities and qualities, and perceived relationships between the sexes as more equitable than their white peers did. However, they still have to negotiate dominant white constructions of femininity within which, as Gargi Bhattacharyya (1997: 250) points out, black females are seen as 'too much skin to be simply girl, too feminine to be just dark'.

## Femininities in education

Helen Wilkinson (1999: 37) argues that male and female values are converging, leading to the emergence of 'a masculinised new woman' at ease with male attributes and 'enjoying the buzz that comes with ambition, drive and success'. There have been significant shifts in the construction of femininity over the past few decades; shifts which have opened up and extended generally held understandings of acceptable female behaviour in both public and private spheres. The 1990s saw the 'post-feminist' assertion of 'girl power' and the notion of an active, powerful femininity which is sexually assertive (Walkerdine *et al.* 2001). Certainly, young women now have freedoms and opportunities unheard of in their mothers' generation, and there has been a welcome expansion of femininity to encompass previously excluded attitudes and practices. But Wilkinson tends to both over-exaggerate the changes and to play down the costs in her enthusiasm about the benefits. Such changes have had a differential impact on the basis of social class, ethnicity, sexuality and age, and the new 'super girls' and 'super women' celebrated in the media often pay a price for their success. As Coppock *et al.* (1995) point out, the underlying realities are far more complicated, destabilizing notions that now 'women and girls can have it all'. It is these complexities and contradictions in relation to new forms of femininity that I discuss below in the sections on female pupils and women teachers.

First it is important to assert that, far from being intrinsic and fixed, a lot of so-called 'female qualities' vary according to differentials of power. Thus it is extremely difficult to disentangle those qualities which develop specifically out of women's position of relative powerlessness and those which women retain regardless of how much power they acquire. Gendered identities are in context more fluid and shifting than they are depicted in many of the texts on women, girls and education. There are many different ways of performing femininity and the particular forms femininity takes are powerfully shaped by the roles women and girls adopt and the context in which they perform these roles (Reay and Ball 2000).

This fluidity of contemporary femininity is evident in other social arenas as well as education. Lisa Adkins (1995: 8), writing about femininity in relation to the labour market, argues:

> those who are concerned with femininity do not assume . . . that femininity pertains only to women. Hence it is not assumed that the aesthetics of femininity concerns only women workers. Rather, the issue to be explored is the ways in which in a range of jobs both women and men are increasingly performing the aesthetics of femininity.

However, I want to argue that within educational contexts, with their growing emphasis on measured outputs, competition and entrepreneurship, it is primarily the assertiveness and authority of masculinity rather than the aesthetics of femininity that is required and rewarded.

## Female pupils

Valerie Hey succintly captures the dilemma of being a female pupil within educational contexts. She argues that the double-bind for girls within schooling is how to become simultaneously the normal school pupil and the proper young woman within the confines of both compulsory schooling and compulsory heterosexuality:

> One institution denies difference while the other is fundamentally invested in producing it so that femininity as sexual difference under terms of subordination is always in play against masculinity in dominance. The difficulty for girls is that of seeking out empowering places within regimes alternatively committed to denying subordination or celebrating it.
>
> (Hey 1997: 132)

Over the last two decades femininity has moved from being equated with poor academic performance to a position at the beginning of the twenty-first century where it is viewed as coterminous with high achievement. While research in the 1970s and 80s found that female pupils avoided displays of cleverness because they felt boys would then find them unattractive (Spender 1982; Lees 1986), today many girls articulate a confidence in female educational abilities (Francis 2000a). Furthermore, disruptive 'failing boys'' behaviour has given girls an unexpected window of opportunity through which some variants of femininities can be valorized over specific pathologized masculinities, particularly in the arena of educational achievement (Epstein *et al.* 1998). However, what is frequently overlooked is that the achieving girls and the underachieving boys do not come from the same constituency. The girls who succeed are overwhelmingly middle class and the boys who fail are working class. What has changed is the gendered composition of middle-class academic success.

What has caused these shifts in relation to middle-class gendered achievement? Walkerdine *et al.* offer one explanation, arguing that over the last 20 years the possibility has opened up 'of making the feminine rational and the rational feminine' (2000: 60). They assert that this has allowed middle-class girls, in particular, to become rational subjects, taking up places in the professions once occupied by men. Indeed, as they point out, when attainment figures are scrutinized, it becomes clear that what is described as girls' 'high performance' is mostly the high performance of girls in 'middle-class' schools (Walkerdine *et al.* 2001).

So we have reached a historical juncture at which middle-class girls, alongside their brothers, have become bearers of what was previously seen to be an exclusively male rationality. Yet, as Walkerdine *et al.* (2001) go on to argue, the entry of middle-class girls into masculine norms of rational academic excellence comes at a price. It is not achieved easily. Powerful associations of cleverness with asexuality (Willis 1977) and unfemininity (Walkerdine 1989) still abound. Middle-class girls are caught up in a delicate balancing act in relation to femininity and cleverness in which being feminine cannot be allowed to interfere with academic success. The melding of middle-class femininity with the rational bourgeois subject requires a huge investment in which femininity has to be struggled over and sexuality sometimes renounced. Indeed, academic success is produced out of the suppression of aspects of femininity and sexuality; a suppression which can generate intense identity crises and has led to a worrying increase in eating disorders such as anorexia and bulimia among, in particular, middle-class teenage girls.

What is happening to working-class girls? Recent research on female students attending secondary schools and further education colleges has stressed the link between class and femininity – specifically the ways in which young, white, working-class women are positioned in relation to discourses about 'appropriate' femininity and sexuality (Sharpe 1976; Lees 1993; Skeggs 1997). It appears that measured against the white bourgeois ideal they can never have the 'right' femininity. Claire Dwyer (1999) reported similar findings among the Muslim female students she interviewed. For these young Asian women, discourses of 'appropriate' femininity were crucially bound up with maintaining respectability and avoiding being labelled as someone who is sexually suspect. However, underlying the commonalities were key class differences:

> While the middle class girls could draw on networks of support and encouragement from teachers and parents to imagine a range of possible future paths, the expectations and encouragement for working class girls were much less in evidence. For these young women there are then considerable divergences in access to repertoires of resources and subjectivities on which they can draw to develop a diversity of new femininities.
>
> (Laurie *et al.*1999: 193)

There is very little research which explores the femininity of primary schoolgirls. A study of predominantly working-class girls' peer group cultures in an inner-city primary school found that girls took up very varied positions in relation to traditional femininities (Reay 2001). Yet, despite widely differentiated practices, all the girls at various times acted in ways which bolstered boys' power at the expense of their own. The 'emphasized' femininity that McRobbie (1978) found among adolescent working-class girls in the 1970s was still evident in the late 1990s, accommodating the interests and enhancing the status of boys in the class. But alongside such compliant forms of femininity were other forms that were more resistant and empowering for girls. Even so, while peer group discourses constructed girls as harder working, more mature and more socially skilled, still the boys and a significant number of the girls adhered to the view that it is better being a boy, suggesting that both girls and boys were still learning many of the old lessons of gender relations which work against gender equity.

Paul Connolly (1998) points out that girls' assertive or disruptive behaviour tends to be interpreted more negatively than similar behaviour in boys, while Robin Lakoff (1975) has described how, when little girls 'talk rough' like the boys do, they will normally be ostracized, scolded or made fun of. For the primary schoolgirls in my study who espoused and tried to practise their own variant of 'girl power', 'doing it for themselves' in ways which ran counter to traditional forms of femininity resulted in them being labelled at various times by teachers in the staff room as 'real bitches', 'a bad influence' and 'little cows'. The tendency Clarricoates found in 1978 for girls' mis-behaviour to be looked upon as a character defect, while boys' misbehaviour is viewed as a desire to assert themselves, was just as evident in teachers' discourses more than 20 years later.

In her study of children in multiracial, mixed social class primary schools, Becky Francis (1998) found that girls constructed a femininity for themselves as selfless and sensible in opposition to the boys' selfish and silly masculinity. Her more recent research (2000a) with secondary-school pupils found that a dominant construction of femininity as sensible and masculinity as silly and selfish was just as evident in secondary-school classrooms, although the sensible/silly construction had been reconfigured as maturity/immaturity. Yet, she concludes that there was still evidence that boys' constructions of masculinity, in particular their 'laddishness' and competitiveness, drew approval from the teachers.

It is perhaps important to remind ourselves that the backdrop to the mani-festation of male power in the classroom, and its discursive reinforcement, lies beyond the classroom. It is a truism to state that men rule the world but they continue to dominate in all 'the corridors of power'. Within the current furore with 'the crisis of masculinity' what often remains masked is the continuing acceptance of white, middle-class masculinity as the ideal all those 'others' (women and girls as well as minority ethnic and white working class males) are still expected to measure themselves against. In the next section I want to explore the continuing conflation of power and rationality with mascu-linity and its consequences for the femininities of women working in education.

## Women teachers

Women teachers across all sectors of schooling are caught up in dominant discursive constructions of the woman teacher as caring and nurturant. That is why traditionally more women secondary teachers than men have been associated with pastoral aspects of the secondary curriculum. However, such discursive constructions have impacted far more powerfully on women primary schoolteachers. Just as the ideal mother embodies all the character-istics of nurturant femininity, so does the ideal female primary schoolteacher. Walkerdine's (1990) thesis is that the capacity for nurturance which historically has come to be seen as grounded in a naturalized femininity has been taken as the basis for women's fitness for the facilitation of knowing and the reproduction of the knower. However this passive role, while supportive of the production of knowledge, is positioned as the opposite of it. As Walkerdine (1990: 137) concludes, 'the production of knowledge is thereby separated from its reproduction and split along a sexual division which renders production and reproduction the natural capacities of the respective sexes'. So the female primary schoolteacher becomes the means through which rational development can occur, a facilitator rather than a producer of knowledge. This discursive construction has had consequences for the ways in which primary schoolteachers are viewed; consequences which both constrict and stereotype. As Carolyn Steedman (1986: 125) comments:

> When I entered that enclosed space, the primary classroom I didn't know about a set of pedagogic expectations, that covertly and mildly – and never using this vocabulary – hoped that I might become a mother. And yet I became one, not knowing exactly what it was that was happening until it was too late.

However, although the school system is still heavily reliant on conventional femininity it is increasingly denigrated in the new evolving educational markets of the 2000s with their technicist emphasis on efficiency and effectiveness, and their marginalization of any schooling outcomes that cannot be measured (MacDonald 2000).

The dominant construction of female teachers, particularly in the primary sector, remains one of 'the surrogate mother'. Yet, within the contemporary educational market-place across all sectors of education an increasing number of women are achieving senior management positions and moving into contexts where traditional nurturant femininity is at odds with the demands of their posts. It is important to look at how their femininity is being reconfigured within educational markets which valorize classic male qualities of competition and individualism.

Connell (1995) argues that both men and women are capable of expressing attitudes and behaviours currently labelled 'masculine' or 'feminine', while Becky Francis (2000a) reasons that 'if the terms "masculinity" and "femininity" cannot be applied to both sexes, the inference is that gendered behaviour is indeed tied essentially to sex' (p. 17). Educational management is commonly conceptualized as 'masculine', concerned with 'male' qualities of rationality and instrumentality (Blackmore 1993; Blackmore and Kenway 1993; Weiner 1994). This would suggest that women (as well as men) promoted to senior management positions within the field of education will aspire to ways of managing which draw on styles widely perceived to be masculine rather than feminine. Judi Marshall (1984: 19) asserts that 'leadership characteristics and the masculine sex role correspond so closely that they are simply different labels for the same concept'.

This conflation of leadership with masculinity has significant implications for women in senior management teams and the ways in which they can (and do) manage, and this is evidenced in various empirical studies. Morrison (1987) found that the psychological profiles of women who succeed in positions of executive leadership may be more like those of their male counterparts than they are like those of women in general, while Schein (1973; 1975) found that female senior managers were often 'more like men than men themselves'. Meta Kruger (1996) found in her study of 98 paired male and female headteachers in Holland that women were no different from their male counterparts in terms of 'internal communication' and 'personnel management'. She also researched whether women were 'more involved with others and less task orientated than men' and found that they were not, concluding that 'Women heads hardly differ from their male colleagues in the way in which they experience power' (p. 454). However, this is not to suggest that promotion into senior management is an easy process for women teachers. Rather, in relation to femininity, these women are caught up in a painful struggle of 'constant reinvention' (Walkerdine *et al.* 2001).

Psychological studies such as those of Snodgrass would support the view that, as women achieve power, qualities normally associated with femininity are modified. Snodgrass found that women were not more sensitive than men overall when status was taken into consideration. Sensitivity varied according to status not sex, with lower status people being significantly more sensitive to the feelings of higher status people than visa versa (Snodgrass 1985; 1992). In contrast, feminist work on women managers has repeated the oversights of mainstream feminisms, largely ignoring the impact of power and status on the construction of the femininity of powerful women. Contrary to such idealized depictions, Kanter (1977) has argued that many of the so-called gender differences in organizational behaviour stem directly from gendered differentials in opportunities and access to power. This would suggest that the acquisition of power within organizations results in women playing out their gendered identity in significantly different ways to those identities realized in normative, socially subordinate femininities. Indeed, female senior managers have to deal with, and act out, a number of contradictory and competing tendencies arising out of the conjunction of a gendered socialization which prepares women for relative powerlessness and a current occupational location invested with power. The negative psychic consequences of playing out a femininity that incorporates qualities traditionally viewed as masculine are just as evident in relation to women educational managers as they are in relation to clever schoolgirls. There is just as much conflict, unease and cost in women's performance of these 'new femininities' in the workplace as there is in schoolgirls' performance of 'new femininities' in the classroom.

Holding power continues to be an 'extraordinary' situation for women in a British labour market (Davidson and Cooper 1992), although increasingly not within education where currently 80 per cent of primary headteachers are female. The literature on women managers typically fails to address their demographic profile in terms of class, race, culture, ethnicity, age and sexual orientation. Women who become senior managers in any sector of the British labour market cannot be deemed to be representative of women in general.

They are largely recruited from a very specific group of women: white, middle or upper class, and in most cases by definition highly credentialled. Furthermore, in addition to particularities of class and ethnicity, exercising power for women is possibly influenced in significant ways by the particular variant of gender socialization experienced in childhood, the culture and ethos of the workplace, earlier role models, personality, and political and philosophical perspectives.

Despite the recent trends in management theory which celebrate a 'feminized' management style, the practice of management, especially in educational institutions, remains an uneasy, paradoxical context for women. While it may be that these style trends have had some impact on some aspects of management behaviour, it is patently unrealistic to argue that there has been a major transformation in management practices and culture, especially not in educational institutions. Indeed, the major transformation that has taken place in educational organizations (i.e. the introduction of the market form) has had the effect of legitimating and encouraging assertive, instrumental and competitive behaviour rather than feminist or feminine ways of working.

As a consequence there remains an inherent paradox in women occupying the upper echelons of educational hierarchies, because such a positioning confounds and contradicts traditional notions of femininity. To be a successful professional near the top of an institutional hierarchy involves at the very least the performance of a markedly different femininity from that inscribed in traditional (or radical) notions of being female (see Tseelon 1995). Within a wider social context in which femininity continues to be denigrated while masculinity is still frequently elevated as manifesting a superior form of development (Archer 1989; Nicholson 1996), it would be surprising for women managers to uncomplicatedly valorize feminine ways of working. The inherent tension between being female and being a leader invariably results in adaptations and adjustments and the assumption of a femininity that is more congruent with leadership than traditional variants of femininity which are grounded in positions of relative powerlessness. Femininity for most women is lived out through paradox in which they are 'simultaneously socially invisible while being physically and psychologically visible, an object of the gaze' (Tseelon 1995: 54). As social visibility is intrinsic to leadership, women in leadership positions inevitably have to develop practices associated with masculinity in order to be seen as authentic leaders. Arguably, career success may be seen as part of a distancing process from normative femininity.

Such a thesis is supported by Tanton's description of women attending a workshop on developing women's presence in senior management. She found that the focus of the group was on positioning women generally as 'the Other' to the characteristics of a male norm with which they themselves identified. Tanton concludes that their complicated positioning 'could be seen as a measure of the depth of the entrenched values within society that even this group of women concentrating their attention on the issue of women's development approached it from the perspective of the "centred male"'

(Tanton 1994: 9). Despite the rhetorics of 'new management' it seems likely that in order to obtain professional success many women at, or near the top of, institutional hierarchies have had to modify some, if not all, of the qualities traditionally associated with femininity (see also Billing and Alvesson 1994). So while there is no uniformity in the femininities performed by women leaders within the field of education, it can be argued, on the basis of the research studies cited here, that on a continuum of femininity and masculinity the femininities they take up and play out as leaders have characteristics in common with those of male peers as well as female subordinates.

This propensity to move between qualities and behaviours traditionally ascribed to one sex or the other was evident among the women headteachers in a research study I carried out with Stephen Ball. Women managers draw on a range of subjectivities, at times as a maternal figure, at times as stereo-typically female, but at other times constructing an identity as a powerful person which cuts across and conflicts with other historically derived aspects of feminine subjectivity. These varied feminine positionings are assumed at different times in different contexts and in relation to different agendas by Mrs Carnegie, one of the headteachers in our study (Reay and Ball 2000: 154). Although others (for example, colleagues and pupils) may interpret her behaviour differently, Mrs Carnegie articulates very clearly where she positions her management style on a continuum of masculinity and femininity. In the excerpt below, she places herself at the point at which 'the feminine and the masculine dovetail':

> and I think that perhaps . . . that's the Margaret Thatcher side of me . . . that my management style is, I don't know that you would differentiate it from a man . . . but it's very focused on women's achievement. I like to think it's not so much feminine or male, I think I would like to think I was the feminine end of the male spectrum to be honest, which I do regard as a thinking, civilised, cultured end. I loathe extremes, I loathe the macho male or the woman who plays the feminine thing so somewhere in the middle and perhaps that is, as I say, where the feminine and the masculine dovetail.

## Conclusion

> 'Being a man' and 'being a woman' are internally unstable affairs. They are always beset by ambivalence precisely because there is a cost in every identification, the loss of some other set of identifications, the forcible approximation of a norm one never chooses, a norm that chooses us, but which we occupy, reverse, resignify to the extent that the norm fails to determine us completely.
>
> (Butler 1993: 126–7)

Performing gender is not straightforward; rather it is confusing. The seduction of binaries such as male: female, boy: girl often prevents us from seeing the full range of diversity and differentiation existing within one gender as well as between categories of male and female. Both females and males are actively involved in the production of gendered identities, constructing gender through a variety and range of social processes (Kerfoot and Knight 1994). Yet, within this 'gender work', social and cultural differences generate the particular toolkit of cultural resources that individuals have available to them.

In the twenty-first century, increasing numbers of girls and women are moving into intellectual and occupational spheres traditionally seen to be masculine (Francis 2000a). These changes involve the performance of new forms of femininity, a distancing from variants traditionally perceived as normative and the adoption of qualities previously viewed as masculine. In particular, middle-class girls and women today are involved in a repositioning and the construction of slightly different variants of femininity which allow the possibility of academic excellence within schooling and leadership within the labour market. They have been more adept than their male peers at assuming the 'gender multiculturalism' which Connell (1995) argues opens up and broadens the possibilities of gender. All this is leading to a positive reconfiguration in which understandings of normative femininity are slowly shifting to include previously excluded behaviours, attitudes and possibilities.

Yet this new reinvented femininity is just as regulated as previous forms of femininity. The 'girls having it all syndrome' and the current preoccupation with boys' underachievement makes it easy to overlook continuing realities in which the pressures on both genders are terrifying (Francis 2000a). Girls and women are clearly paying a price for their success, as women develop illnesses of stress previously only seen in men, and eating and other obsessive-compulsive disorders continue to grow among female students (see Walkerdine *et al.* 2001). The downside of female 'success' is apparent in the double and sometimes triple shift of many female managers juggling work, child care and further study, while younger female students are caught up in a different juggling act between high academic achievement and positioning themselves as attractive and desirable to male peers. However, despite the complexities of these changes there is still much to celebrate. In contrast, the situation for working-class girls and women remains less positive. They are often marginalized and excluded from the more positive shifts in constructions of femininity experienced by their middle-class peers. There has been no parallel melding of white or black working-class femininity with rational, bourgeois subjectivity. Transformations in the way femininity is lived for girls and women continue to be mediated by the intransigence of class.

# 12 Typical boys? Theorizing masculinity in educational settings

*Christine Skelton*

## Introduction

From the middle of the 1990s headlines began to appear in national newspapers in the UK claiming that schools were letting boys down. For example, *'The failing sex'* (*Guardian* 12.3.96.); *'Where did we go wrong?'* (*Times Educational Supplement* 14.2.97.); *'Classroom rescue for Britain's lost boys'* (*Independent* 5.1.98.). The government have also expressed concern about boys' attitudes towards schooling and their performance in assessment tests (Woodhead 1996; Blunkett 2000). Boys are portrayed as being poorly motivated towards school work and underperforming generally in relation to girls, but particularly in terms of literacy skills, with this disaffection leading to truancy and exclusion. A consequence of government and media concern about Britain's 'failing boys' is a proliferation of articles, books and reports exploring the 'gender problem' of the late twentieth and twenty-first centuries – boys' underachievement. However, reading through much of this literature it is possible to conclude that little has been learned from feminist understandings of gender and schooling, and similarly there is no apparent recognition of the more recent theories of masculinity and schooling.

This chapter aims to provide a context for the current high profile given to the problems of boys and education by raising questions about how concepts of 'masculinity' have been, and are, theorized in the literature. As this is a book written mainly by feminists or by writers who engage with issues raised by feminism, it seems appropriate to begin with feminists' views on investigating boys and masculinities. The chapter will then go on briefly to look at how boys were constructed in studies of schooling from the 1960s to the 1970s. The chapter then moves on to outline ways of theorizing masculinities in the latter part of the twentieth century, and how these have been informed by research on, and intervention strategies into boys' schooling. The final section looks at contemporary reflections on masculinity/gender theorizing in relation to education.

Before exploring these issues a few words need to be said about the boys' underachievement debate. There is not the space here to go into a detailed discussion of the criticisms made of this debate (see, instead, Epstein *et al.* 1998; Delamont 1999; Salisbury *et al.* 1999; Skelton 2001) but, briefly, the main critique has centred around the narrow parameters of the argument whereby it has been projected that *all* boys, irrespective of social class, ethnicity and so on are underachieving. Thus, feminists have observed that the notion of boys' underachievement has focused specifically on statistical information (Kenway and Willis 1998; Raphael Reed 1999) and pointed out that the complexity of gender and achievement cannot simply be 'read off' crude, basic data (see Chapter 2).

Another concern about the boys' underachievement debate has involved a questioning of where the focus is leading, especially in the light of the fact that girls' apparently superior academic performance does not follow through into the workplace where women's average salary remains lower than that of men (Equal Opportunities Commission 2000). Also, one suggestion offered by government and the media to explain boys' disinclination towards academic work is the feminization of education – that is, because schools are predominantly female in terms of teaching staff this is seen by some to result in a privileging of female learning styles and forms of assessment as well as teachers' bias towards girls' behaviours as learners (Biddulph 1998; Pollack 1998). Remediation strategies to address boys' underachievement have included both single-sex groupings and mixed gender seating; increasing the number of men teachers and male mentors; and using teaching styles which accommodate what are considered to be boys' preferred approaches to learning. However, in focusing on boys as a group and on what are adjudged to be boys' needs, educationalists have warned that:

- advocating such strategies as single-sex grouping might reinforce traditional gender stereotypes (Sukhnandan *et al.* 2000);
- teachers will put all their efforts into making the learning environment 'boy friendly' while girls are not provided with the requisite opportunities to fulfil their potential (Arnot *et al.* 1998b);
- a self-fulfilling prophecy may come into effect if teachers are constantly told that girls are more effective as learners than boys (Younger *et al.* 1999).

## Feminists' views on investigating boys and masculinities

The immediate years following the Sex Discrimination Act 1975 saw the publication of books written by feminists on the ways in which education processes discriminated against girls. This does not mean to say that feminists simply shifted the foci away from boys onto girls, thereby replicating the 'gender blind' practices of much of the earlier educational research (see next section) – rather, the nature, processes and experiences of girls' education were seen in relation to that of boys' education (Mahony 1985). Indeed, some feminists directly wrote about boys and education (Arnot 1984; Askew and Ross 1988), but the marginalization of females in previous research investigations meant there was an understandable reluctance to undertake empirical research which looked explicitly at boys.

Although second wave feminism generated a corresponding men's movement (particularly in the USA, see Farrell 1974; Pleck and Sawyer 1974), the literature on masculinity was more limited and did not attract the attention of feminists. However, in the late 1980s and early 90s there was an upsurge of interest in issues of masculinity in the UK and elsewhere to the extent that feminists began to respond to the resulting literature (Hagan 1992). Although, as will be discussed later, there are multiple perspectives on masculinity (Carrigan *et al.* 1985), two perspectives in particular were noted: that identified as 'the new men's studies' (Brod 1987; Kimmel 1987) and that referred to as the 'study of men' (Hearn and Morgan 1990), more recently labelled as 'pro-feminist' writing. An immediate concern for feminists was that the men who included their writing and research as part of 'the new men's studies' argued that their work was akin to women's studies. For example, Harry Brod (1987: 265) claimed that women's studies had succeeded in 'adding supplemental or compensatory knowledge to the traditional curriculum'. However, this was a serious misreading of women's studies which is about much more than just 'adding women on' to existing knowledge (O'Brien 1982). It is not simply concerned with individual experiences of femininity in interpersonal relationships but with issues of social power and powerlessness (Hanmer 1990). Also, much of 'the new men's studies' canon was characterized by omissions or distortions of fundamental elements of feminism (Griffin and Wetherell 1992).

The second perspective can be categorized as 'pro-feminist' in that it 'recognizes the broad imbalances of economic, cultural, political, sexual and educational power between males and females and males and males. It emphasizes the different ways of being male that arise from different cultural groups (ethnic, class, sexual, age) and the connections between them' (Kenway 1997b: 58). Although pro-feminist work could be seen to actively engage with feminist theories, perspectives, methodologies and epistemologies as part of its research agenda, the concern remained that turning attention towards masculinity could result in any available funding on gender being directed towards this area (Canaan and Griffin 1990). Of even greater concern was that investigations into masculinities by male researchers would sidestep feminist concerns while appearing to pay lip-service to them. Thus, at the beginning of the 1990s there were understandable reservations by feminists about the growth of interest in studies of masculinity. Indeed, it is evident from some of the arguments put forward within the boys' underachievement debate that these were well-founded fears (Skelton 1998, 2001).

In recent years, shifts in the way in which gender is theorized have highlighted a need to make conceptualizations of femininity and masculinity much more problematic (Butler 1990) and this has been incorporated into research designs. For example, feminists researching young children in classrooms have identified how girls and boys construct their gender positions by adopting attitudes and behaviours which are in opposition to each other – that is, gender as relational (Davies 1989; Francis 1998). It continues to be the case that much of the literature which focuses more directly on masculinities[1] and schooling comes from male sociologists who adopt a pro-feminist perspective (Walker 1988; Mac an Ghaill 1994; Swain 2000), but feminists have also been involved in looking more closely at masculinity issues, specifically in considering the problems of gender for those boys from marginalized groups – for example, homophobic bullying (Epstein and Johnson 1998) and the exclusion of black boys from school (Wright *et al.* 1998). This work can be seen as part of the ongoing development of the ways in which perspectives on gender have become less fixed to a person's biological sex (see Chapter 1). However, the emergence of a moral panic in the mid-1990s about boys' underachievement brought about feminist involvement in debates on boys and schooling (Kenway 1995b; Yates 1997; Epstein *et al.* 1998).

To summarize: the recent focus on boys and the interest in theorizing masculinities should not obscure the fact that feminists have always recognized boys/masculinities in their work on females' experiences of education and schooling. At the same time, there has been an understandable reluctance to look more closely at how males construct masculinities in educational settings. There are two possible explanations for this. First, feminism is about placing women/girls' experiences at the centre of any exploration and analysis. (And the burgeoning literature on masculinity posed a threat in terms of attracting research funding, publishing deals and even jobs.) Second, for the majority of feminists working in education, gender is seen as relational; therefore, in order to explain and understand gender processes, it is necessary to look at the ways in which girls (and boys) take up constructions of their social identity as opposite to the other sex. This has been referred to as 'male-female' dualism or the 'gender dichotomy' (Davies 1989; Walkerdine 1990).

### 'Boys' in studies of schooling (1960s–1970s)

Many of the early sociological studies of schools and classrooms tended to be 'gender blind', so findings of explorations of boys' experiences of schooling and/or all male institutions were unproblematically generalized to all pupils (see, for example, Hargreaves 1967; Lacey 1970; Willis 1977; Corrigan 1979). Importantly, even the research which explicitly focused on boys took as self-evident what 'being a boy' was all about (Mungham and Pearson 1976). One example of the taken for granted nature of 'boys' appears in the index of Parker's (1974) book *View from the Boys* where one entry reads 'Sex: see Girls'. At the same time, the theoretical positions researchers adopted did provide information about *differences between* groups of boys.

Both Hargreaves (1967) and Lacey's (1970) studies of, respectively, boys in a secondary modern and a grammar school drew on ethnomethodological understandings, whereby what is important is to recognize how we, as members of social groups, construct social reality. In the case of both schools, Hargreaves and Lacey focused on the opposing positions towards schooling taken up by the pupils (boys) which, they argued, were informed by home factors, school organization and the effects of differences in cultural resources between working-class and middle-class families. Social class differences between boys also underpinned the work of researchers committed to radical schooling who were influenced by neo-Marxist ideology. The most famous of these is Willis' (1977) study of a group of 'lads' in a secondary school, *Learning to Labour*. Here, Willis drew parallels between the counter-school culture of the 'lads' to that of workers on the factory floor. In a similar vein Paul Corrigan's (1979) study, *Schooling the Smash Street Kids*, documented the ways in which a group of white, working-class, heterosexual boys in the North-East of England resisted the perceived repressive authority of the school. The point here is that although this research provided insights into how schooling was experienced by white boys from different social classes there was no attempt to theorize their gender identities or the gendered nature of their position. The attention to such issues came with the second wave of feminism in the 1970s.

## Theorizing masculinity/ies

The influence of the 'new sociology of education' – of which the work of Hargreaves and Lacey were examples – 'focused attention on the social construction of action and knowledge *within* schools and classrooms (as opposed to being ' "determined" by external forces') – Woods 1996: 6. This new sociology rapidly divided into various strands: a Marxist oriented route and those informed by interactionism – that is, ethnomethodology, phenomenology and symbolic interactionism. Feminists researching females' experiences of schooling were particularly drawn to symbolic interactionism not least because it privileges the accounts of the participants. Symbolic interactionism as a general theory of society has three basic foci: meaning, process and interaction (Blumer 1969). Symbolic interactionists argue that people 'perform' on the basis of meanings and understandings which they develop through interaction with others. Through these interactions individuals are believed to develop a concept of 'self'; this is generated through their interpretations of the responses of others to their own actions. Consequently, the 'self' is not seen as static but as constantly being refined.

Another influential explanation for how girls and boys learned their gendered identities through interactions with others was offered by sex-role and socialization theories.

*Sex-role and socialization theories*

Many of the early feminist accounts of girls and schooling drew to some extent on sex-role theories (Sharpe 1976; Lobban 1978; Delamont, 1980; Whyte *et al.* 1985). Role theories argue that children learn 'appropriate' ways of relating to the world around them through observation and/or experiencing a system of rewards and sanctions which reinforce such behaviours (Gregory 1969). So in terms of sex roles this means females learning and internalizing such traits as caring, nurturing and selflessness, and so on, while males acquire and demonstrate characteristics such as aggression, independence and competitiveness (Oakley 1972; Seidler 1989). The same kind of emphasis on sex-role/socialization theories to explain gender differences could also be found in the literature associated with the 'men's movement' of the same period (Farrell 1974).

Such was the importance attributed to socialization theories that they formed the basis of many of the remediation strategies aimed at redressing gender inequalities in schooling (for example, changing school texts, establishing 'gender fair' teaching styles, offering non-traditional role models and unbiased careers advice). However, it was later argued that such approaches towards gender identity formation and assumptions about the nature of stereotyping were inappropriate in that 'these strategies although designed to widen girls' and boys' horizons, and give them more opportunities in life were somewhat idealistic in intention and naive in approach' (Arnot 1991: 453). This was because such approaches assumed that young girls and boys would want to take up curriculum subjects, leisure activities and so on conventionally associated with the 'other' sex once they were given the opportunities. What such perspectives neglected to recognize was that boys and girls invest heavily in demonstrating that they belong to their 'own' gender and the last thing that the majority want to do is to appear not to fit in with their same-sex peer group. While feminists, among others, have argued that remediation strategies based on sex-role socialization theories are inadequate, it is evident that they continue to influence some of the current strategies for addressing issues of masculinity in schooling. This can be seen by considering the main theoretical influences in the boys/masculinities and schooling debates.

*'Men's rights' versus 'pro-feminists'*

Various feminist perspectives were in evidence in the 1970s with liberal, Marxist-socialist, radical, and (later) black feminism paying particular attention to educational issues. Among masculinity theorists there is no definite agreement on the number of different perspectives: Clatterbaugh (1990) writes of six positions on masculinity (conservative, men's rights, spiritual, pro-feminist, socialist, group specific); Messner (1997) identifies eight approaches (men's liberation, men's rights, radical feminist men, socialist feminist men, men of colour, gay activists, the mythopoetic men's movement, and the Promise Keepers); Lingard and Douglas (1999) note four groupings (men's rights, pro-feminism, masculinity therapy and conservative), acknowledging that their categorizations omit the perspectives of gay men (which are encapsulated in the other categories). The two approaches most evident in the discussions on boys, masculinities and schooling are the 'men's rights' and 'pro-feminist' perspectives. The 'men's rights' approach has its roots in what was referred to earlier as 'the new men's studies'.

One of the main characteristics of the men's rights perspective is that it positions boys as a homogenous group who share common experiences of schooling. Hence, no recognition is given to differences between boys because of social class, ethnicity, culture, sexuality, religion, age and so on. Indeed it is the men's rights perspective which appears to have gained the support of both the media and government. For example, the proponents of men's rights share a belief in the *essential* nature of 'man' and see schooling as restricting or oppressing this 'maleness'. This means of conceptualizing gender identity and inequality is attractive because of its simplicity. Hence, newspaper headlines can easily condense what are actually complex issues to straightforward binary opposites, as in 'Girls trounce the boys in examination league table' (*The Times*, 3.9.94.); 'Now let's give boys a boost' (*Daily Telegraph* 7.12.94.); and 'Girls doing well while boys feel neglected' (*Guardian*, 26.8.95.). Such unambiguous positionings of boys as victims while girls are school successes elicits apparently self-evident solutions. The more conservative advocates of this perspective argue that changes to schooling made to rectify discriminatory practices inhibiting girls' educational experiences have been detrimental to boys and policies which focus exclusively on boys should now be pursued (Redwood 1994; Pollack 1998). This would mean schools adopting traditional forms of organization, enforcing stricter discipline measures and reintroducing competition (Moir and Moir 1999). Alternatively, Biddulph (1998) suggests that as boys mature later than girls, they should start school a year later. The more middle of the road supporters of men's rights argue that the problems boys' experience in school need to be tackled within a gender equity framework (Lingard and Douglas 1999). It would seem from this that there would be agreement between the men's rights and pro-feminist perspective. However, if we compare the former's position with that of feminists then obvious contrasts emerge.

Although there are differences between the various feminist perspectives they all share the view that schools are masculinizing agencies and that they privilege maleness over femaleness. Proponents of men's rights start from the opposing stance: that schools are feminizing agencies. The argument here is that schools are staffed predominantly by women who employ 'girl-centred' teaching styles and classroom management practices (Noble 1998; Mason 1999). Thus, for supporters of men's rights a gender equity framework involves adopting practices such as mixed-sex seating arrangements, mentoring and ensuring an increased number of male role models, particularly in the primary years. However, these could be seen as strategies which draw on girls' apparent strengths to support boys' learning. For example, it has been suggested that teachers should consider 'pairing boys with girls in group work to expose them to the "feminine" skills of language and reflection' (Bleach *et al.* 1996: 25). (Interestingly the converse argument is also used, that boys do better in single-sex classes – Thomas 1998.)

The problems of the contemporary men's rights perspective in looking at boys and schooling have been usefully summarized by Kenway (1996: 510):

> This strand of thought draws its inspiration from social psychology rather than sociology and therefore its focus tends to be on the personal, interpersonal and small scale. It tends not to attend to broad social structures, to matters of power or social complexity and dynamics or indeed the social role of emotion. Neither does it have a relational understanding of gender and therefore it fails to attend to the undeniable broad structural inequalities between males and females. Also it has tended to set itself up alongside rather than in co-operation with feminism. It has therefore not tended to draw its insights from the best and most recent feminist theory and research about gender. Neither has it attended to the ways in which boys and men are a problem for women and girls or, particularly, to the ways some males are a problem for other males.

An alternative masculinity perspective that engages with boys and schooling and problematizes the issues in the ways suggested by Kenway is that referred to as 'pro-feminist'. This is where there is a recognition of imbalances in power between males and females, and males and males (Mac an Ghaill 1994; Connolly 1998). Here the focus is on broader social structures and the different ways of being male that emerge from different cultural groups through the influence of social class, age, ethnicity and sexuality as well as the connections between them. One of the most influential discussions on the construction of masculinities has been offered by Connell (1987, 1995, 1997), notably his discussion on 'hegemonic masculinity'.

### Hegemonic masculinity

Connell's theory of masculinities is based on the idea that there are many modes of masculinity but that it is possible to identify certain configurations of masculinity on the basis of general social, cultural and institutional patterns of power and meaning, and to discern how they are constructed in relation to each other. These masculinities are defined as *hegemonic, complicitous, subordinate* and *marginal*. In order to explore these various configurations Connell argues for a threefold model of the structure of gender relations, which distinguish relations of *power, production* and *cathexis* (emotional attachment). In drawing on all three areas Kenway (1997b: 59) explains that 'masculine identities are not static but historically and spatially situated and evolving. They arise through an individual's interaction with both the dynamisms and contradictions within and between immediate situations and broader social structures'. This model provides a means of considering power relations that exist between men and men as well as between males and females.

Hegemonic masculinity is a concept used to describe the mode of masculinity which at any one point is 'culturally exalted' (Connell 1995) – that is, it refers to those dominant and dominating modes of masculinity which claim the highest status and exercise the greatest influence and authority. Hegemonic masculinity is a position which is achieved as a result of collective cultural and institutional practices, and asserts its authority through these practices, particularly through the media and the state (Kenway 1997b). At the same time, it is not 'fixed'; it is in a constant state of flux and constantly needs to be achieved by dominating, not obliterating, alternative patterns and groups. Of particular significance is that hegemonic masculinity is constructed in relation to women and subordinated masculinities, and is heterosexual. As such, hegemonic masculinity structures dominant and subordinate relations across and between the sexes, as well as legitimizing patriarchy. Kenway and Fitzclarence (1997: 121) have suggested that 'hegemonic masculinity mobilizes around physical strength, adventurousness, emotional neutrality, certainty, control, assertiveness, self-reliance, individuality, competitiveness, instrumental skills, public knowledge, discipline, reason, objectivity and rationality'. Importantly, there is no *one* form of hegemonic masculinity although all forms may draw upon, exaggerate, modify and distort these aspects.

Hegemonic masculinity defines what it means to be a 'real' man or boy, and other forms of masculinity are seen in relation to this form. However, hegemonic masculinity is not something embodied within individual male personalities but is the public face of male power. So while the construction and positioning of the 'lads' by themselves and the authors of the 1970s research into schooling were redolent of ascribed traditional, dominant forms of white, working-class masculinity, it was not necessarily the case that the boys themselves lived out this 'way of being' (Willis 1977; Robins and Cohen 1978; Corrigan 1979). At the same time, it is fair to say that the 'lads' in these studies were constructing masculine identities which placed them in what Connell (1995: 79) has termed 'the frontline troops of patriarchy'.

Of course, not all men or boys attempt to engage with, or even wish to aspire to, the rigorous standards demanded by hegemonic masculinity. At the same time, all men benefit from the *patriarchal dividend* (Connell 1995: 79) which is the advantage men gain from the overall subordination of women without actually being at the forefront of the struggles involved with hegemonic masculinity. Connell uses the term '*complicitous* masculinities' to indicate that cluster of masculinities whereby men reap the benefits of hegemonic masculinity without actively seeking or supporting it. Also evident in the various ways of 'being male' in school settings are '*subordinate* masculinities' which stand in direct contrast to hegemonic masculinity (for example, gay masculinity). Furthermore, the interrelationship of gender with other major social structures such as social class and 'race' creates further complex associations between masculinities. To explain masculinities at the intersection of gender, 'race' and social class, Connell (1995) uses the concept of *'marginalized* masculinities'. He refers here to the relations between dominant and subordinated classes or ethnic groups. Marginalized masculinities are contingent upon the sanctioning of the hegemonic masculinity of the dominant group (see Connell 1995 for a detailed explanation of these ideas).

The more complex analyses of masculinities offered by Connell and others (see Brittan 1989; Hearn and Collinson 1990; Morgan 1992) made their appearance in the literature on masculinities and schooling in the UK around the mid-1990s (Mac an Ghaill 1994; Connolly 1995b; Parker 1996). A brief sweep of the titles of articles adopting this more sophisticated form of analysis provides an indication of the multiplicity of masculinities to be found in school settings. In relation to studies in secondary school we find: *'Cool guys, swots and wimps: the interplay of masculinity and education'* (Connell 1989); *'"Cool boys", "party animals", "squids" and "poofters": interrogating the dynamics and politics of adolescent masculinities in school'* (Martino 1999); and the identification in Mac an Ghaill's (1994) study of masculinities of the 'macho lads', the 'academic achievers', the 'new enterprisers' and the 'real Englishmen'. Then there are the accounts of primary schooling where Connolly (1998) compares the positioning of the 'bad boys' to that of South Asian boys, and Warren's (1997) naming of the 'princes of the park' and 'working-class kings'. Importantly, these research studies did not talk of masculinity as something only relevant to interpersonal interactions but highlighted the relationship between masculinities and institutional life; 'It is not too strong to say that *masculinity is an aspect of institutions, and is produced in institutional life: as much as it is an aspect of personality* or produced in interpersonal transactions' (Connell 1997: 608). Thus this research into masculinities and schooling explores how schools develop dominant images of masculinity and how boys construct, negotiate and reconstruct their identities in relation to these through their own histories (intersected as they are by class, ethnicity, culture, religion, sexuality and so on).

## Putting theory into (school) practice

While the conceptualizations of masculinities offered by these theorists reflect the complexity of gender constructions, they offer little in terms of providing schools and teachers with practical strategies and guidance. This obviously contrasts with the numerous strategies offered to schools by those writing from within the men's rights perspective but, as was said earlier, its conceptualization of boys/masculinity is limited and limiting. Some programmes based on pro-feminist theorizing do exist (in Australia) but they tend to be couched in ways that make boys feel guilty about being boys and/or present alternative images of masculinity which boys do not find appealing (Lingard and Douglas 1999). For example, in order to look at broader structural inequalities they are heavily reliant on discussion-based activities (journal writing, brainstorming, role play exercises) and are more appropriate for secondary pupils. *Boys-Talk,* an Australian programme, is based on ten topics focusing on the construction of gender, relationships, sexuality and violence, thereby placing emphasis on interpersonal behaviours.

It is fairly clear that there are problems with programmes based on both men's rights and pro-feminist perspectives. First, as has just been said, they both centralize interpersonal relationships (Lingard and Douglas 1999). As such they are not going to help teachers tackle those issues which have attracted the most attention – namely, boys disinclination towards literacy-based activities and their aggressive behaviours. Nor will these programmes help in getting children to try out and become comfortable with a range of learning styles or to take up activities they associate with the opposite sex such as girls playing football or boys choosing home corner play. Second, programmes based on either pro-feminist or men's rights perspectives locate boys as the problem and the subjects of change. We already have the situation in the UK whereby local education authorities have increased the number of strategies targeting boys specifically from 14 per cent prior to 1995 to 41 per cent in 1997–8, while those aimed at boys and girls fell from 71 per cent to 52 per cent during the same period (Sukhnandan 1999). But more importantly, focusing on boys does not provide opportunities for the school to identify their own contribution in constructing and maintaining dominant images of masculinity with which boys and girls negotiate.

The question is: what initiatives can be implemented which are informed by pro/feminist theories *and* which tackle the issues teachers have identified as a problem such as boys and literacy, misbehaviour and negative attitudes to school? For this we need to turn to contemporary feminist thinking and practice.

## Towards gender equity in schooling

It has already been observed that the concept of hegemonic masculinity has proved useful and has certainly influenced studies of masculinities and schooling (Mac an Ghaill 1994; Skelton 1996; Sewell 1997; Gilbert and Gilbert 1998). However, it is not an unproblematic concept and it has lent itself to being used in problematical ways. There are a number of points which need to be made here:

- Connell did point out that women and gay men can also perform hegemonic masculinity but this idea has generally been overlooked (Cheng 1996; Heywood 1997).
- Hegemonic masculinity has evoked the use of typologies or categories of masculinity such as 'cool guys', 'lads' and 'party animals' (thus helping to 'fix' gender identity, whereas Connell talks of masculinities as more fluid). This can be seen to be a misrepresentation of Connell's theory.
- However, speaking of hegemonic masculinity as constructed in relation to women and to subordinated masculinities implies a hierarchy which in itself suggests that gender identity is fixed. Also, it does not allow for the notion that individuals occupy multiple, contradictory subject positions.

- Hegemonic masculinity is that which is the most 'culturally exalted' (Connell 1995: 77). Therefore, by definition, it is the most powerful. This causes a problem for poststructuralism which does not regard 'power' as a commodity that can be held by any person or group.

The last point highlights the main difficulty in devising appropriate gender equity programmes: what is or are the most appropriate theoretical frameworks to build upon? It would seem that the two theoretical positions which have the most to offer are those that draw on (hegemonic) masculinity and poststructuralism, but as shown there are major tensions between the two. Francis (2000a) has argued a strong case for a theory which has the capacity to recognize the multiple positions we inhabit *and* that accounts for the importance we place on ourselves as coherent human beings (indeed the absence of the latter is seen to result in psychotic illnesses such as schizophrenia). This form of theorizing would allow for a retention of the notion of difference but recognize collective interests. Some of the contributors to this book are instrumental in the development of such theories but these have still to become more widely adopted (see Part 2). In the meantime there are specific issues which we know of and which can be built upon in order to develop gender equity programmes.

We know that children work hard to demonstrate their gender identity (Francis 1998) and are not swayed by 'alternative' images. For example, young children were positively hostile to characters in feminist fairytales such as the assertive princess and a boy interested in ballet dancing (Davies 1989). This suggests that simply *presenting* various images of masculinity/ femininity is not enough; rather, children need to *question* conventional gendered characterizations. In order to put together a relevant gender equity programme, schools need to develop their own policies, particular to their own needs, which could be ascertained by exploring four key questions (see Skelton 2001 for a detailed discussion). Briefly these are:

- What images of masculinity and femininity are children bringing with them into school and what types are they acting out in the classroom and playground?
- What are the dominant images of masculinity and femininity that the school itself reflects to the children?
- What kinds of role model does the school want and expect of its teachers?
- What kinds of initiatives/strategies/projects should teachers be undertaking with children to question gender categories?

These kinds of question are the ones being posed by feminists in their work in schools – that is, the emphasis is not on 'boys' or 'girls' but on 'boys *and* girls' (Francis 2000a; MacNaughton 2000; Marsh 2000; Skelton 2001).

## Conclusion

This chapter has set out to chart the ways in which boys have been theorized in educational literature and the critiques of these perspectives by feminists. Prior to the second wave of feminism in the 1970s studies of schooling took the 'male as norm', so investigations focusing on boys in boys' schools were unquestioned, although findings were generalized to all pupils. Equally, where studies explicitly considered the school experiences of boys, the gendered nature of these experiences went unremarked. The interest and concern generated by feminists over girls in the educational system predominated in discussions of gender until the mid-1990s when boys' underachievement grabbed the attention of the media, the government, and subsequently schools. It has been shown here how the majority of intervention initiatives are informed by one theoretical perspective: men's rights – which seems not to build upon feminist understandings and, as such, marginalizes girls' needs. An alternative means of theorizing masculinity in school settings (pro-feminist) has developed programmes which, although recognizing feminist work, nevertheless reduce complex issues to ones of interpersonal relationships and focus on boys. It was finally argued that the development of appropriate gender equity programmes requires new forms of theorizing which are based on gender as relational, which incorporate notions of difference and agency, and which recognizes the insights provided by both feminist and masculinity perspectives.

## Note

1 The use of the term masculinit*ies* is indicative of a particular theoretical perspective which recognizes the multiplicity of ways of being and 'maleness'. It recognizes that individuals take up and perform various modes of masculinities in different times, places and so on. At the same time, the concept of masculinities has been criticized for reasons including its wide variety of uses, its imprecision nad its propensity for essentialism (Hearn 1996; Kerfoot and Whitehead 1998; Francis 2000a).

# 13 | Social class, gender and schooling

*Helen Lucey*

## Introduction

In this chapter I will be looking at the relationship between social class, gender and education. The dynamic between the structures and processes of these cannot be viewed in isolation from the profound transformations that have already taken place and continue to take place at all levels of the individual, family and social world – local, national and global. At the heart of all of these changes are subjects – girls and boys, men and women – who have had to transform *themselves* in order to cope and survive in a maelstrom of change. As if that were not challenging enough, it turns out that the 'new social order' of the twenty-first century retains some distinctly 'old order' features which even the shiniest meritocratic rhetoric of 'can do', 'can have' and 'excellence' cannot entirely banish. While some attempted to celebrate the 'death of class' in the 1980s and 90s (Gorz 1982), we find in the new century that the power of class never went away after all and that, alongside gender, race and ethnicity, class continues to be a vital factor in determining the educational experiences, achievements and trajectories of girls and boys.

There is no doubt that viewed from a distance the overall educational achievements of all girls as compared to boys would seem to have improved significantly over the last 20 or so years. But as with any distant object, moving closer reveals details which appear insignificant or are invisible to the distant view, the macro gaze. What appear to be tiny specks on an otherwise smooth surface turn out to be towering mountains of hierarchy; hairline cracks become huge fissures of difference. So it is with gender, social class and educational achievement. Working-class girls *are* doing better at school and gaining more qualifications at higher grades than working-class boys, but this improvement in no way challenges the vastly and consistently superior examination performance of the overwhelming majority of girls *and* boys from the various sections of the professional middle classes.

Now, it would be easy to demonstrate working-class educational failure against middle-class success and leave it at that, but there is a lot more to the story of contemporary schooling than this. Questions of identity or self are at the very heart of education and as such must be considered in any discussion of how success and failure come to be so predictably produced for the majority of girls and boys of different classes. Drawing on the findings from a number of research studies that I have been involved with I will explore the social, structural and emotional, and individual processes through which some (mainly working-class) pupils fail, while other (mainly middle-class) pupils maintain their educational success.

## Girls and boys: progress and panic

Debates about educational performance and gender have shifted dramatically over the last three decades. In the wake of second-wave feminism[1] of the 1970s a great deal of concern was expressed about the relative underachievement of girls, especially in maths and science subjects (Sutherland 1983; Whyte 1986). Since then, girls' increased examination success and participation in post-compulsory education has for some signalled a 'closing of the gender gap' (Arnot *et al.* 1999). In the mid-1990s however, in an educational context in which girls were now viewed as doing very well and a social and economic context which had undergone profound change, it was boys' newly perceived underachievement which provoked a moral panic (Sammons 1995; Epstein *et al.* 1998; Lucey and Walkerdine 2000).

The story of boys' underachievement and girls' success as it has emerged during the last decade is a complex one. Arnot *et al.* (1999), in their in-depth exploration of gender patterns in education, conclude that girls have made major strides in reducing the overall lead of boys in assessments and examinations. For instance, in 1995 the number of girls achieving five or more A* to C grades at GCSE stood at 48 per cent of girls compared with 39 per cent of boys (Arnot *et al.* 1999: 15). At A/AS level, girls have continued to do as well and in some cases better than boys; a trend that has had a knock-on effect on the proportion of girls staying in education after they are 18. Slightly more girls than boys now take up training and further education courses and enter higher education. Arnot *et al.* identify girls' consistent and continuing advantage in English and their improvement in maths and science as the two main factors in the progress of girls over the last ten years. Available data does point to significant gender differences in English, where the performance gap between boys and girls is widest and evident from an early age (Equal Opportunities Commission/Ofsted 1996; Arnot *et al.* 1998a). Explanations for this disparity are various but tend to involve facets of the concept of 'feminization'. The feminized environment of the primary school is seen to be problematic for boys (Shaw 1995) and there are suggestions that this can result in the formation of damaging attitudes towards English in adolescence (Ofsted 1993; Millard 1997). Not only this, but just as science was previously thought of as a male subject, literacy and English are regarded as 'naturally' female, requiring practices in the classroom – such as introspection, empathy, self-disclosure and the creative description of emotions – which are perceived to be more suited to girls' than boys' constructions of gender (Davies 1993).

Girls have not only maintained their advantage in English, but by 1995 they had almost caught up with boys in maths and science. However, despite getting off to a good start in primary school, boys' advantage in these subjects is evident at age 11 and continues on to GCSE and A/AS level in both numbers entered and grades achieved (Arnot *et al.* 1999). In their research, Arnot *et al.* identify the introduction of the National Curriculum (with its set of compulsory subjects) and the GCSE as playing a 'key role in reducing the sex segregation of subjects up to the age of sixteen' (1999: 18). However, once subject choice is in the hands of the student they tend to choose gender-typed subjects and courses, with young women more likely to choose arts and humanities courses and young men to choose science and technical courses at degree and A level. These trends have an ongoing influence on the kinds of job which young men and women take up and help produce a highly gendered labour impact (Furlong and Cartmel 1997).

## Class differences

It is very important to highlight the gains made by girls in education, not least because they have been, and continue to be, so hard fought for by feminists, educationalists and girls and young women themselves. But there is a danger that concentrating on gender differences may help to suppress deep and enduring class differences between boys and girls. Arnot *et al.* (1999) stress that social class remains a 'key factor' in educational success and that 'Gender differences appeared narrowest where students have the greatest cultural and material advantages and sharpest where their parents were more socially advantaged' (1999: 28). Data from the Office for Standards in Education shows that schools in deprived areas do worse in inspections than those in wealthy areas, and failing primary schools are overwhelmingly in areas where poverty levels are high. Other research demonstrates that social class inequalities in education remain substantial and persistent, not only in the UK (Reid 1994; Smith and Noble 1995; Hillman and Pearce 1998), but across Europe (Muller and Karle 1993; Shavit and Blossfeld 1993). Gillian Plummer (2000) states categorically that the educational failure of working-class girls is hidden by an interpretation of statistics whereby middle-class girls' rise in achievement is extrapolated to mean *all* girls. She argues that a different examination of the available data reveals that the gender gap is nowhere near as severe as the class gap.

Changing patterns of schooling and the introduction of new forms of credentials and vocational courses since the late 1970s have had a significant impact on the qualification profiles of school-leavers. In 1970, 44 per cent of pupils left school without any graded exams (prior to 1972 many left school at 15 without even having sat any exams). By 1991, unqualified school-leavers made up only 6 per cent of the 16-year-old cohort. Despite the rapid overall increases in GCSE qualifications, the gap between different social groups is widening (Sammons 1995; Smith and Noble 1995). At the same time as credentials have gone up, there are still grave concerns about the number of young adults leaving school with only a poor grasp of literacy and numeracy (Bynner and Steedman 1995). Vocational options have grown but are largely taken up by working-class pupils in lower attainment bands, leaving intact the traditional academic curriculum followed by middle-class pupils (Brown 1987). What is also clear is that the effects of social class can shape the patterns of performance of different groups of ethnic minority pupils (Gillborn and Gipps 1996).

*Post-compulsory education*

There have been dramatic increases in the last 20 years in the number of young people who stay on in education beyond the minimum school-leaving age of 16 years. Where previously the main pattern for working-class children was to leave education at the minimum school-leaving age, far fewer now leave school at 16 and most school-leavers continue to receive formal education or training on a part-time or block release basis (Furlong 1992). In 1973/4 approximately 33 per cent of 16-year-old males and 37 per cent of females were in full-time education. More working-class girls than boys had traditionally stayed on at school and this difference remained into the 1990s: in 1993/4 70 per cent of males and 76 per cent of females were in full-time education. But despite the increase in post-compulsory education, participation rates are still low and education underfunded in comparison with many other developed countries (Furlong and Cartmel 1997). Furthermore, comparative research shows that when compared to other countries, the UK has a greater proportion of low-achieving pupils and a wider distribution of achievement (Reynolds and Farrell 1996).

*Higher education*

The expansion of universities since the 1960s as well as the restructuring of higher education in 1990s has had an effect on working-class people's participation in higher education. Once the domain of a small minority, university has become part of the educational experience of a growing number. Since the post-war period, women's participation has steadily increased so that their numbers are equal to men (Reay *et al.*, in press). In fact, the biggest change in higher education has been its take-up by women. In the 1960s higher education was male dominated with women tending to be steered towards teacher training colleges (Crompton 1992). However, class inequalities persist, with little change over the years in the proportion of entrants to higher education who come from working-class families (National Commission on

Education 1993). Older, more prestigious universities are still the preserve of the children of managers and professionals, and overall the biggest increases in participation have been among the middle classes, not the working classes (Egerton and Halsey 1993). Plummer (2000) reports that in 1998 women in social class V got 1.6 per cent of places at university (boys from same class got 2 per cent), a rise of 0.4 per cent over ten years. And Furlong and Cartmel (1997: 34) state that 'Despite an apparent increase in the possibilities to continue full-time education or embark on a course of training, young people from advantaged positions in the socio-economic hierarchy have been relatively successful in protecting privileged access to the most desirable routes'.

## The effects of marketization in education

Within the policy arena of education, dominant discourses have shifted dramatically over the last 20 years, not only in Britain but also in Australia, Canada and the USA. Various educational reforms imposed by Conservative and New Labour administrations since 1979 have done little to reduce social class inequalities in attainment. Legislation such as that allowing for local management of schools (LMS) whereby schools can 'opt out' of the local education authority; the introduction of Standard Assessment Tasks (SATs); schools' selection procedures; setting; and primary and secondary school performance league tables have resulted in the production of school markets in which education is presented as a commodity and parents as consumers.

The idea that families are 'free to choose' has been shown to be a fiction which masks the persistence of old inequalities (Gewirtz *et al.* 1995; Reay and Ball 1997; Noden *et al.* 1998). In a study of children's transitions to secondary school,[2] Diane Reay and I found that there is a world of difference between making and getting your choice of secondary school. Working-class children are less likely to get their first choice of school than middle-class children, with black working-class boys faring most badly in this (Lucey and Reay 1999; see also Bagley 1996). In Bourdieu's terms it would seem that in these new school markets, those with the most 'capital' – financial, social and cultural – are the most powerful consumers, and that the education system privileges the already privileged (McCulloch 1998).

There is evidence that such an emphasis on performance within and between schools has increased rather than helped reduce some pupils' disaffection with schooling. More and more schools have introduced setting as a means of selection, a process which 'for many . . . boys would confirm their failure to succeed in what were perceived as other people's educational designs . . . by raising the stakes in terms of compliance to a school culture that was class oriented, schools were more rather than less likely to be viewed as hostile institutions' (Arnot *et al.* 1999: 143). Certainly the rising rate of school exclusions experienced in the 1990s is closely associated with this intensely competitive ethos. This is a point which official statistics clearly bear out in relation to ethnic minority pupils, with African-Caribbean pupils six times more likely to be excluded than white pupils (Gillborn and Gipps 1996).

## Excellence

New Labour have gathered rhetoric and policy behind the concept of 'excellence' – a powerful notion which consciously insists on the eradication of failure across the schooling system. The White Paper *Excellence in Schools* (DfEE 1997) acknowledged that the main problem of the education system had been its failure to cater for the 'majority of pupils' and that this failure had 'deep and historic roots'. But there are some processes which cannot be allowed for or even contemplated in this discourse of excellence. First, excellence is produced within dynamic relation to its opposite and therefore depends upon the continued presence rather than eradication of failure (Schostack 2000). Critics of the Excellence in Cities programme argue that, despite it costing £350 million and being designed to help urban schools, it is likely to exacerbate polarization through the status symbols of specialist and beacon schools and learning centres (Johnson 1999). Elements of this programme such as 'Gifted and Talented' schemes are based on the merito-cratic notion that 'able' working-class children will be 'chosen' for a limited number of privileged places on these schemes (just like the eleven-plus). However, research carried out with Diane Reay suggests that middle-class children are more likely than working-class children to be chosen for such acceleration and enrichment programmes (Lucey and Reay 2000). For those not deemed clever enough to be chosen, such schemes are about a painful exclusion. This leads the 'mass' failure of working-class children to gain places on such programmes and be 'accelerated' alongside middle-class peers to be interpreted as explained by their lack of ability, rather than lack of opportunity.

Second, in the current 'performance culture' of education and within celebratory discourses of girls' achievement there is no room to explore what might be the emotional costs for those mainly middle-class children, who far from being low achievers are the ones who must and consistently do produce excellent attainment.

## Project 4: 21

Together with June Melody and Valerie Walkerdine, I conducted a longi-tudinal study of two groups of working-class and middle-class girls and young women. One group of 30 girls, born in 1972/3 was first studied by Barbara Tizard and Martin Hughes (1984) when they were 4 years old at home with their mothers and at nursery school. This data was re-analysed by Valerie Walkerdine and myself and the girls also followed up in school when they were 10 years old (Walkerdine and Lucey 1989). Another smaller group of eight girls, born in 1978, also took part in the study when they were 6 years old. Ten years later we followed up both groups when they were 16 and 21 years old (Walkerdine *et al.* 2001).

What we found at this last stage of the research, when one group were beyond compulsory education and the other were just making decisions about whether or not to stay in school, truly shocked us. First, class differences in educational performance present when the girls were 6 and 10 years old had become deeply entrenched at 16 and 21. High standards of examination success characterized the majority of middle-class girls' educational experience to such an extent that in some of their families and the schools they attended, anything less than 'excellent' performance was viewed as tantamount to failure. Meanwhile, the examination achievements of even the 'good' working-class girls were simply not of the same order as those of the middle-class girls. Second, while the middle-class girls followed straightforward educational trajectories, from GCSE to A levels to higher education at degree level, the working-class girls' educational histories were far more diversified, chequered and fragmented. While all but one of the middle-class girls had gone on to higher education only four of the working-class girls had managed to get there and even then by very circuitous routes.

How was it that such homogeneity of success was produced in one group while the other took such diverse routes, leading to comparatively poor educational achievement (although the latter was not true of *all* the working-class girls). This question is particularly pertinent bearing in mind that higher education has supposedly been opened up to make it more accessible to young working-class women (Ainley 1993; Smithers and Robinson 1995). The sameness of the middle-class girls' educational pathways would seem to contradict theories of individualization which assert that we can no longer understand educational experiences in terms of class-based divisions (Beck 1992). Educational experiences may have become more diverse, but this is a diversification which has impacted most powerfully on the working-class girls. Meanwhile, the educational pathways of the middle-class girls are so strictly circumscribed that it seems as if most of them are on a conveyor belt, smoothly progressing towards graduate and then professional status.

But things are not as smooth as they first appear. Middle-class girls who routinely produced high attainment in formal examinations simultaneously presented us with deep anxieties about that very performance. Looking back at various stages in the research it was clear that these anxieties had been around since the middle-class girls were 10 years old when, despite the evidence of their success, feelings of not being good enough began to surface (Walkerdine and Lucey 1989). This is also consistent with findings from research with Diane Reay in which we found similar patterns of anxiety alongside the production of extremely high performance among middle-class 11-year-old girls (Lucey and Reay 2000). The actuality of the educational achievements of the middle-class girls makes a puzzle of the level of their anxieties over that performance – enough of a puzzle for us to understand that there are some complex emotional dynamics bound in up this.

Beck (1992), Giddens (1991) and other 'individualization' theorists empha-size the positive possibilities contained in the idea that one can be the author of one's own biography. For Beck *et al.* (1994) it is women who are symbolic of all the social changes that have occurred – it is women who embody the new subjectivity required by the 'global, risk society' (p. 7). This is a view supported by Wilkinson and Mulgan (1995) who report that it is younger women in particular who presented as 'setting the pace' of change, showing a desire for autonomy, self-fulfilment in work and family and a valuing of risk, excitement and change. Giddens argues that everything is presented as a possibility today. But this also means that individuals are increasingly held accountable for their own fate. The middle-class girls are compelled to succeed educationally, for this is the basis on which their future subjectivities as bourgeois feminine subjects depend (Evans 1995). Power *et al.* (1998) argue that by the 1980s there was a crisis of confidence in professionalism, and success for middle-class pupils was no longer a guaranteed given. They also suggest that recent anxiety about boys' educational performance may well reflect the frustrations and ambitions of middle-class parents for their sons. Pat Allatt (1993) discusses the critical 'domestic transition' (Bourdieu 1984) whereby privilege is not automatically transmitted, but depends upon 'con-stant purposeful activity' in the family directed towards the maintenance of class position and the prevention of downward mobility. Middle-class families are now investing similar cultural, economic, social and emotional capital in the maintenance and reproduction of their daughters' (as well as their sons') élite class position. It is through their impeccable academic credentials that middle-class girls have been able to join their brothers and fathers as pro-fessionals (Arnot *et al.* 1999). Black feminist writers have argued that in the UK black people are viewed as automatically working class, a homogenizing view which prevents class differences from emerging (Reynolds 1997; Sudbury 1998). However, what I have found, in this research and other studies, is that the drive towards high attainment in professional middle-class black, Asian and non-white ethnic families is undisturbed by ethnicity (Lucey and Walkerdine 2000).

These clever, accomplished young women look like the 'I can have every-thing girls' of popular discourses, the kind of perfect subject who has managed the psychological transformation required of the new social order. But noth-ing is allowed to threaten the production of the academic success on which they depend. Failure is simply not an available option. Not being allowed to fail, but never feeling good enough, placed middle-class girls in our sample in an emotional dilemma. It is not surprising that there were a number of cases of middle-class girls displaying chronic symptoms of anxiety such as pulling out hair, anorexia and insomnia.

It's also crucially important to pay attention to those others who live in the shadow of the giddy, privileged, high octane 'normality' of the middle-class girls; all of the working-class girls and their families who do not succeed at school, or whose qualifications are considered second rate, or those who find that, having struggled to reach the government definition of exam 'success', the goalposts have been moved and a new definition holds sway, always and forever beyond their grasp. Until we find that even ten grade A* GCSEs and high predictions for A levels are not enough to get you into a top university – if you come from a comprehensive school.

For the working-class girls in particular the combination of individual responsibility and accountability on the one hand and vulnerability and lack of control on the other puts them in an impossible situation. The experiences of young people have undoubtedly changed radically over the last 20 years, but life chances and processes of social reproduction remain highly structured: 'Blind to the existence of powerful chains of inter-dependency, young people frequently attempt to resolve collective problems through individual action and hold themselves responsible for their inevitable failure' (Furlong and Cartmel 1997: 114). However, against all odds, a small number of working-class girls from our study managed to succeed in education. Trying to explain the educational success of working-class girls defies current conventional explanations of success and failure. There were no guarantees or predictors whatsoever of good educational outcomes; no easy or straightforward correlations.

There is a large and historic literature dating from the 1950s which looks at the relationship between families and schools and identifies parenting and family practices as a key factor in the continued educational failure of working-class children. Most of these accounts are underpinned by a deficit model of working-class families. Policies aimed at improving working-class children's attainment push responsibility further into the family and away from considerations of sociality (Vincent and Warren 1998).

Our research clearly demonstrates that for working-class girls and boys, having aspirational parents who 'do all the right things' is no guarantee of the kind of educational success routinely achieved by middle-class children (Walkerdine and Lucey 1989; Lucey and Reay 2000). Furthermore, it is useless to compare working- and middle-class practices for the production of educational success because they are operating in very different circumstances and with quite different dynamics. It is not by being like middle-class girls that working-class girls succeed, but rather via a complex mixture of determination to live a different kind of life from that of their peers and the emotional support of their parents which is not upset by the parents' distress at the difficulties their daughter has to face – bringing up, as they do, memories of their own failure. Chris Mann (1998), in her research on the processes of working-class family relationships and their contribution to the educational success of their daughters, found that in terms of emotional support, mothers are the most significant people in the lives of working-class achieving girls. Fathers, however, were viewed quite differently and were seen as 'inhibiting', destructive and damaging influences on their daughters' aspirations. Gillian Plummer's complex evocation of working-class fathers is of men who are far more supportive though still conflicted in relation to their daughters' educational success. She argues that it is against the idealized middle-class father that the working-class father is found wanting, and notes that it is the educated daughters of working-class fathers who have begun to challenge these accounts: 'They have come to their father's defence, high-lighting both the harshness of his life as an oppressed worker – there is no romanticised notion of the working class here – and his weakness as oppres-sive ogre or overly dependent man in the home' (Plummer 2000: 63).

Mann (1998: 215) found a much clearer commitment to education in homes where some family members are in transition from traditional working-class culture:

> Adults may have reviewed their earlier lives in the light of later experi-ence, including changing relationships in the home and/or changing employment patterns. Such changes may be initiated by, or may trigger, adult learning experience, itself a potent catalyst for re-assessing values and aspirations.

While Mann found that it is working-class mothers who have begun to transform themselves in this way who are most positively influential on their daughters, June Melody, Valerie Walkerdine and I found that fathers were key figures for educationally successful working-class girls (Walkerdine *et al.* 2001). Pilling (1990), in her analysis of data from the National Child Development Study, concludes that one of the central reasons for the success at school of disadvantaged children was not so much the practices of the parents as what the children *believed*. These children believed that their parents wanted them to do well, to do better than they had done. While working-class parents' dreams and desires of a 'better life' for their children are part of the psychological underpinnings which support and sustain educa-tional success, this too has profound emotional consequences. Wanting some-thing better, something more, speaks primarily of the pain of *not having*, the struggles involved in not having enough. Very few accounts, apart from those feminist academics who come from working-class families themselves, speak of the emotional consequences of their success (Reay 1997; Mahony and Zmroczek 1997; Plummer 2000). Here I am referring to often uncon-scious, hard to acknowledge feelings of envy and resentment on the part of the parent; of rejection and contempt on the part of daughters who dream of escape; of betrayal; of the 'survival guilt' of daughters who feel that others have been sacrificed for them to succeed.

Educational debates have always assumed that working-class children and their families will have an unproblematic relationship to school success. How-ever, I want to stress that while achieving academic success in order to follow a well-trodden path towards university and a professional career is central to middle class subjectivity, for most working-class children, doing well at school is to be profoundly *different* from the overwhelming majority of the children and adults in their families and social milieu, and therefore inevitably becomes 'intertwined with the pain of difference, separation and therefore loss' (Lucey and Walkerdine 2000: 43).

These aspects of educational success seem to be beyond the imaginations of successive policy makers, who fail to see the transformation of identity that maintaining high school performance requires for most working-class children. Most seriously, educationalists are left without an adequate framework in which to understand and work with the disabling responses such as ambivalence and 'resistance' which many working-class children develop as defences against the prospect of such difference. However, such a framework must be able to incorporate the complexities of the unconscious and appreciate it not only as an abstract theory but as a driving force, able to produce real, material effects. Only then can its 'creative significance' to 'our practices as teachers and researchers' be fully realized (Raphael Reed 1995b).

## Conclusion

The story of social class, gender and schooling at the turn of the century is a complex and contradictory one. In the face of the unprecedented social, economic and personal change of the last decades of the twentieth century, 'meta narratives' of class became woefully inadequate, unable to make sense of the material and psychological upheaval of the UK's transition to a post-industrial economy. The Right and the Left have been keen to distance themselves from the very notion of social class, pushing it off the educational and political agenda and variously proclaiming its disappearance and death. This period was one of massive transformation for the social fabric of Britain, but this transformation has left patterns of inequality, differently, but no less starkly, organized.

If we look at educational trends over the last 20 or so years, it is clear that, overall, girls have made great strides in their attainment. Indeed, *some* girls are achieving as well or even better than *some* boys who are doing very badly. But it is when we try to decipher who the girls who are doing well and the boys who are doing badly actually *are* that we come face to face with the very thing that is supposed to have disappeared and died – something that it is difficult to call by any other name than 'class' (Walkerdine *et al.* 2001).

Popular representations of girls and women revolve around notions of endless potential for fun, achievement and fulfilment – possibilities which have been opened up because of changes at the economic and social levels. But while popular discourses stress the gains in the 'remaking' that young women in Britain have had to do in the face of these changes, for fewer discourses engage with the very complex emotional and social costs that these transformations have also brought. Working-class and middle-class girls and young women watch their mothers struggle to combine work and family and are only too aware of how exhausting this can be. They don't want to have to always work this hard but know that if they want a family of their own, then this is precisely the future they face (Walkerdine *et al.* 2001). Indeed, more than that, working-class women may also have to cope with men who are taking the loss of previous modes of masculinity very hard. In these circumstances, it would be difficult to say that the female future is simply rosy.

## Notes

1  As opposed to the 'first wave' of feminists who campaigned for women's legal and political rights around the turn of the twentieth century.
2  'Secondary School Transfer: children as consumers of education', ESRC Research Grant No. R00237900.

# Endnotes: gender, school policies and practices

*Christine Skelton and Becky Francis*

## Introduction

In bringing together the work of the authors in this book we have provided a snapshot of gender, theory and education at the turn of the twenty-first century. The contributors to Part 3 have explored the interrelationship of gender, theory and education for particular aspects of social identity. And while our intention has been to chart theoretical developments, we recognize that readers may well be interested in what these theories 'look like' in terms of school policy and classroom practices. In this concluding chapter we briefly outline where and how 'gender issues' feature in educational policy and provision.

## Education policy and 'equal opportunities: gender'

Many contributors to this book have referred to the media and government furore over boys' 'underachievement'. The concern for some commentators has been to not only identify ways in which boys' underachievement can be tackled by schools, but also to locate the reasons why they are 'failing'. As was shown in Chapter 12, some have blamed the rise of second-wave feminism in the 1960s and 70s and the subsequent passing of various civil rights parliamentary acts for the (perceived) underachievement of boys. The debates and misconceptions around boys' underachievement have been widely discussed (see Epstein *et al.* 1998; Raphael Reed 1999; Skelton 2001), but it is worth looking at educational policy regarding gender in recent decades and asking whether the implementation of equal opportunities initiatives could have contributed towards these current concerns over boys.

The equal opportunities strategies implemented in schools in the 1970s referred only to gender rather than to 'race' and/or social class. This was largely due to the Equal Opportunities Commission having been set up specifically to implement and monitor the tenets of the Sex Discrimination Act (1975) (the Commission for Racial Equality was established to do the same thing via the Race Relations Act 1976). Latterly, the concept of equal educational opportunities took on a more encompassing definition (Weiner 1994). Thus the initial focus in school and local education authority equal opportunity policies was on encouraging, motivating and addressing the unequal and discriminatory experiences of girls in schools. The question today for some observers is whether this focus resulted in a disadvantaging of boys (Pollack 1998; Hoff Sommers 2000). In their detailed analysis of education policy and social change, Arnot et al. (1999) make it clear that any transformations in gender patterns and educational achievement are more likely to be a result of related broader societal changes than simply the implementation of equal opportunities policies in schools. They argue a number of important points:

- Girls' current success in terms of academic achievement cannot be accounted for solely by 'educational actions' such as new forms of assessment or changes to examination systems. Rather, the various issues affecting school performance are more complex, and include the impact of feminism as well as economic and social change.
- The implementation of national equity strategies (see, for example, the Sex Discrimination Act 1975 and the Race Relations Act 1976) did not instigate the changes to gender patterns in education. Instead such changes were the result of a combination of a decentralized system of education and social changes (the latter of which led to changed expectations on the part of girls – see Francis 2000a). Teacher professionalism and autonomy also played a role, allowing some teachers space to challenge conventional notions of femininity with their pupils.
- Shifts in economic and societal trends throughout the 1980s and 90s have held implications for the place of schooling in boys' lives. The period saw a decline in the availability of traditional industrial work and apprenticeships for male school-leavers. Yet studies suggest that many boys have little recognition of such social and workplace changes (Francis 2000a), and, irrespective of social class and ethnicity, often retain traditional notions of male and female roles in the family and the labour market (Mahony 1998).

Of particular significance in terms of 'equal opportunities' classroom strategies is the point that 'the shift in girls' aspirations resulted from the postwar welfare state which suggested that individuals could be uncoupled from their class fates' (Arnot et al. 1999: 153). It was this increasing emphasis on 'individualization' which was to be the hallmark of New Right government legislation on issues of educational equality (social justice). For example, during the 1980s there were moves towards a centralization of education culminating in the Education Reform Act 1988. Here the government established its control of the curriculum while simultaneously devolving power to parents as consumers of education. The themes of this period were choice, vocationalism and marketization. Although there was a place for the notion of 'equity' in government discourses, this was presented in the form of 'entitlements' at the level of the individual and, as such, replaced the idea of education as important to the development of social justice and equality of opportunity among social groups (Haywood and Mac an Ghaill 1996). The arrival of the New Labour government has not marked any fundamental shift in this approach and, as Salisbury and Riddell (2000) have indicated, social justice issues are increasingly fused with those relating to performance, standards and improvement in government policy discourse. The discourse of social responsibility, which places responsibility for educational development with the individual rather than with society (hence disguising inequalities between broader social groups), is clearly evident in policy material concerning lifelong learning (Ainley 1998; Ball 1999). As Ball (1999) observes, the discourse of lifelong learning collapses educational policy into economic policy, and conflates issues of 'social inclusion' with economic efficiency and productivity.

As contributors to this book have demonstrated, during this same period there was an increasing interest among educational researchers in interrogating ideas about homogenous groups (such as male/female, middle class/ working class, ethnic majority/minority and so on). What emerged was the notion of *difference* as a means of exploring individual subjectivities (Davies 1989; Jones 1993). Thus, at the end of the twentieth century we had a situation whereby, albeit as a result of different ideological positions, both educational policy and educational research were emphasizing the individual and individual differences. So what implications has this had for school policies and classroom practices on gender and other social justice issues?

## School policy

In terms of their official responsibility for equal opportunities, a school governing body has to ensure that policies on sex and race discrimination are in place. Inspections by the Office for Standards in Education include a consideration of equal opportunities. In terms of gender, three areas are inspected:

- the relative achievements of boys and girls (to identify whether there are any significant variations);
- access to the curriculum (to ascertain whether certain aspects are restricted or closed to one gender or the other);
- the extent to which leadership and management promote access to the full range of opportunities for achievement that the school provides (Orr 2000: 22).

However, it may well be that many inspectors do not understand the concerns around social justice and certainly the majority of school inspection reports 'do not deal with equality in any meaningful way and the issue is rarely included in key points for action' (Myers 2000: 224). This is perhaps not surprising when one considers that the complexity of the issues has increased. As was noted above, there has been an move among educational researchers to look more closely at 'difference', hence paying attention to regional, local and site-specific concerns. For example, Riddell and Salisbury (2000: 6) observe that different facets of equality 'achieve prominence in different parts of the UK, depending on which aspects of social identity are seen as having greatest salience'. They cite the example of Northern Ireland where the focus is on equality for those from different religious groups, and Wales where the issues are to do with Welsh culture and identity. At the same time, the Department for Education and Employment (DfEE) have splintered the issues which were at one time covered by a school's equal opportunities policy, and repackaged them as part of the move towards greater monitoring and accountability. For example, on their website the DfEE provide the following guidance on sexual and racial equality matters:

- *Headteachers have a legal duty* to draw up procedures to prevent bullying among pupils and to bring these procedures to the attention of staff, parents and pupils. Effective anti-bullying strategies should form part of a school's discipline and behaviour policy. The three main types of bullying are:
    physical (e.g. hitting, kicking, theft)
    verbal (e.g. name-calling, racist remarks)
    indirect (e.g. spreading rumours, excluding someone from social groups).
- *The legal framework for school discipline.* The governing body should advise the headteacher of their views on specific measures for promoting good behaviour. Those might include such issues as bullying, racial or sexual harassment, and maintaining regular attendance. The governing body also has a general duty to ensure the school follows policies to promote good behaviour and discipline among pupils.
- *Management and finance: equal opportunities (employment).* Heads have a responsibility to ensure that they do not commit unlawful discriminatory acts and that the governing body's equal opportunities policy is implemented in the school.
- *Equal opportunities for pupils.* Parents and pupils should know that the school has an equal opportunities policy and is committed to equality of opportunity for all pupils. Headteachers should monitor the impact of their policies and procedures on different groups (by race, gender and disability) and the effectiveness of such policies should be assessed at governors' meetings.
- Key documents providing more detailed guidance on equal opportunities include:

Circular 10/99: *Social Inclusion: Pupil Support*
*Sex Discrimination Act: a Guide to the Sex Discrimination Act 1975* (DfEE
Publications)
*Sexual Harassment in the Workplace: A Guide for Employers* (DfEE
Publications)
*Sexual Harassment in the Workplace: The Facts Employees Should Know*
(DfEE Publications)
Circular 20/99 *What the Disability Discrimination Act (DDA) 1995 Means
for Schools and LEAs*

The point being made here is that the splintering and repackaging of issues
which were once clearly identified as 'equal opportunities' adds to the burden
on teachers who are having to cope with a wide range of demands to drive up
standards. In the White Paper *Excellence in Schools*, the chapter on Standards
and Accountability states with regard to ethnic minority children that
'Targeted action is required to break the cycle of disadvantage and create
genuinely equal opportunities for all' (DfEE 1997: 11). Given the diversity of
schools and differing situations of school populations, the question is precisely
what shape does that 'targeted action' take? Although some of the equal
opportunities policies adopted by many local education authorities and
schools in the late 1980s and 90s were based on (simplistic) sex-role theories
and sat awkwardly alongside antiracist initiatives (Williams 1987), they
nevertheless offered clear guidance to teachers as to what might be implemented at a practical level in the classroom.

## Classroom policies and strategies

Developing and implementing strategies that promote social justice is clearly
not straightforward when there is an evident tension between the need to
recognize *differences* between individuals while retaining an awareness of,
and responsibility to, collective concerns. Take, for example, sexual harassment policies. These were notoriously difficult to devise given that what is
defined as sexual harassment is largely reliant on how a behaviour is perceived and experienced by its recipient (Thomas and Kitzinger 1997; Francis
and Skelton 2001). Also, at an earlier period the issue of homophobia was
played down (if not ignored) in school sexual harassment policies (Epstein
1994). We now know that a relatively large percentage of gay and lesbian
students leave school because of homophobic harassment; that they are
amongst the high risk groups for suicide; and that 'gay bashing' is predominantly carried out by young people (Epstein and Johnson 1998; Gilbert and
Gilbert 1998). These and other studies suggest that boys often invest in homophobic behaviours as a means of constructing heterosexual masculinities (for
example, Salisbury and Jackson, 1996). Such processes are also reflected in
boys' attempts to regulate and control girls' sexual behaviours, and in their
sexual harassment of girls (Mahony 1985; Lees 1986; 1993; Herbert 1989).
A simple response would be to 'target action' on boys' behaviours. However,

the picture is more complex than this. As Epstein and Johnson (1998) discuss, gay boys' positioning is not unitary, with some taking pleasure (rather than just protection) in adopting heterosexual personas. Further, as Mary Jane Kehily clearly demonstrates in Chapter 8, girls contribute towards the policing of each others' heterosexual identities (see also Lees 1993; Hey 1997). Therefore, strategies aimed at changing such behaviour must address both genders and indeed the whole construction of gender as oppositional (Davies 1989; Francis 1998), rather than simply focusing on boys.

As we said in the introduction to this book, recent shifts in focus around the theorization and study of gender and education, caused by social and policy changes, encouraged us to put together an update of theoretical developments and cutting-edge research around different issues within the field. The fragmentation of social justice issues in government educational policy and in the subsequent instructions to schools, together with parallel (if ideologically different) shifts in educational researchers' theoretical conceptualizations of social identity, demand the development of new approaches with which teachers might address these issues in the classroom. At the moment, the emphasis on raising standards and achievement has resulted in an apparent quest for quick-fix, mono-focused 'solutions'. As Arnot *et al.* (1998b: 222) have discovered in their study ascertaining the number and kind of equality initiatives in operation in schools and local education authorities, 'the most significant finding was the current primacy of *"'improving boys' achievement"* projects . . . 40 were targeted on boys only . . . only three projects were specifically targeted at girls'. As we have discussed elsewhere (Francis 2000a; Skelton 2001), many of the 'pragmatic' strategies aimed at improving boys' achievement actually compound the construction of gender difference and stereotypes, and sometimes risk marginalizing girls. How do the projects focused exclusively on 'improving boys' achievements' fit alongside the introduction of citizenship education which offers the potential for broader based considerations of social justice issues alongside those of social identity?

It is outside the remit of this chapter to discuss in any detail the ways in which recent theories of social identity can be deployed in classroom practices. Briefly, an equity policy in schools and classrooms would involve, first, a recognition and awareness of the constructions of identity pupils bring with them into the classroom and act out on a daily basis. Teachers would then use the pupils' knowledge, understanding and experience to challenge traditional and conventional perceptions and beliefs about gender, culture, social class and so on. A critical element is the involvement of pupils in analysis, evaluation and discussion. For example, in terms of challenging gender constructions, Francis (1998) suggests that using anti-sexist stories is a good starting point with children in the primary school. A discussion of any differences children could identify between feminist and traditional fairytales could lead into a fuller debate about gender roles generally. Another example would be challenging particular expressions of masculinity and femininity: for example, boys' laddish behaviours – bearing in mind that 'laddish' boys are often popular with children and adults and that such behaviour enables individuals to present themselves as 'proper boys'. Rather than simply offering pupils stories or images of alternative forms of expression (such as the assertive female, or the gentle, caring male), which they may not relate to, teachers might talk with pupils about which gender constructions they find desirable and why; explore with them the difficulties involved in different ways of being masculine or feminine; expose the occasions when pupils make choices about how to be boys or girls and the knock-on effects of those choices; and curtail those boys who are violent and aggressive and help them to develop definitions of masculinity that redefine what it means to be brave, strong, admirable and so on (MacNaughton 2000: 159).

Innovative practices in enabling school pupils to examine conventional gender identities and challenge traditional social *in*justice have frequently emerged from collaborative projects devised by educational researchers and teachers (Frith and Mahony 1994; Salisbury and Jackson 1996; Arizpe and Arnot 1997; MacNaughton 2000). Classroom interventionist strategies are not developed in a vacuum but are based on specific theoretical beliefs. For example, the majority of equal opportunities policies of the 1980s were based upon liberal feminism which was informed by sex-role socialization theories, while anti-sexist policies of the same period were based on radical feminism which was concerned with gender-power dynamics. The contributors to this book have mapped out the current theoretical terrain and it is these theories, informed both by postmodernism and by notions of collective social identity, that will inform the next cycle of interventionist strategies in schools.

# References

Acker, S. (1981) No-woman's-land: British sociology of education 1960–79, *Sociological Review*, 29(1): 77–104.

Acker, S. (1994) *Gendered Education*. Buckingham: Open University Press.

Acker, S. and Feurverger, G. (1997) Doing good and feeling bad: the work of women university teachers, *Cambridge Journal of Education*, 26(3): 401–22.

Adkins, L. (1995) *Gendered Work: Sexuality, Family and the Labour Market*. Buckingham: Open University Press.

Afshar, H. and Maynard, M. (1994) The dynamics of 'race' and gender, in H. Afshar and M. Maynard (eds) *The Dynamics of 'Race' and Gender*. London: Taylor & Francis.

Ahmed, S. (1997) It's a sun-tan, isn't it? Autobiography as an identificatory practice, in H. Mirza (ed.) *Black British Feminism*. London: Routledge.

Ainley, P. (1993) *Class and Skill: Changing Divisions of Knowledge and Labour*. London: Cassell.

Ainley, P. (1998) Towards a learning or a certified society? Contradictions in the New Labour modernisation of lifelong learning, *Journal of Education Policy*, 13(4): 559–73.

Allatt, P. (1993) Becoming privileged: the role of family processes, in I. Bates and G. Riseborough (eds) *Youth and Inequality*. Buckingham: Open University Press.

Anderson, A. (1998) Debatable performances: restaging contentious feminisms, *Social Text*, 54, 16(1): 1–24.

Angelou, M. (1988) In conversation with Rosa Guy, in M. Chamberlain (ed.) *Writing Lives – Conversations Between Women Writers*. London: Virago.

Anthias, F. (1996) Rethinking social divisions: or what's so important about gender, ethnicity, 'race' and social class? Inaugural lecture, 15 February, University of Greenwich.

Anthias, F. and Yuval-Davis, N. (1992) *Racialized Boundaries: Race, Nation, Gender, Colour and Class and the Anti-Racist Struggle*. London: Routledge.

Apple, M. W. (1996) Power, meaning and identity: critical sociology of education in the United States, *British Journal of Sociology of Education*, 17(2): 125–44.

APU (Assessment of Performance Unit) (1980) *Mathematical Development: Primary Survey Report No. 1*. London: HMSO.

Archer, J. (1989) Childhood gender roles: structure and development, *The Psychologist*, 9: 367–70.

Archer, L., Hutchings, M. and Leathwood, C. (2000) Beyond cross-cutting and Intersections. Paper presented at the PCET Research Seminars series, University of Greenwich, 6th November.

Arizpe, E. and Arnot, M. (1997) The new boys of the '90s: a study of the reconstruction of masculinities in relation to economic change. Paper presented at Gender and Education Conference, University of Warwick, 16–18 April.

Arnot, M. (1984) How shall we educate our sons?, in R. Deem (ed.) *Co-education Reconsidered*. Buckingham: Open University Press.

Arnot, M. (1991) Equality and democracy: a decade of struggle over education, *British Journal of Sociology of Education*, 12(4): 447–66.

Arnot, M. and Weiner, G. (eds) (1987) *Gender and the Politics of Schooling*. London: Hutchinson.

Arnot. M. and Weiler, K. (1993) *Feminism and Social Justice in Education: International Perspectives*. London: Falmer.

Arnot, M., David, M. and Weiner, G. (1996) *Educational Reforms and Gender Equality in Schools*. Manchester: Equal Opportunities Commission.

Arnot, M., Gray, J., James, M. and Rudduck, J. (1998a) *A Review of Recent Research on Gender and Educational Performance*, Ofsted Research Series. London: HMSO.

Arnot, M., Millen, D. and Maton, K. (1998b) *Current Innovative Practice in Schools in the United Kingdom*, final report. Cambridge: University of Cambridge for the Council of Europe.

Arnot, M., David, M. and Weiner, G. (1999) *Closing the Gender Gap*. Cambridge: Polity Press.

Askew, S. and Ross, C. (1988) *Boys Don't Cry: Boys and Sexism in Education*. Buckingham: Open University Press.

Assiter, A. (1996) *Enlightened Women: Modernist Feminism in a Postmodern Age*. London: Routledge.

Back, L. (1996) *New Ethnicities and Urban Culture: Racism and Multiculture in Young People's Lives*. London: UCL Press.

Bagley, C. (1996) Black and white unite or fight? The racialised dimension of schooling and parental choice, *British Educational Research Journal*, 22(5): 569–80.

Bakhtin, M. (1981) *The Dialogic Imagination*. Austin, TX: University of Texas Press.

Balbus, I. (1987) Disciplining women: Michel Foucault and the power of feminist discourse, in S. Benhabib and D. Cornhill (eds) *Feminism as Critique*. Cambridge: Polity Press.

Ball, S. (1999) Labour, learning and the economy: a 'policy sociology' perspective, *Cambridge Journal of Education*, 29(2): 195–206.

Ball, S. and Gewirtz, S. (1997) Girls in the education market: choice, competition and complexity, *Gender and Education*, 9(2): 207–23.

Ball, S., Bowe, R. and Gold, A. (1992) Reforming Education and Changing Schools: Case Studies in Policy Sociology. London: Routledge.

Barker, M. (1989) *Comics: Ideology, Power and the Critics*. Manchester: Manchester University Press.

Barnes, C. (1991) *Disabled People and Discrimination*. London: Hurst & Co.

Baron, S., Wilson, A. and Riddell, S. (1999) The secret of eternal youth, *British Journal of Sociology of Education*, 20(4): 483–99.

Barrett, M. (1980) *Women's Oppression Today: Problems in Marxist Feminist Analysis.* London: Verso.

Barthes, R. (1990) *The Pleasure of the Text.* Oxford: Basil Blackwell.

Barton, L. (ed.) (1994) *Disability and Society: Some Emerging Issues and Insights.* London: Longman.

Beck, U. (1992) *Risk Society: Towards a New Modernity.* London: Sage

Beck, U., Giddens, A. and Lash, S. (1994) *Reflexive Modernisation.* Cambridge: Polity Press.

Berger, P. and Luckman, T. (1966) *The Social Construction of Reality.* Harmondsworth: Penguin.

Bernstein, B. (1977) *Class Codes and Control,* 3rd edn. London: Routledge & Kegan Paul.

Bernstein, B. (1978) Class and pedagogies: visible and invisible, in J. Karabel and A. Halsey (eds.) *Power and Ideology in Education.* Oxford: Oxford University Press.

Bhattacharyya, G. (1997) The fabulous adventures of the mahogany princess, in H. Mirza (ed.) *Black British Feminism.* London: Routledge.

Biddulph, S. (1998) *Manhood.* Stroud: Hawthorn.

Billig, M., Condor, S., Edwards, D. *et al.* (1988) *Ideological Dilemmas.* London: Sage.

Billing, Y.D. and Alvesson, M. (1994) *Gender, Managers and Organisations.* Berlin: De Gruyter.

Blackmore, J. (1993) In the shadow of men: an historical construction of administration as a 'masculinist' enterprise, in J. Blackmore and J. Kenway (eds) *Gender Matters in Educational Administration and Policy: A Feminist Introduction.* London: Falmer.

Blackmore, J. (1997) The gendering of skill and vocationalism in twentieth-century Australian education, in A. Halsey, H. Lauder, P. Brown and A. Wells (eds) *Education: Culture, Economy, Society.* New York: Oxford University Press.

Blackmore, J. (1999) *Troubling Women: Feminism, Leadership and Educational Change.* Buckingham: Open University Press.

Blackmore, J. and Kenway, J. (eds) (1993) *Gender Matters in Educational Administration and Policy: A Feminist Introduction.* London: Falmer.

Blair, M. (1995) Race, class and gender in school research, in J. Holland, M. Blair and S. Sheldon (eds) *Debates and Issues in Feminist Research and Pedagogy.* Clevedon: Multilingual Matters.

Blair, M. and Holland, J. (eds) (1995) *Identity and Diversity.* Clevedon: Multilingual Matters.

Blaxter, L. and Hughes, C. (2000) Social capital: a critique, in J. Thompson (ed.) *Politics and Practice of Widening Participation in Higher Education.* Leicester: NIACE.

Bleach, K. with Blagden, T., Ebbutt, D. *et al.* (1996) *What Difference Does it Make? An Investigation of Factors Influencing the Motivation and Performance of Year 8 Boys in a West Midlands Comprehensive School.* Wolverhampton: Educational Research Unit, University of Wolverhampton.

Bloch, H. (1992) *Medieval Misogyny and the Introduction of Western Romantic Love.* Chicago: University of Chicago Press.

Blumer, H. (1969) *Symbolic Interactionism: Perspective and Method.* Englewood Cliffs, NJ: Prentice-Hall.

Blunkett, D. (2000) quoted in 'Single sex classes to help failing boys', the *Observer,* 20 August: 4.

Bonnet, A. (1996) Anti-racism and the critique of white identities, *New Community,* 22(1): 97–110.

Bordo, S. (1990) Feminism, postmodernism and gender scepticism, in L. Nicholson (ed.) *Feminism/Postmodernism.* London: Routledge.

Bourdieu, P. (1984) *Distinction: A Social Critique of the Judgement of Taste.* London: Routledge & Kegan Paul.

Bourdieu, P. and Passeron, J.C. (1977) *Reproduction in Education, Society and Culture.* London: Sage.

Bowe, R., Ball, S.J. and Gold, A. (1992) *Reforming Education and Changing Schools.* London: Routledge.

Bowles, S. and Gintis, H. (1976) *Schooling and Capitalist America.* London: Routledge & Kegan Paul.

Bradley, H. (1996) *Fractured Identities: Changing Patterns of Inequality.* Cambridge: Polity Press.

Brah, A. (1996) *Cartographies of Diaspora: Contesting Identities.* London: Routledge.

Brah, A. (1999) The scent of memory: 'Strangers', 'Our own' and 'Others', *Feminist Review*, 60(4): 25.

Brah, A. and Minhas, R. (1985) Structural racism or cultural difference: schooling for Asian girls, in G. Weiner (ed.) *Just a Bunch of Girls: Feminist Approaches to Schooling.* Buckingham: Open University Press.

Brannen, J. (1988) Research note: the study of sensitive subjects: notes on interviewing, *Sociological Review*, 36(3): 552–63.

Brittan, A. (1989) *Masculinity and Power.* Oxford: Blackwell.

Brod, H. (ed.) (1987) *The Making of Masculinities: The New Men's Studies.* London: Allen & Unwin.

Brown, P. (1987) *Schooling Ordinary Kids: Inequality, Unemployment and the New Vocationalism.* London: Tavistock.

Brown, P. (1997) The 'third wave': education and the ideology of parentocracy, in A. Halsey, H. Lauder, P. Brown, and A. Wells (eds) *Education: Culture, Economy, Society.* New York: Oxford University Press.

Bruner, J. (1986) *Actual Minds, Possible Worlds.* Cambridge, MA: Harvard University Press.

Brynner, J. and Steedman, J. (1995) *Difficulties with Basic Skills.* London: Basic Skills Agency.

Burman, E. (1994) *Deconstructing Developmental Psychology.* London: Routledge.

Burman, E. and Parker, I. (1993) Introduction: discourse analysis – the turn to the text, in E. Burman and I. Parker (eds) *Discourse Analytical Research.* London: Routledge.

Butler, J. (1990) *Gender Trouble.* New York: Routledge.

Butler, J. (1993) *Bodies That Matter: On the Discursive Limits of 'Sex'.* London: Routledge.

Byrne, E. (1978) *Women and Education.* London: Tavistock.

Callender, C. and Wright, C. (2000) Discipline and democracy: race, gender, school sanctions and control, in M. Arnot and J. Dillabough (eds) *Challenging Democracy: International Perspectives on Gender, Education and Citizenship.* London: Routledge.

Canaan, J. (1986) Why a 'slut' is a 'slut': cautionary tales of middle class teenage girls' morality, in H. Varenne (ed.) *Symbolising America.* Lincoln, NE: University of Nebraska Press.

Canaan, J. and Griffin, C. (1990) The new men's studies: part of the problem or part of the solution? in J. Hearn and D. Morgan (eds) *Men, Masculinities and Social Theory.* London: Unwin Hyman.

Carby, H. (1982) Schooling in Babylon, in Centre for Contemporary Cultural Studies (eds) *The Empire Strikes Back.* London: Hutchinson.

Carmichael, S. and Hamilton, C. (1967) *Black Power: The Politics of Liberation in America.* Harmondsworth: Penguin.

Carrigan, T., Connell, B. and Lee, J. (1985) Toward a new sociology of masculinity, *Theory and Society*, 14: 551–604.

Carter, J. (l997) Post-Fordism and the theorisation of educational change: what's in a name? *British Journal of Sociology of Education*, 18(1): 45–62.

Cealey Harrison, W. and Hood-Williams, J. (1998) More varieties than Heinz: social categories and sociality in Humphries, Hammersley and beyond, *Social Research Online*, 3(1) (http://www.socresonline.org.uk/socresonline/3/1/8.htm).

Cealey Harrison, W. and Hood-Williams, J. (2001) *Beyond Sex and Gender*. London: Sage.

Cheng, C. (ed.) (1996) *Masculinities in Organizations*. London: Sage.

Chisholm, L. and Du Bois Reymond, M. (1993) Youth transitions, gender and social change, *Sociology*, 27(2): 259–79.

Cixous, H. (1981) Castration or decapitation? *Signs*, 7(1): 41–55.

Clarricoates, K. (1978) Dinosaurs in the classroom: a re-examination of some aspects of the 'hidden' curriculum in primary schools, *Women's Studies International Forum*, 1: 353–64.

Clarricoates, K. (1980) The importance of being Ernest . . . Emma . . . Tom . . . Jane. The perception and categorization of gender conformity and gender deviation in primary schools, in R. Deem (ed.) *Schooling for Women's Work*. London: Routledge & Kegan Paul.

Clatterbaugh, K. (1990) *Contemporary Perspectives on Masculinity: Men, Women and Politics in Modern Society*. Washington: Westview Press.

Coard, B. (1971) *How the Black Child is Made Educationally Subnormal in the British School System*. London: New Beacon Books.

Coard, B. (1982) What the British school system does to the black child, in A. James and R. Jeffcoate (eds) *The School in the Multicultural Society*. London: Harper & Row.

Cohen, P. (1993) 'It's racism what dunnit': Hidden narratives in theories of racism, in J. Donald and A. Rattansi (eds) *'Race', Culture and Difference*. London: Sage.

Cohen, P. (1997) *Rethinking the Youth Question*. Basingstoke: Macmillan.

Coles, F. (1994–5) Feminine charms and outrageous arms, *Trouble and Strife*, 29/30: 67–72.

Combahee River Collective ([1977] 1997) A black feminist statement, in L. Nicholson (ed.) *The Second Wave: A Reader in Feminist Theory*. New York: Routledge.

Connell, R.W. (1987) *Gender and Power*. London: Routledge.

Connell, R.W. (1989) Cool guys, swots and wimps: the interplay of masculinity and education, *Oxford Review of Education*, 15(3): 291–303.

Connell, R.W. (1995) *Masculinities*. London: Polity Press.

Connell, R.W. (1996) Teaching the boys: new research on masculinity, and gender strategies for schools, *Teachers College Record*, 98: 206–35.

Connell, R.W. (1997) The big picture: masculinities in recent world history, in A.H. Halsey, H. Lauder, P. Brown and A. Stuart Wells (eds) *Education: Culture, Economy and Society*. Oxford: Oxford University Press.

Connolly, P. (1995a) Boys will be boys? Racism, sexuality and the construction of masculine identities among infant boys, in J. Holland and M. Blair (eds) *Equality and Difference: Debates and Issues in Feminist Research and Pedagogy*. Clevedon: Multilingual Matters.

Connolly, P. (1995b) Racism, masculine peer-group relations and the schooling of African/Caribbean infant boys, *British Journal of Sociology of Education*, 16(1): 75–92.

Connolly, P. (1998) *Racism, Gender Identities and Young Children*. London: Routledge.

Coppock, V., Hayden, D. and Richter, I. (1995) *The Illusions of 'Post-Feminism'*. London: Taylor & Francis.

Corrigan, P. (1979) *Schooling the Smash Street Kids*. London: Macmillan.

Cowie, C. and Lees, S. (1987) Slags or Drags? in Feminist Review (eds) *Sexuality: A Reader*. London: Virago.

Cox, E. (1996) *Leading Women: Tactics for Making the Difference*. Sydney: Random House.

Crompton, R. (1992) Where did all the bright girls go? in N. Abercrombie and A. Warde (eds) *Social Change in Modern Britain*. Cambridge: Polity Press.

Daniels, H., Hey, V., Leonard, D. and Smith, M. (1994) Gendered practice in special educational needs in J. Holland (ed.) *Equality and Inequality in Education Policy*. Clevedon: Multilingual Matters.

David, M. (1980) *Women, Family and Education*. London: Routledge.

David, M. (2001) Gender equity issues in educational effectiveness in the context of global, social and family life changes. Plenary paper presented to the 14th International Congress for School Effectiveness and Improvement, Toronto, Canada, 5–9 January.

David, M. and Woodward, D. (1998) *Negotiating the Glass Ceiling*. London: Falmer.

David, M., West, A. and Ribbens, J. (1994) *Mother's Intuition? Choosing Secondary Schools*. London: Falmer.

Davidson, M.J. and Cooper, C.L. (1992) *Shattering the Glass Ceiling: The Woman Manager*. London: Paul Chapman.

Davies, B. (1989) *Frogs and Snails and Feminist Tales*. London: Allen & Unwin.

Davies, B. (1993) *Shards of Glass: Children Reading and Writing Beyond Gendered Identities*. Sydney: Allen & Unwin.

Davies, B. (1997) Constructing and deconstructing masculinities through critical literacy, *Gender and Education*, 9(1): 9–30.

de Beauvoir, S. (1972) *The Second Sex*. Harmondsworth: Penguin

Deem, R. (1978) Women and schooling, in R. Deem (ed.) *Schooling for Women's Work*. London: Routledge & Kegan Paul.

Deem, R. (ed.) (1980*) Schooling for Women's Work*. London: Routledge & Kegan Paul.

Delamont, S. (1980) *Sex Roles and the School*. London: Methuen.

Delamont, S. (1999) Gender and the discourse of derision, *Research Papers in Education*, 14(1): 3–21.

Delphy, C. (1984) *Close to Home: A Materialist Analysis of Women's Oppression*. London: Hutchinson.

DES (Department of Education and Science) (1985) *Education for All* (the Swann Report). London: HMSO.

DES (Department of Education and Science) (1981) *West Indian Children in Our Schools* (the Rampton Report). London: HMSO.

Derrida, J. (1976) *Of Grammatology*. Baltimore, MD: Johns Hopkins University Press.

DfEE (Department for Education and Employment) (1997) *Excellence in Schools*. London: HMSO.

DfEE (Department for Education and Employment) (1999) *Education and Training Statistics for the UK*. London: HMSO.

Dillabough, J. (1999) Gender politics and conceptions of the modern teacher: women, identity and professionalism, *British Journal of Sociology of Education*, 20(3): 373–94.

Dillabough, J. (2001) Gender, social change and the study of impoverished youth in Ontario schools. Social Sciences and Humanities Research Council Grant Proposal, under review. Ottawa: Canada.

Dillabough, J. and Arnot, M. (2001) Feminist sociology of education: dynamics, debates, directions, in J. Demaine (ed.) *Sociology of Education Today.* London: Macmillan.

Dillabough, J. and Arnot, M. (in press) Feminist perspectives in the sociology of education: continuity and transformation in the field, in D. Levinson, A. Sadovnik and P. Cookson (eds) *Encyclopaedia: Sociology of Education.* New York: Garland.

Doane, M. (1988) Masquerade reconsidered: further thoughts on the female spectator, *Discourse: Journal for Theoretical Studies in Media and Culture,* 11: 42–54.

Donaldson, M. (1992) *Human Minds: An Exploration.* Harmondsworth: Penguin Books.

Driver, G. (1980a) How West Indians do better at school (especially the girls), *New Society,* 17 January.

Driver, G. (1980b) *Beyond Underachievement.* London: Commission for Racial Equality.

Driver, G. (1982) Classroom stress and school achievement: West Indian adolescents and their teachers, in A. James and. R. Jeffcoate (eds) *The School in the Multicultural Society.* London: Harper & Row/The Open University.

Dubberley, W.S. (1988) Social class and the process of schooling, in A. Green and S. Ball (eds) *Progress and Inequality in Comprehensive Education.* London: Routledge & Kegan Paul.

Dwyer, C. (1999) Negotations of femininity and identity for young British Muslim Women, in N. Laurie, C. Dwyer, S. Holloway and F. Smith (eds) *Geographies of New Femininities.* Harlow: Longman.

Eagleton, T. (1996) *The Illusions of Post Modernism.* Oxford: Blackwell.

Edley, N. and Wetherell, M. (1995) *Men in Perspective: Practice, Power and Identity.* London: Prentice Hall.

Egerton, M. and Halsey, A.H. (1993) Trends in social class and gender in access to higher education in Britain, *Oxford Review of Education,* 9(2): 183–96.

Eliot, J., Foster, T., Hood, C. and Raphael Reed, L. (1996) Gossip, cake and wine: methodological challenges for feminist and dialogic research in cross-cultural settings. Paper presented at British Educational Research Association Conference, Lancaster, 12–15 September.

Epstein, C. (1988) *Deceptive Distinctions: Sex, Gender and the Social Order.* New Haven, CT: Yale University Press.

Epstein, D. (ed.) (1994) *Challenging Gay and Lesbian Inequalities in Education.* Buckingham: Open University Press.

Epstein, D. (1997) Boyz' own story: masculinities and sexualities in schools, *Gender and Education,* 9(1): 105–16.

Epstein, D. (1998) Real boys don't work: 'underachievement', masculinity and the harassment of 'sissies', in D. Epstein, J. Elwood, V. Hey, and J. Maw (eds) *Failing Boys? Issues in Gender and Achievement.* Buckingham: Open University Press.

Epstein, D. and Johnson, R. (1998) *Schooling Sexualities.* Buckingham: Open University Press.

Epstein, D., Elwood, J., Hey, V. and Maw, J. (eds) (1998) *Failing Boys? Issues in Gender and Achievement.* Buckingham: Open University Press.

Equal Opportunities Commission (1997) *Briefings on Women and Men in Britain.* Manchester: Equal Opportunities Commission.

Equal Opportunities Commission (2000) *Some Facts About Men and Women.* Manchester: Equal Opportunities Commission.

Equal Opportunities Commission/Ofsted (Office for Standards in Education) (1996) *The Gender Divide: Performance Differences Between Boys and Girls at School.* London: HMSO.

Espie, C., Curtice, L., Morrison, J. *et al.* (1999) *The Role of the NHS in Meeting the Health Needs of People with Learning Disabilities*, Report to the Scottish Executive. Glasgow: University of Glasgow.

Evans, M. (1995) Culture and Class, in M. Blair and J. Holland with S. Sheldon (eds) *Identity and Diversity: Gender and the Experience of Education*. Buckingham: Open University Press.

Evetts, J. (1990) *Women in Primary Teaching*. London: Unwin Hyman.

Fanon, F. ([1952] 1970) *Black Skin White Masks*. London: Paladin.

Fanon, F. (1993) The fact of blackness, in J. Donald and R. Rattansi (eds) *Race, Culture and Difference*. London: Sage.

Farrell, W. (1974) *The Liberated Man*. New York: Random House.

Fausto-Sterling, A. (1989) Life in the XY corral, *Women's Studies International Forum*, 12(3): 319–31.

Finch, J. and Groves, D. (1983) *A Labour of Love: Women, Work and Caring*. London: Routledge & Kegan Paul.

Fish, S. (1987) Interpreting the Variorum, in R. Rylance (ed.) *Debating Texts*. Buckingham: Open University Press.

Fogarty, M.P. with Rapoport R. and Rapoport R. (eds) (1972) *Women and Top Jobs: The Next Move*. London: Heinemann.

Foster, P., Gomm, R. and Hammersley, M. (1996) *Constructing Educational Inequality*. London: Falmer.

Foster, P., Hammersley, M. and Gomm, R. (2000) Case studies as spurious evaluations: the example of research on educational inequalities, *British Journal of Educational Studies*, 48(3): 215–30.

Foucault, M. (1977) *Discipline and Punish*. Harmondsworth: Penguin.

Foucault, M. (1978) *The History of Sexuality, Volume One*. Harmondsworth: Penguin.

Foucault, M. (1980) *Power/Knowledge: Selected Interviews and Other Writings, 1972–1977*. New York: Pantheon.

Foucault, M. (1988a) *Politics, Philosophy, Culture: Interviews and Other Writings 1977–1984*. London: Routledge.

Foucault, M. (1988b) Technologies of the self, in L. Martin, H.Gutman and P. Hutton (eds) *Technologies of the Self: A Seminar with Michel Foucault*. London: Tavistock.

Francis, B. (1998) *Power Plays*. Stoke-on-Trent: Trentham Books.

Francis, B. (1999) Modernist reductionism or poststructuralist relativism: can we move on? An evaluation of the arguments in relation to feminist educational research, *Gender and Education*, 11(4): 381–94.

Francis, B. (2000a) *Boys, Girls and Achievement: Addressing the Classroom Issues*. London: Routledge/Falmer.

Francis, B. (2000b) The gendered subject: students' subject preferences and discussions of gender and subject ability, *Oxford Review of Education*, 26(1): 35–48.

Francis, B. (forthcoming) Relativism, realism and feminism, *Journal of Gender Studies*.

Francis, B. and Skelton, C. (2001) Men teachers and the construction of heterosexual masculinity in the classroom, *Sex Education*, 1(1): 1–17.

Fraser, N. (1989) *Unruly Practices: Power, Discourse and Gender in Contemporary Social Theory*. Cambridge: Polity Press.

Freud, S. (1905) *Three Essays on the Theory of Sexuality*, standard edn, 7: 125–245.

Frith, R. and Mahony, P. (1994) *Promoting Quality and Equality in Schools*. London: David Fulton.

Frosh, S., Phoenix, A. and Pattman, R. (2001) *Young Masculinities: Understanding Boys in Contemporary Society*. London: Palgrave.

Fuller, M. (1980) Black girls in a London comprehensive school, in R. Deem (ed.) *Schooling for Women's Work*. London: Routledge & Kegan Paul.

Fuller, M. (1982) Young, female and black, in E. Cashmore and B. Troyna (eds) *Black Youth in Crisis*. London: Allen & Unwin.

Fuller, M. (1983) Qualified criticism, critical qualifications, in L. Barton and S. Walker (eds) *Race, Class and Education*. Beckenham: Croom Helm.

Furlong, A. (1992) *Growing Up in a Classless Society? School to Work Transitions*. Edinburgh: Edinburgh University Press.

Furlong, A. and Cartmel, F. (1997) *Young People and Social Change: Individualization and Risk in Late Modernity*. Buckingham: Open University Press.

Gewirtz, S. (1997) Post-welfarism and the reconstruction of teachers' work in the UK, *Journal of Educational Policy*, 12(4): 217–31.

Gewirtz, S., Ball, S.J. and Bowe, R. (1995) *Markets, Choice and Equity in Education*. Buckingham: Open University Press.

Giddens, A. (1991) *Modernity and Self Identity: Self and Society in the Late Modern Age*. Oxford: Polity Press.

Gilbert, R. and Gilbert, P. (1998) *Masculinity goes to School*. London: Routledge.

Gillborn, D. (1990) *'Race', Ethnicity and Education: Teaching and Learning in Multi-ethnic Schools*. London: Unwin Hyman/Routledge.

Gillborn, D. (1995) *Racism and Antiracism in Real Schools*. Buckingham: Open University Press.

Gillborn, D. (1996) Student roles and perspectives in antiracist education: a crisis of white ethnicity? *British Educational Research Journal*, 22(2): 165–79.

Gillborn, D. and Gipps, C. (1996) *Recent Research on the Achievements of Ethnic Minority Pupils*, report for Ofsted. London: HMSO.

Gillborn, D. and Mirza, H. (2000) *Educational Inequality: Mapping Race, Class and Gender – A Synthesis of Evidence*. London: Ofsted.

Gilroy, P. (1987) *There Ain't No Black in the Union Jack*. London: Hutchinson.

Giroux, H. (1997a) Rewriting the discourse of racial identity: towards a pedagogy and politics of whiteness, *Harvard Educational Review*, 67(2): 285–319.

Giroux, H. (1997b) Racial politics and the pedagogy of whiteness, in M. Hill (ed.) *Whiteness: A Critical Reader*. New York: New York University Press.

Gitlin, A. (ed.) (1994) *Power and Method: Political Activism and Educational Research*. London: Routledge.

Gorard, S. (1999) Keeping a sense of proportion: the 'politician's error' in analysing school outcomes, *British Journal of Educational Studies*, 47(3): 235–46.

Gorard, S. (2000) *Education and Social Justice: The Changing Composition of Schools and its Implications*. Cardiff: University of Wales Press.

Gorard, S., Rees, G. and Salisbury, J. (1999) Reappraising the apparent underachievement of boys at school, *Gender and Education*, 11(4): 441–54.

Gordon, T., Holland, J. and Lahelma, E. (2000) *Making Spaces: Citizenship and Difference in Schools*. London: Macmillan.

Gore, J. (1993) *The Struggle for Pedagogies: Critical and Feminist Discourses as Regimes of Truth*. London: Routledge.

Gorz, A. (1982) *Farewell to the Working Class*. London: Pluto.

Gramsci, A. (1971) *Selections from the Prison Notebooks of Antonia Gramsci*. London: Lawrence & Wishart.

Gregory, R. (1969) *A Shorter Textbook of Human Development*. Maidenhead: McGraw-Hill.

Griffin, C. (1985) *Typical Girls?* London: Routledge & Kegan Paul.

Griffin, C. and Wetherell, M. (1992) Feminist psychology and the study of men and masculinity, Part II: politics and practices, *Feminism and Psychology*, 2(2): 133–68.

Griffiths, M. (1995a) *Feminisms and the Self: The Web of Identity*. London: Routledge.

Griffiths, M. (1995b) Making a difference: feminism, post-modernism and the methodology of educational research, *British Educational Research Journal*, 21(2): 219–35.

Hagan, K. (ed.) (1992) *Women Respond to the Men's Movement*. San Francisco: Harper-Collins.

Hall, S. (1992) Cultural studies: two paradigms, in L. Grossberg, C. Nelson and P. Treichler (eds) *Cultural Studies*. New York: Routledge.

Hall, S. (1993) New Ethnicities, in J. Donald and A. Rattansi (eds) *'Race', Culture and Difference*. London: Sage.

Hammersley, M. (1990). An evaluation of two studies of gender imbalance in primary classrooms, *British Educational Research Journal*, 16(2): 125–43.

Hammersley, M. (1996) *Education and Inequality*, Unit 1, EU208 'Exploring Educational Issues'. Buckingham: The Open University.

Hammersley, M. and Woods, P. (eds) (1976) *The Process of Schooling: A Sociological Reader*. London: Routledge & Kegan Paul.

Hanmer, J. (1990) Men, power and the exploitation of women, in J. Hearn and D. Morgan (eds) *Men, Masculinities and Social Theory*. London: Unwin Hyman.

Hansot, E. and Tyack, D. (1981) *The Dream Deferred: A Golden Age for Women School Administrators*, policy paper No. 81. Palo Alto, CA: Stanford University.

Harding, S. (ed.) (1987) *Feminism and Methodology*. Buckingham: Open University Press.

Harding, S. (1990) Feminism, science and the anti-Enlightenment critiques, in L. Nicholson (ed.) *Feminism/Postmodernism*. London: Routledge.

Hargreaves, A. (1982) Resistance and relative autonomy theories: problems of distortion and incoherence in recent Marxist theories of education, *British Journal of Sociology of Education*, 3(2): 107–26.

Hargreaves, D.H. (1967) *Social Relations in a Secondary School*. London: Routledge & Kegan Paul.

Hartley, L.P. (1958) *The Go-Between*. Harmondsworth: Penguin.

Hartsock, N. (1990) Foucault on power: a theory for women?, in L. Nicholson (ed.) *Feminism/Postmodernism*. London: Routledge.

Hawkes, T. (1977) *Structuralism and Semiotics*. London: Methuen.

Hayek, F. (1976) *Law, Legislation and Liberty, Vol. 2: Rules and Order*. London: Routledge & Kegan Paul.

Haywood, C. and Mac an Ghaill, M. (1996) Schooling masculinities, in M. Mac an Ghaill (ed.) *Understanding Masculinities*. Buckingham: Open University Press.

Hearn, J. (1996) Is masculinity dead? A critique of the concept of masculinity/masculinities, in M. Mac an Ghaill (ed.) *Understanding Masculinities*. Buckingham: Open University Press.

Hearn, J. and Collinson, D. (1990) Unities and differences between men and masculinities: the categories of men and the case of sociology. Paper presented to British Sociological Association Conference, 'Social Divisions and Social Change', University of Surrey, 2–5 April.

Hearn, J. and Morgan, D. (eds) (1990) *Men, Masculinities and Social Theory*. London: Unwin Hyman.

Heath, S. (1989) Joan Riviere and the masquerade, in V. Burgin, J. Donald and C. Kaplan (eds) *Formations of Fantasy*. London: Routledge.

Hebdige, D. ([1979] 1995) *Subculture: The Meaning of Style*. London: Routledge.

Hekman, S.J. (1995) *Moral Voices, Moral Selves: Carol Gilligan and Feminist Moral Theory*. Cambridge: Polity Press.

Herbert, L. (1989) *Talking of Silence – The Sexual Harassment of Schoolgirls*. London: Falmer.

Hewitt, R. (1996) *Routes of Racism*. London: Centre for Multicultural Education, Institute of Education.

Hey, V. (1997) *The Company She Keeps: An Ethnography of Girls' Friendship*. Buckingham: Open University Press.

Hey, V. (1999) Troubling the auto/biography of the questions: re/thinking rapport and the politics of social class in feminist participant observation. Paper presented at Gender and Education Second International Conference, University of Warwick, 29–31 April.

Heywood, J. (1997) The object of desire is the object of contempt: representations of masculinity in *Straight to Hell* magazine, in S. Johnson and U.H. Meinhof (eds) *Language and Masculinity*. Oxford: Blackwell.

Hill-Collins, P. (1990) *Black Feminist Thought: Knowledge, Consciousness, and the Politics of Empowerment*. Boston, MA: Unwin Hyman.

Hillman, J. and Pearce, N. (1998) *Wasted Youth*. London: IPPR.

Hoff Sommers, C. (2000) *The War Against Boys*. New York: Simon & Schuster.

Hood-Williams, J. (1996) Goodbye to sex and gender, *Sociological Review*, 44(1): 1–16.

Hood-Williams, J. (1998) Stories for sexual difference, *British Journal of Sociology of Education*, 18(1): 81–99.

hooks, b. (1981) *Ain't I a Woman? Black Women and Feminism*. Boston, MA: South End Press.

hooks, b. (1989) *Talking Back: Thinking Feminist, Thinking Black*. Boston, MA: South End Press.

hooks, b. (1991) *Yearning: Race, Gender and Cultural Politics*. London: Turnaround.

hooks, b. (1993) *Black Looks*. New York: Routledge.

Hull, G., Scott P., Bell. A. and Smith, B. (1982) *All the Women are White, all the Blacks are Men, but Some of Us are Brave*. New York: The Feminist Press.

Johnson, M. (1999) *Failing School Failing City*. London: Jon Carpenter.

Johnston, L. (1996) Flexing femininity: female body-builders refiguring 'the body', *Gender, Place and Culture*, 3(3): 327–40.

Jones, A. (1993) Becoming a 'girl': poststructuralist suggestions for educational research, *Gender and Education*, 5(2): 157–66.

Jones, A. (1997) Teaching poststructuralist feminist theory in education: student resistances, *Gender and Education*, 9(3): 261–9.

Jung, C.G. (1957) *The Collected Works of C.G. Jung*. London: Routledge & Kegan Paul.

Kanter, R. (1977) *Men and Women of the Corporation*. New York: Basic Books.

Kehily, M.J. (1995) Self-narration, autobiography and identity construction, *Gender in Education*, 7(1): 23–32

Kehily, M.J. (1999a) *'Learning sex and doing gender: cultures of heterosexuality in the secondary school'*, unpublished PhD thesis. Institute of Education, University of London.

Kehily, M.J. (1999b) More sugar? Teenage magazines, gender displays and sexual learning, *European Journal of Cultural Studies*, 2(1): 65–89.

Kehily, M.J. and Nayak, A. (1996) The Christmas kiss: sexuality, story-telling and schooling, *Curriculum Studies*, 4(2): 211–27.

Kehily, M.J. and Nayak, A. (1997) Lads and laughter: humour and the production of heterosexual hierarchies, *Gender and Education*, 9(1): 69–87.

Kelly, L., Burton, S. and Regan, L. (1994) Researching women's lives or study-ing women's oppression? Reflections on what constitutes feminist research, in M. Maynard and J. Purvis (eds) *Researching Women's Lives from a Feminist Perspective*. London: Taylor & Francis.

Kenway, J. (1995a) Having a postmodernist turn or postmodernist *angst*: a disorder experienced by an author who is not yet dead or even close to it, in R. Smith and P. Wexler (eds) *After Postmodernism: Education, Politics and Identity*. London: Falmer.

Kenway, J. (1995b) Masculinities in schools: under siege, on the defensive and under reconstruction, *Discourse*, 16(1): 59–79.

Kenway, J. (1996) Review of *The Making of Men: Masculinities, Sexualities and Schooling, British Journal of Sociology of Education*, 17(4): 509–13.

Kenway, J. (1997a) Taking stock of gender reform policies for Australian schools: past, present, future, *British Educational Research Journal*, 23(3): 329–44.

Kenway, J. (1997b) Point and counterpoint: boys' education in the context of gender reform, *Curriculum Perspectives*, 17(1): 57–61.

Kenway, J, and Epstein, D. (eds) (1996) Introduction: the marketisation of school education: feminist studies and perspectives, *Discourse*, 17(3): 301–14.

Kenway J. and Fitzclarence, L. (1997) Masculinity, violence and schooling: challenging 'poisonous pedagogies', *Gender and Education*, 9(1): 117–33.

Kenway, J. and Willis, S. (1998) *Answering Back*. London: Routledge.

Kerfoot, D. and Knight, D. (1994) Into the realm of the fearful: identity and the gender problematic, in H.L. Radtke and H.J. Stam (eds) *Power/Gender: Social Relations in Theory and Practice*. London: Sage.

Kerfoot, D. and Whitehead, S. (1998) Whither hegemonic masculinity? Paper presented at Gendering the Millennium conference, University of Dundee, 11–13 September.

Kessler, S. and McKenna, W. (1978) *Gender: An Ethnomethodological Approach*. Chicago: University of Chicago Press.

Kimmel, M. (ed.) (1987) *Changing Men*. London: Sage.

Kruger, M. (1996) Gender issues in school headship: quality versus power? *European Journal of Education*, 31(4): 447–62.

Lacan, J. (1977) *The Signification of the Phallus in Ecrits: A Selection*. New York: W.W. Norton.

Lacey, C. (1970) *Hightown Grammar*. Manchester: Manchester University Press.

Lakoff, R. (1975) *Language and Woman's Place*. New York: Harper & Row.

Lambart, A. (1976) The sisterhood, in M. Hammersley and P. Woods (eds) *The Process of Schooling*. London: Routledge.

Lambart, A. (1982). Expulsion in context: a school as a system in action, in R. Franken-berg (ed.) *Custom and Conflict in British Society*. Manchester: Manchester University Press.

Lambart, A. (1997) Mereside: a grammar school for girls in the 1960s, *Gender and Education* 9(4): 441–56

Laqueur, T. (1990) *Making Sex: Body and Gender from the Greeks to Freud*. Cambridge, MA: Harvard University Press.

Lather, P. (1986) Research as praxis, *Harvard Educational Review*, 56(3): 257–77.

Laurie, N., Dwyer, C., Holloway, S. and Smith, F. (1999) *Geographies of New Femininities*. Harlow: Longman.

Le Guin, U. (1989) *Dancing at the Edge of the World: Thoughts on Words, Women, Places*. London: Paladin.

Ledger, S., McDonagh, J. and Spencer, J. (eds) (1994) *Political Gender: Texts and Contexts.* Hemel Hempsted: Harvester Wheatsheaf.

Lee, A. (1980) Together we learn to read and write: sexism and literacy, in D. Spender and E. Sarah (eds) *Learning to Lose.* London: The Women's Press.

Lees, S. (1986) *Losing Out: Sexuality and Adolescent Girls.* London: Hutchinson.

Lees, S. (1993) *Sugar and Spice.* Harmondsworth: Penguin.

Lenskyj, H. (1987) Female sexuality and women's sport, *Women's Studies International Forum*, 10(4): 381–6.

Lewis, M.G. (1993) *Without a Word: Teaching Beyond Women's Silence.* London: Routledge.

Lingard, B. and Douglas, P. (1999) *Men Engaging Feminisms.* Buckingham: Open University Press.

Lobban, G. (1978) The influence of the school on sex-role stereotyping, in J. Chetwynd and O. Hartnett (eds) *The Sex Role System.* London: Routledge & Kegan Paul.

Lucey, H. and Reay, D. (1999) First choice or second best? The impact on children of not getting their first choice of secondary school. Paper presented at British Educational Research Association annual conference, University of Sussex, 2–5 September.

Lucey, H. and Reay, D. (2000) Carrying the beacon of excellence: pupil performance, gender and social class. Paper presented at British Educational Research Association annual conference, University of Cardiff, 7–11 September.

Lucey, H. and Walkerdine, V. (2000) Boys' under-achievement: social class and changing masculinities, in T. Cox (ed.) *Combating Educational Disadvantage.* London: Falmer.

Luke, C. and Gore, J. (eds) (1992) *Feminisms and Critical Pedagogy.* London: Routledge.

Lyotard, J.F. (1979). *The Postmodern Condition: A Report on Knowledge.* Manchester: Manchester University Press.

Mac an Ghaill, M. (1988) *Young, Gifted and Black.* Milton Keynes: Open University Press.

Mac an Ghaill, M. (1994) *The Making of Men.* Buckingham: Open University Press.

Mac an Ghaill, M. and Haywood, C. (1997) The end of anti-oppressive education? A differentialist critque, *International Studies in Sociology of Education*, 7(1): 21–34.

McCulloch, G. (1998) *Failing The Ordinary Child.* Buckingham: Open University Press.

MacDonald, B. (2000) How education became nobody's business, in H. Altrichter and J. Elliott (eds) *Images of Educational Change.* Buckingham: Open University Press.

MacDonald, I., Bhavani, R., Khan, L. and John, G. (1989) *Murder in the Playground: the Burnage Report.* London: Longsight.

MacDonald, M. (1980) Schooling and the reproduction of class and gender relation, in L. Barton, R. Meighan and S. Walker (eds) *Schooling, Ideology and the Curriculum.* Lewes: Falmer.

Mackinnon, D. (1984) From everyday experience to academic study, Unit 2, *E200 Contemporary Issues in Education.* Buckingham: The Open University.

MacNaughton, G. (2000) *Rethinking Gender in Early Childhood Education.* London: Paul Chapman.

McNay, L. (2000) *Gender and Agency.* Cambridge: Polity Press.

Macpherson, W. (1999) *The Stephen Lawrence Inquiry*, CM 4262–1. London: HMSO.

McRobbie, A. (1978) Working class girls and the culture of femininity, in Women's Studies Group Centre for Contemporary Cultural Studies, University of Birmingham (Eds) *Women Take Issue: Aspects of Women's Subordination.* London: Hutchinson.

McRobbie, A. and Garber, G. (1982) Girls and subcultures, in S. Hall and T. Jefferson (eds) *Resistance through Rituals: Youth Subcultures in Post-war Britain.* London: Hutchinson.

McWilliam, E. (1996) Touchy subjects: a risky inquiry into pedagogical pleasure, *British Educational Research Journal,* 22(3): 305–17.

Mahony, P. (1983) How Alice's chin really came to be pressed against her foot: sexist processes of interaction in mixed sexed classrooms, *Women's Studies International Forum,* 16(1): 107–15.

Mahony, P. (1985) *Schools for the Boys: Coeducation Reassessed.* London: Hutchinson.

Mahony, P. (1997) The underachievement of boys in the UK: old tunes for new fiddles? *Social Alternatives,* 16(3): 44–50.

Mahony, P. (1998) Girls will be girls and boys will be first, in D. Epstein, J. Elwood, V. Hey and J. Maw (eds) *Failing Boys? Issues in Gender and Achievement.* Buckingham: Open University Press.

Mahony, P. and Hextall, I. (1997). Sounds of silence: the social justice agenda of the teacher training agency, *International Studies in Sociology of Education,* 7(2): 137–57.

Mahony, P. and Zmroczek, C. (eds) (1997) *Women and Social Class.* London: Taylor & Francis.

Mann, C. (1996) *'Finding a favourable front: the contribution of the family to working-class girls' achievement',* unpublished PhD dissertation. University of Cambridge.

Mann, C. (1998) The impact of working class mothers on the educational success of their adolescent daughters at a time of social change, *British Journal of Sociology of Education,* 19(2): 211–26.

Marsh, J. (2000) 'But I want to fly too!': girls and superhero play in the infant classroom, *Gender and Education,* 12(2): 209–20.

Marshall, J. (1984) *Women Managers: Travellers in a Male World.* Chichester: Wiley.

Martino, W. (1999) 'Cool boys', 'party animals', 'squids' and 'poofters': interrogating the dynamics and politics of adolescent masculinities in school, *British Journal of Sociology of Education,* 20(2): 239–63.

Mason, R. (1999) Giant steps for mankind, *Times Educational Supplement,* 14 May: 19.

Measor, L. (1999) Looking back at the boys: reflections on issues of gender in classroom data, in M. Hammersley (ed.) *Researching School Experience.* London: Falmer.

Measor, L. and Sikes, P. (1992) *Gender and Schooling.* London: Cassell.

Measor, L. and Woods, P. (1984) *Changing Schools.* Milton Keynes: Open University Press.

Meehan, D. (1999) The under-representation of women managers in higher education: are there issues other than style? in S. Whitehead and R. Moodley (eds) *Transforming Managers.* London: UCL Press.

Messner, M.A. (1997) *Politics of Masculinities: Men in Movements.* London: Sage.

Middleton, S. (1995) Doing feminist educational theory: a post-modern perspective, *Gender in Education,* 7(1): 87–100.

Miles, R. (1995) *Racism.* London: Routledge.

Millard, E. (1997) *Differently Literate: Boys, Girls and the Schooling of Literacy.* London: Falmer.

Miller, A. (1987) *The Drama of Being a Child and the Search for the True Self.* London: Virago.

Milner, M. (1987) *Eternity's Sunrise: A Way of Keeping a Diary.* London: Virago.

Mirza, H. (1992) *Young, Female, and Black.* Buckingham: Open University Press.

Mirza, H. (1993) The social construction of black womenhood in British educational research: towards a new understanding, in M. Arnot and K. Weiler (eds) *Feminism and Social Justice in Education: International Perspectives.* London: Falmer.

Mirza, H. (1995a) The myth of underachievement, in L. Dawtrey, J. Holland and M. Hammer with S. Sheldon (eds) *Equality and Inequality in Education Policy*. Clevedon: Multilingual Matters.

Mirza, H. (1995b) Some ethical dilemmas in fieldwork: feminist and antiracist methodologies, in M. Griffiths and B. Troyna (eds) *Anti-Racism, Culture and Social Justice in Education*. Stoke-on-Trent: Trentham Books.

Mirza, H. (ed.) (1997) *Black British Feminism*. London: Routledge.

Mirza, H. and Reay, D. (2000) Redefining citizenship: Black women educators and the 'third space', in M. Arnot and J. Dillabough (eds) *Challenging Democracy: International Perspectives on Gender, Education and Citizenship*. London: Routledge.

Modood, T. (1988) 'Black', racial equality and Asian identity, *New Community*, 14(3): 397–404.

Moir, A. and Moir, B. (1999) *Why Men Don't Iron*. London: HarperCollins.

Money, J. and Ehrhardt, A.A. (1972). *Man and Woman, Boy and Girl: The Differentiation and Dimorphism of Gender Identity from Conception to Maturity*. Baltimore, MD: Johns Hopkins University Press.

Morgan, D. (1992) *Discovering Men*. London: Routledge.

Morris, J. (1993) *Pride Against Prejudice: Transforming Attitudes to Disability*. London: The Women's Press.

Morrison, A. (1987) *Breaking the Glass Ceiling*. Reading, MA: Addison Wesley.

Mortimore, P., Owen, C. and Phoenix, A. (1997) Higher educational qualifications, in V. Karn (ed.) *Ethnicity in the 1991 Census. Volume Four: Employment, Education and Housing Among the Ethnic Minority Populations of Britain*. London: HMSO.

Muller, W. and Karle, W. (1993) Social selection in education systems, *European Sociological Review*, 9(1): 1–23.

Mungham, G. and Pearson, G. (1976) *Working Class Youth Culture*. London: Routledge & Kegan Paul.

Murphy, P. and Gipps, C. (eds) (1996) *Equity in the Classroom: Towards an Effective Pedagogy for Girls and Boys*. London: Falmer.

Myers, K. (ed.) (2000) *Whatever Happened to Equal Opportunities in Schools?* Buckingham: Open University Press.

National Commission on Education (1993) *Learning to Succeed: A Radical Look at Education Today and a Strategy for the Future*, report of the Paul Hamlyn Foundation National Commission on Education. London: Heinemann.

Nayak, A. (1997) Tales from the darkside: negotiating whiteness in school arenas, *International Studies in Sociology of Education*, 7(1): 57–79.

Nayak, A. (1999) White English ethnicities: racism, antiracism and students' perspectives, *Race, Ethnicity and Education* 2(2): 177–202.

Nayak, A. and Kehily, M.J. (1996) Playing it straight: masculinities, homophobias and schooling, *Journal of Gender Studies*, 5(2): 211–30.

Nebeker, K.C. (1998) Critical race theory: a white graduate student's struggle with this growing area of scholarship, *Qualitative Studies in Education*, 11(1): 25–41.

Nelson, M.B. (1996) *The Stronger Women Get, the More Men Love Football*. London: The Women's Press.

Nicholson, L. (1994) Interpreting gender, *Signs*, 20(1): 79–105.

Nicolson, P. (1996) *Gender, Power and Organisation*. London: Routledge.

Noble, C. (1998) Helping boys do better in their primary schools, in K. Bleach (ed.) *Raising Boys' Achievement in Schools*. Stoke-on-Trent: Trentham Books.

Noden, P., West, A., David, M. and Edge, A. (1998) Choices and destinations at transfer to secondary schools, *Journal of Education Policy*, 13(2): 221–36.

Norquay, N. (1990) Life history research: memory, schooling and social difference, *Cambridge Journal of Education*, 20(3): 14–17.

O'Brien, M. (1982) The commatisation of women: patriarchal fetishism in the sociology of knowledge. Paper presented at the British Sociological Association Conference on 'Gender and Society', University of Manchester, 14–17 May.

Oakley, A. (1972) *Sex, Gender and Society*. London: Temple Smith.

Oakley, A. (1981) Interviewing women: a contradiction in terms, in H. Roberts (ed.) *Doing Feminist Research*. London: Routledge & Kegan Paul.

Ofsted (Office for Standards in Education) (1993) *Boys and English: A Report from the Office of Her Majesty's Chief Inspector of Schools*. London: Ofsted.

Ofsted (Office for Standards in Education) (1999) *Raising the Attainment of Minority Ethnic Pupils: School and LEA Responses*. London: Ofsted.

Ogilvy, C., Boath, E., Cheyne, W., Jahoda, G. and Schaffer, H.R. (1990) Staff attitudes and perceptions in multi-cultural nursery school, *Early Child Development and Care*, 64: 1–13.

Ogilvy, C., Boath, E., Cheyne, W., Jahoda, G. and Schaffer, H.R. (1992) Staff-child interaction styles in multi-ethnic nursery schools, *British Journal of Developmental Psychology*, 10: 85–97.

Oliver, M (1990) *The Politics of Disablement*. Basingstoke: Macmillan.

Orr, P. (2000) Prudence and progress: national policy for equal opportunities (gender) in schools since 1975, in K. Myers (ed.) *Whatever Happened to Equal Opportunities in Schools?* Buckingham: Open University Press.

Oudshoorn, N. (1994) *Beyond the Natural Body: An Archaeology of Sex Hormones*. London: Routledge.

Paechter, C. (1993) What happens when a school subject undergoes a sudden change of status? *Curriculum Studies*, 1(3): 349–64.

Paechter, C. (1996) Power, knowledge and the confessional in qualitative research, *Discourse*, 17(1): 75–84.

Paechter, C. (1998a) *Educating the Other: Gender, Power and Schooling*. London: Falmer.

Paechter, C. (1998b) Investigating power in the staffroom: issues in the study of power and gender relations in a professional group, *Cambridge Journal of Education*, 28(1): 97–111.

Paechter, C. (2000) *Changing School Subjects: Power, Gender and Curriculum*. Buckingham: Open University Press.

Paechter, C. and Head, J. (1995) Power and gender influences on curriculum implementation. Paper presented at American Educational Research Association Annual Meeting, San Francisco, 22–26 April.

Paechter, C. and Head, J. (1996) Power in the staffroom, *British Educational Research Journal*, 22(1): 57–69.

Paechter, C. and Weiner, G. (1996) Editorial of special issue: post-modernism and post-structuralism in educational research, *British Educational Research Journal*, 22(3): 267–72.

Palmgren, C., Lövgren, K. and Göran, B. (eds) (1992) *Ethnicity in Youth Culture*. Stockholm: Stockholm University.

Parker, A. (1996) The construction of masculinity within boys' physical education, *Gender and Education*, 8(2): 141–57.

Parker, G. (1993) *With this Body: Caring and Disability in Marriage*. Buckingham: Open University Press.

Parker, H.J. (1974) *View from the Boys*. Newton Abbot: David & Charles.

Pattman, R., Phoenix, A. and Frosh, S. (1998) Lads, machos and others: developing 'boy-centred' research, *Journal of Youth Studies*, 1(2): 125–42.

Patton, C. (1993) Tremble, hetero swine!, in M. Warner (ed.) *Fear of a Queer Planet, Queer Politics and Social Theory*. Minneapolis, MN: University of Minnesota Press.

Patton, P. (1979). Of power and prisons, in M. Morris and P. Patton (eds) *Michel Foucault: Power, Truth, Strategy*. Sydney: Feral Publications.

Phoenix, A. (1987) Theories of gender and black families, in G. Weiner and M. Arnot (eds) *Gender Under Scrutiny: New Inquiries in Education*. London: Hutchinson.

Pilling, D. (1990) *Escape from Disadvantage*. London: Falmer.

Pleck, J.H. and Sawyer, J. (eds) (1974) *Men and Masculinity*. Englewood Cliffs, NJ: Prentice Hall.

Plewis, I. (1996) Young children at school: inequalities and the National Curriculum, in B. Bernstein and J. Brannen (eds) *Children, Research and Policy*. London: Taylor & Francis.

Plummer, G. (2000) *Failing Working-Class Girls*. Stoke-on-Trent: Trentham Books.

Pollack, W. (1998) *Real Boys*. New York: Owl Books.

Power, S., Edwards, A., Whitty, G. and Wigfall, V. (1998) Schoolboys and schoolwork: gender identification and academic achievement, *Journal of Inclusive Education*, (2)2: 135–53.

Purvis, J. (1991) *A History of Women's Education in England*. Buckingham: Open University Press.

Putnam, R.D. (2000) *Bowling Alone: The Collapse and revival of American Community*. New York: Simon & Schuster.

Pyke, K.D. (1996) Class-based masculinities: the interdependence of gender, class and interpersonal power, *Gender and Society*, 10: 527–49.

Raphael Reed, L. (1995a) Working with boys: a new research agenda, *The Redland Chapters*, 3: 71–8.

Raphael Reed, L. (1995b) Reconceptualising equal opportunities in the 1990s: a study of radical teacher culture in transition, in M. Griffiths and B. Troyna (eds) *Anti-racism, Culture and Social Justice in Education*. Stoke-on-Trent: Trentham Books.

Raphael Reed, L. (1996) Re-searching, re-finding, re-making: exploring the unconscious as a pedagogic and research practice. Paper presented at the British Educational Research Conference, University of Lancaster, 12–15 September.

Raphael Reed, L. (1997) Troubling boys and disturbing discourses on masculinity and schooling. Paper presented at the 'Gender in Education' conference, Warwick, April.

Raphael Reed, L. (1999) Troubling boys and disturbing discourses on masculinity and schooling: a feminist exploration of current debates and interventions concerning boys in school, *Gender and Education*, 11(1): 93–110.

Rattansi, A. (1993) Changing the subject? Racism, culture and education, in J. Donald and A. Rattansi (eds) *'Race', Culture and Difference*, 2nd edn. London: Sage/Open University Press.

Rattansi, A. (1994) 'Western' racisms, ethnicities and identities in a 'postmodern' frame, in A. Rattansi and S. Westwood (eds) *Racism, Modernity and Identity*. Cambridge: Polity Press.

Reay, D. (1997) The double bind of the working class feminist academic: the success of failure or the failure of success? in P. Mahony and C. Zmroczek (eds) *Class Matters: Working Class Women's perspectives on Social Class*. London: Taylor & Francis.

Reay, D. (1998) *Class Work: Mothers' Involvement in their Children's Schooling*. London: UCL Press.

Reay, D. (2001) 'Spice girls', 'nice girls', 'girlies' and tomboys: gender discourses, girls' cultures and femininities in the primary classroom, *Gender and Education*, 13(2): 153–66.

Reay, D. and Ball, S.J. (1997) 'Spoilt for choice': the working classes and education markets, *Oxford Review of Education*, 23(1): 89–101.

Reay, D. and Ball, S.J. (2000) Essentials of female management: women's ways of working in the education marketplace? *Educational Management and Administration*, 28(2): 145–59.

Reay, D., David, M. and Ball, S.J. (in press) Choices of degree or degrees of choice?: Class, 'race' and the higher education choice proces', *Sociology*.

Redman, P. and Mac an Ghaill, M. (1996) Schooling sexualities: heterosexual masculinities, schooling and the unconscious, *Discourse*, 17(2): 243–56.

Redman, P. and Mac an Ghaill, M. (1997) Educating Peter, in D.L. Steinberg, D. Epstein and R. Johnson (eds) *Border Patrols: Policing the Boundaries of Heterosexuality*. London: Cassell.

Redwood, F. (1994) Now let's give boys a boost, *Daily Telegraph*, 7 December: 23.

Rees, T. (1999) *Mainstreaming Equality in the European Union*. London: Routledge.

Reid, I. (1994) *Inequality, Society and Education*. Loughborough: Loughborough University of Technology.

Reynolds, D. and Farrell, S. (1996) *Worlds Apart: A Review of International Surveys of Education and Achievement Involving England*. London: Ofsted.

Reynolds, T. (1997) Class matters, 'race' matters, gender matters, in P. Mahony and C. Zmroczek (eds) *Women and Social Class*. London: Taylor & Francis.

Rhodes, D. (1992) The politics of paradigms: gender difference and gender disadvantage, in G. Bock and S. James (eds) *Beyond Equality and Difference: Citizenship, Feminist Politics and Female Subjectivity*. London: Routledge.

Rich, A. (1980) Compulsory heterosexuality and lesbian existence, *Signs*, 5(4): 631–60.

Rich, A. (1986) *Of Woman Born: Motherhood as Experience and Institution*. New York: Norton & Co.

Riddell, S. (1996) Gender and special educational needs, in G. Lloyd (ed.) *Making Progress Unsatisfactory*. Edinburgh: Moray House Publications.

Riddell, S. and Salisbury, J. (2000) Introduction: educational reforms and equal opportunities programmes, in J. Salisbury and S. Riddell (eds) *Gender, Policy and Educational Change*. London: Routledge.

Riddell, S., Baron, S., Stalker, K. and Wilkinson, H. (1997) The concept of the learning society for adults with learning difficulties: human and social capital perspectives, *Journal of Education Policy*, 12(6): 473–83.

Riddell, S., Baron, S. and Wilkinson, H. (1998) Training from cradle to grave: social justice and training for people with learning difficulties, *Journal of Education Policy*, 13(4): 531–44.

Riddell, S., Baron, S. and Wilson, A. (1999) Social capital and people with learning difficulties, *Studies in the Education of Adults*, 31(1): 49–66.

Riddell, S., Baron, S. and Wilson, A. (2001a) The significance of the learning society for women and men with learning difficulties, *Gender and Education*, (13)1: 57–75.

Riddell, S., Baron, S. and Wilson, A. (2001b) *People with Learning Difficulties and the Learning Society*. Bristol: Policy Press.

Riley, D. (1988) *'Am I That Name?' Feminism and the Category of 'Women' in History*. London: Macmillan.

Robins, D. and Cohen, P. (1978) *Knuckle-Sandwich: Growing Up in the Working-Class City*. Harmondsworth: Penguin.

Rogers, C. (1983) *Freedom to Learn for the 80s*. New York: Merrill.

Rosen, H. (1993) *Troublesome Boy*. London: English and Media Centre.

Rosser, E. and Harre, R. (1976) The meaning of trouble, in M. Hammersley and P. Woods (eds) *The Process of Schooling, A Sociological Reader*. London: Routledge & Kegan Paul.

Rudberg, M. (1996) The researching body: the epistemopholic project, *The European Journal of Women's Studies*, 3: 285–305.

Said, E. (1986) Foucault and the imagination of power, in D. Couzens Hoy (ed.) *Foucault, a Critical Reader*. Oxford: Basil Blackwell.

Salisbury, J. and Jackson, D. (1996) *Challenging Macho Values*. London: Falmer.

Salisbury, J. and Riddell, S. (2000) *Gender, Policy and Educational Change*. London: Routledge.

Salisbury, J., Rees, G. and Gorard, S. (1999) Accounting for the differential attainment of boys and girls at school, *School Leadership and Management*, 19(4): 403–26.

Sammons, P. (1995) Gender, ethnic and socio-economic differences in attainment and progress: a longitudinal analysis of student achievement over nine years, *British Educational Research Journal*, 21(4): 465–85.

Samuel, R. (1982) Local history and oral history, in R.G. Burgess (ed.) *Field Research: A Sourcebook and Field Manual*. London: Allen & Unwin.

Samuel, R. and Thompson, P. (1990) *The Myths We Live By*. London: Routledge.

Schein, V. (1973) Relationships between sex role stereotypes and requisite management characteristics, *Journal of Applied Psychology*, 57(2): 95–100.

Schein, V. (1975) Relationships between sex role stereotypes and management characteristics among female managers, *Journal of Applied Psychology*, 60(3): 340–4.

Schmuck, P. (1996) Women's place in educational administration: past, present and future, in K. Leithwood (ed.) *International Handbook of Educational Leadership and Administration*. Dordrecht, Netherlands: Kluwer Academic Press.

Schostak, J. (2000) Developing under developing circumstances: the personal and social development of students and the process of schooling, in H. Altrichter and J. Elliott (eds) *Images of Educational Change*. Buckingham: Open University Press.

Schuman, J. (1999) The ethnic minority populations of Great Britain – latest estimates, *Population Trends*, 96: 33–43.

Schutz, A. (1964) The stranger, in B.R. Cosin, I.R. Dale, G.M. Esland, D. MacKinnon and D.F. Swift (eds) *School and Society*. London: Routledge & Kegan Paul.

Scottish Executive (2000) *Statistical Bulletin: Summary Results of the September 1999 School Census* Edinburgh: Scottish Executive.

Sears, J. (ed.) (1992) *Sexuality and the Curriculum: The Politics and Practices of Sexuality Education*. New York: Teachers' College Press.

Segal, L. (1990) *Slow Motion: Changing Masculinities, Changing Men*. London: Virago.

Seidler, V. (1989) *Rediscovering Masculinity*. London: Routledge.

Sellar, A. (1994) Should the feminist philosopher stay at home? in J. Lennon and C. Whitford (eds) *Knowing the Difference: Feminist Perspectives in Epistemology*. London: Routledge.

Sewell, T. (1997) *Black Masculinities and Schooling*. Stoke-on-Trent: Trentham Books.

Sex Education Forum (1995) *The Effectiveness of Sex Education* (Sex Education Forum Occasional Parliamentary Briefing Paper, no. 1.) London: National Children's Bureau.

Sex Education Forum (1997) *Supporting the Needs of Boys and Young Men in Sex and Relationships Education*. London: National Children's Bureau.

Shakespeare, T., Gillespie-Sells, K. and Davies, D. (1996) *The Sexual Politics of Disability: Untold Desires*. London: Cassell.

Sharpe, S. (1976) *Just Like a Girl*. Harmondsworth: Penguin.

Shavit, Y. and Blossfeld, H-P (1993) *Persistent Inequality: Changing Educational Achievement in Thirteen Countries*. Boulder, CO: Westview Press.

Shaw, J. (1995) *Gender, Education and Anxiety*. London: Taylor & Francis.

Shilling, C. (1993) *The Body and Social Theory*. London: Sage.

Shotter, J. (1989) Social accountability and the social construction of 'You', in J. Shotter and K. Gergen (eds) *Texts of Identity*. London: Sage.

Shuard, H. (1981) Mathematics and the ten-year-old child, *Times Educational Supplement*, 27 March.

Shuard, H. (1982) Differences in mathematical performance between girls and boys, in Department of Education and Science, *Mathematics Counts: Report of the Committee of Enquiry into the Teaching of Mathematics in Schools* (the Cockroft Report). London: HMSO.

Signell, K. (1990) *Wisdom of the Heart: Working with Women's Dreams*. London: Rider.

Singh, P. (1995) Voicing the 'Other', speaking for the 'Self', disrupting the meta-narratives of educational theorizing with poststructural feminisms, in R. Smith and P. Wexler (eds) *After Postmodernism: Education, Politics and Identity*. London: Falmer.

Skeggs, B. (1991) Challenging masculinity and using sexuality, *British Journal of Sociology of Education*, 12(2): 127–39.

Skeggs, B. (1997) *Formations of Class and Gender*. London: Sage.

Skelton, C. (1996) Learning to be 'tough'; the fostering of maleness in one primary school, *Gender and Education*, 8(2): 185–97.

Skelton, C. (1997) Primary boys and hegemonic masculinities, *British Journal of Sociology of Education*, 18(3): 349–70.

Skelton, C. (1998) Feminism and research into masculinities and schooling, *Gender and Education*, 10(2): 217–27.

Skelton, C. (2001) *Schooling the Boys: Masculinities and Primary Education*. Buckingham: Open University Press.

Smith, C. and Lloyd, B. (1978) Maternal behavior and perceived sex of infant: revisited, *Child Development*, 49: 1263–5.

Smith, T. and Noble, M. (eds) (1995) *Education Divides: Poverty and Schooling in the 1990s*. London: CPAG.

Smithers, A. and Robinson, P. (1995) *Post-18 education: Growth, Change, Prospect*. London: Council for Industry and Higher Education.

Snodgrass, S.E. (1985) Women's intuition: the effect of subordinate role in interpersonal sensitivity, *Journal of Personality and Social Psychology*, 55 (1): 146–55.

Snodgrass, S.E (1992) Further effects of role versus gender in interpersonal sensitivity, *Journal of Personality and Social Psychology*, 62(1): 154–8.

Sonuga-Barke, E., Minocha, K., Taylor, E. and Sandberg, S. (1993) Inter-ethnic bias in teachers' ratings of childhood hyperactivity, *British Journal of Developmental Psychology*, 11: 187–200.

Soper, K. (1990) *Troubled Pleasures*. London: Verso.

Soper, K. (1993a) Productive contradictions, in C. Ramazanoglu (ed.) *Up Against Foucault*. London: Routledge.

Soper, K. (1993b) Postmodernism, subjectivity and the question of value, in J. Squires (ed.) *Principled Positions: Postmodernism and the Rediscovery of Value*. London: Routledge.

Spender, D. (1980) *Man Made Language*. London: Routledge & Kegan Paul.

Spender, D. (1982) *Invisible Women: The Schooling Scandal*. London, Writers' and Readers' Publishing Collective.

Spender, D. (1983) 'Telling how it is': language and gender in the classroom, in M. Marland (ed.) *Sex Differentiation and Schooling*. London: Heinemann.

Spivak, G.C. (1990) *The Post-Colonial Critic. Interviews, Strategies, Dialogues*. London: Routledge.

Spretnack, C. (1993) *States of Grace*. London: HarperCollins.

Stanley, L. and Wise, S. (1993) Breaking Out Again: Feminist Ontology and Epistemology. London: Routledge.

Stanworth, M. (1981) *Gender and Schooling: A Study of Sexual Divisions in the Classroom*. London: Women's Research and Resources Centre Publications Collective.

Steedman, C. (1985) 'The mother made conscious': the historical development of primary school pedagogy, *History Workshop Journal*, 20: 149–63.

Steedman, C. (1986) *Landscape for a Good Woman*. London: Virago.

Sudbury, J. (1998) *'Other Kinds of Dreams': Black Women's Organisations and the Politics of Transformation*. London: Routledge.

Sukhnandan, L. (1999) *An Investigation into Gender Differences in Achievement. Phase 1: A Review of Recent Research and LEA Information on Provision*. Slough: National Foundation for Educational Research.

Sukhnandan, L., Lee, B. and Kelleher, S. (2000) *An Investigation into Gender Differences in Achievement. Phase 2: School and Classroom Strategies*. Slough: National Foundation for Educational Research.

Sutherland, M. (1983) Anxiety, aspirations and the curriculum, in M. Marland (ed.) *Sex Differentiation and Schooling*. London: Heinemann.

Swain, J. (2000) 'The money's good, the fame's good, the girls are good': the role of playground football in the construction of young boys' masculinity in a junior school, *British Journal of Sociology of Education*, 21(1): 95–109.

Tanton, M. (ed.) (1994) *Women in Management: A Developing Presence*. London: Routledge.

Thomas, A. (1998) French and the single-sex classroom, Times Educational Supplement, 9 October.

Thomas, A. and Kitzinger, C. (eds) (1997) *Sexual Harassment*. Buckingham: Open University Press.

Thomas, C. (1999) *Female Forms: Experiencing and Understanding Disability*. Buckingham: Open University Press.

Thorne, B. (1993) *Gender Play*. Buckingham: Open University Press.

Tizard, B. and Hughes, M. (1984) *Young Children Learning*. London: Fontana.

Tizard, B., Blatchford, P., Burke, J., Farquhar, C. and Plewis, I (1988) *Young Children at School in the Inner City*. London: Lawrence Erlbaum.

Tomlinson, S. (1984) *A Sociology of Special Education*. London: Routledge & Kegan Paul.

Trenchard, L. and Warren, H. (1984) *Something to Tell You: The Experiences and Needs of Young Lesbians and Gay Men in London*. London: Gay Teenage Group.

Troyna, B. (1994) Blind Faith? Empowerment and educational research, *International Studies in Sociology of Education*, 4(1): 3–24.

Troyna, B. and Hatcher, R. (1992a) *Racism in Children's Lives*. London: Routledge.

Troyna, B. and Hatcher, R. (1992b) It's only words: understanding 'racial' and racist incidents, *New Community*, 18(3): 493–6.

Tseelon, E. (1995) *The Masque of Femininity*. London: Sage.

Unterhalter, E. (2000) Transnational visions of the 1990s: contrasting views of women, education and citizenship, in M. Arnot and J. Dillabough (eds) *Challenging Democracy: International Perspectives on Gender, Education and Citizenship*. London: Routledge Falmer.

van Dijk, T. (1993) *Elite Discourse and Racism*. London: Sage.

Vincent, C. and Warren, S. (1998) Becoming a 'better' parent? Motherhood, education and transition, *British Journal of Sociology of Education*, 19(2): 177–94.

Volosinov, V. (1973) *Marxism and the Philosophy of Language*. New York: Seminar Press.

Walker, A. (1984) *In Search of our Mothers' Gardens*. London: The Women's Press.

Walker, J. (1988) *Louts and Legends*. Sydney: Allen & Unwin.

Walker, S. and Barton, L. (eds) (1983) *Gender, Class and Education*. Lewes: Falmer.

Walkerdine, V. (1981) Sex, power and pedagogy, *Screen Education*, 38: 14–24.

Walkerdine, V. (1985) On the regulation of speaking and silence, in C. Steedman, C. Urwin and V. Walkerdine (eds) *Language, Gender and Childhood*. London: Routledge & Kegan Paul.

Walkerdine, V. (1988) *The Mastery of Reason*. Cambridge: Routledge & Kegan Paul.

Walkerdine, V. (1989) *Counting Girls Out*. London: Virago.

Walkerdine, V. (1990) *Schoolgirl Fictions*. London: Verso.

Walkerdine, V. and Lucey, H. (1989) *Democracy in the Kitchen: Regulating Mothers and Socialising Daughters*. London: Virago.

Walkerdine, V., Lucey, H. and Melody, J. (2000) Class, attainment and sexuality in late twentieth-century Britain, in C. Zmroczek and P. Mahony (eds) *Women and Social Class – International Feminist Perspectives*. London: UCL Press.

Walkerdine, V., Lucey, H. and Melody, J. (2001) *Growing Up Girl: Psychosocial Explorations of Gender and Class*. London: Macmillan.

Ward, M. (1979) *Mathematics and the 10-year-old: The Report of the Schools Council Project, Primary School Mathematics – Evaluation Studies*. London: Evans/Methuen.

Ware, V. (1991) *Beyond the Pale: White Women, Racism, and History*. London: Verso.

Warren, S. (1997) Who do these boys think they are?: an investigation into the construction of masculinities in a primary classroom, *International Journal of Inclusive Education*, 1(2): 207–22.

Warrington, M. and Younger, M. (2000) The other side of the gender gap, *Gender and Education*, 12(4): 493–507.

Weedon, C. (1987) *Feminist Practice and Poststructuralist Theory*. Oxford: Blackwell.

Weiner, G. (1994) *Feminisms in Education: An Introduction*. Buckingham: Open University Press.

Weiner, G. and Arnot, M. (eds) (1987) *Gender Under Scrutiny*. London: Hutchinson.

Weir, A. (1997) *Sacrificial Logics: Feminist Theory and the Critique of Identity*. New York: Routledge.

Westwood, S. (1990) Racism, black masculinity and the politics of space, in J. Hearn and D. Morgan (eds) *Men, Masculinities and Social Theory*. London: Unwin Hyman.

Wexler, P. (1995) Postmodernism: a new age social theory in education, in R. Smith and P. Wexler (eds) *After Postmodernism: Education, Politics and Identity*. London: Falmer.

Whitehead, H. (1981) The bow and the burden strap: a new look at institutionalised homosexuality in native North America, in S.B. Ortner and H. Whitehead (eds) *Sexual Meanings: The Cultural Construction of Gender and Sexuality*. Cambridge: Cambridge University Press.

Whitehead, J. (1996) Sex stereotypes, gender identity and subject choice at 'A' level, *Educational Research*, 38(2): 147–60.

Whitehead, S. (2001) *Men and Masculinities*. Cambridge: Polity Press.

Whitty, G. (1985) *Sociology and School Knowledge: Curriculum Theory, Research and Politics*. London: Methuen.

Whyte, J. (1986) *Girls into Science and Technology: The Story of a Project*. London: Routledge & Kegan Paul.

Whyte, J., Deem, R., Kant, L. and Cruickshank, M. (eds) (1985) *Girl Friendly Schooling*. London: Methuen.

Wilkinson, H. (1996) Mothers marketing work: the experiences of mothers making choices for children with special needs, *Discourse*, 17(3): 315–24.

Wilkinson, H. (1999) The Thatcher legacy: power feminism and the birth of girl power, in N. Walters (ed.) *On the Move: Feminism for a New Generation*. London: Virago.

Wilkinson, H. and Mulgan, G. (1995) *Freedom's Children: Work, Relationships and Politics for 18–34 Year Olds in Britain Today*. London: Demos.

Wilkinson, R. (1999) The social environment, in D. Gordon, M. Shaw, D. Dorling and G. Davey Smith (eds) *Inequalities in Health: The Evidence Presented to the Independent Inquiry into Inequalities in Health, Chaired by Sir Donald Acheson*. Bristol: The Policy Press.

Williams, J. (1987) The construction of women and black students as educational problems: re-evaluating policy on gender and 'race', in M. Arnot and G. Weiner (eds) *Gender and the Politics of Schooling*. London: Unwin Hyman.

Williams, W. (1986) *The Spirit and the Flesh: Sexual Diversity in American Indian Culture*. Boston, MA: Beacon Press.

Willis, P. (1977) *Learning to Labour*. Aldershot: Saxon House.

Wilson, A., Lightbody, P. and Riddell, S. (2000) *A Flexible Gateway to Employment? An Evaluation of Enable Service's Traditional and Innovative Forms of Work Preparation*. Glasgow: Strathclyde Centre for Disability Research.

Wolpe, A. (1976) The official ideology of education for girls, in M. Flude and J. Ahier (eds) *Educability, Schools and Ideology*. London: Croom Helm.

Woodhead, C. (1996) quoted in the *Times Educational Supplement*, 15 March.

Woods, P. (1996) *Researching the Art of Teaching: Ethnography for Educational Use*. London: Routledge.

Wright, C. (1992) *Race Relations in the Primary School*. London: David Fulton.

Wright, C., Weekes, D., McGlaughlin, A. and Webb, D. (1998) Masculinised discourses within education and the construction of black male identities amongst African Caribbean youth, *British Journal of Sociology of Education*, 19(1): 75–87.

Yates, L. (1992) Postmodernism, feminism and cultural politics: or, if master narratives have been discredited, what does Giroux think he is doing?, *Discourse*, 13(1): 124–33.

Yates, L. (1997) Gender equity and the boys debate: what sort of challenge is it? *British Journal of Sociology of Education*, 18(3): 337–47.

Younger, M., Warrington, M. and Williams, J. (1999) The gender gap and classroom interactions: reality and rhetoric? *British Journal of Sociology of Education*, 20(3): 352–42.

Yuval-Davis, N. (1994) Women, ethnicity and empowerment, *Feminism and Psychology*, 4(1): 179–97.

# Index

**WHATEVER HAPPENED TO EQUAL OPPORTUNITIES IN SCHOOLS?**

**Kate Myers (ed.)**

*Whatever Happened to Equal Opportunities in Schools?* is an edited book which makes an important contribution to the current debate about equal opportunities. Today the dominant concern is about boys' achievement but it was not always thus. Contributors trace events relating to schools since the introduction of the Sex Discrimination Act and the establishment of the Equal Opportunities Commission in the mid-1970s. Prior to the advent of the National Curriculum it was common practice for boys and girls to take different subjects and be offered very different opportunities and experience through the overt and covert school curriculum. Initiatives emerging from central government, quangos, trade unions, local education authorities, and individual schools are described. The book discusses: how much has really changed; the extent to which credit should be given to earlier initiatives concerned with the raising of girls' aspirations and achievement; what we can learn from these initiatives; and what we should really be concerned about now. The book also addresses the question of boys' achievement both past and present and will be important reading for all educators with an interest in promoting gender equality in schools.

## Contents

*How did we get here? – Part I Country-wide initiatives – Prudence and progress: national policy for equal opportunities (gender) in schools since 1975 – Challenging inequalities in the classroom: the role and contribution of the Equal Opportunities Commission – Equal to the task? The role of the NUT in promoting equal opportunities in schools – Part II Local education authorities – An episode in the thirty years war: race, sex and class in the ILEA 1981–90 – Now you see it, now you don't: gender equality work in Brent 1982–8 – Did it make a difference? The Ealing experience 1987–9 – Part III Projects – Was there really a problem? The Schools Council Sex Differentiation Project 1981–3 – Has the mountain moved? The Girls Into Science and Technology Project 1979–83 – Working with boys at Hackney Downs School 1980–4 – Teachers. Femocrats and academics: activism in London in the 1980s – Part IV Whatever happened to . . . – A black perspective – When Ms Muffet fought back: a view of work on children's books since the 1970s – Part V Conclusion – Lessons learned? – Index.*

256pp     0 335 20303 5 (Paperback)     0 335 20304 3 (Hardback)

## SCHOOLING THE BOYS
MASCULINITIES AND PRIMARY EDUCATION

### Christine Skelton

This book explores where masculinity is in primary schools. It has been argued by some commentators that a contributory factor to boys' underachievement is the predominance of women teachers in primary schools which has led to classroom management and teaching styles which 'favour' girls. As this book shows, primary schools produce a range of masculinities for pupils to draw on. A number of questions are raised: what are the tensions for boys between what the school expects from them as 'school pupils' and how they are drawn to behave as a 'boy'? How does a primary school produce certain masculine styles in its day-to-day routines? In what ways do girls respond to male practices and behaviours in the primary school classroom? The book aims to provide readers with an understanding of the background literature on boys and schooling, an insight into 'masculinity-making' in primary schools, and to offer strategies for developing gender-relevant programmes.

### Contents

224pp     0 335 20695 6 (Paperback)     0 335 20696 4 (Hardback)

# WHAT ABOUT THE BOYS?
ISSUES OF MASCULINITY IN SCHOOLS

## Wayne Martino and Bob Meyenn (eds)

- How can teachers address the challenge of educating boys for life in the twenty-first century?
- What aspects of schooling are particularly problematic for boys?
- How do issues of class, race and sexuality impact upon boys' educational experiences?

This edited collection brings together leading researchers from Australia, the United Kingdom and the United States to explore issues of boys, schooling and masculinities within the context of the current concern about the education of boys. The contributors draw on detailed empirical research to highlight some important issues that are not addressed in public debates about boys in the media. Chapter topics include international perspectives on debates about boys; teaching boys; programmes for boys in schools; boys and risk taking; boys and discipline; boys and sexuality; African-American boys; indigenous boys in Australian schools; boys and reading; boys and maths; boys, dance and sport; boys and science; and girls' talk about boys. The book will be important and compelling reading for all teachers concerned with the education of boys.

## Contents
*'What about the boys?' an overview of the debates – The significance of teaching English boys: exploring social change, modern schooling and the making of masculinities – Rethinking masculinities: new ideas for schooling boys – Pushing it to the max: interrogating the risky business of being a boy – Challenging boys: addressing issues of masculinity within a gender equity framework – 'Powerful people aren't usually real kind, friendly, open people!' Boys interrogating masculinities at school – Boyz' own stories: masculinities and sexualities in schools – 'Learning to laugh': a study of schoolboy humour in the English secondary school – Sad, bad or sexy boys': girls' talk in and out of the classroom – Transgressing the masculine: African American boys and the failure of schools – 'Someone has to go through': indigenous boys, staying on at school and negotiating masculinities – Naughty boys at school: perspectives on boys and discipline – Boys will be boys (if they pay attention in science class) – Maths talk is boys' talk: constructing masculinity in school mathematics – Boys, books and breaking boundaries: developing literacy in and out of school – 'I like smashing people, and I like getting smashed myself': addressing issues of masculinity in physical education and sport – Index.*

## Contributors
*Lori Beckett, Anne Chapman, Martin Coles, Angela Creese, Harry Daniels, James Earl Davis, Debbie Epstein, Shaun Fielding, Victoria Foster, Michael Gard, Christine Hall, Chris Haywood, Valerie Hey, Mary Jane Kehily, Michael S. Kimmel, Diana Leonard, Will Letts, Máirtín Mac an Ghaill, Mark McFadden, Wayne Martino, Bob Meyenn, Martin Mills, Geoff Munns, Anoop Nayak, Judith Parker, Michael C. Reichert, Lee Simpson, Christine Skelton.*

256pp     0 335 20623 9 (Paperback)     0 335 20624 7 (Hardback)